Metaphor and Dialectic in Managing Diversity

Also by Christina Schwabenland

PARTICIPATION NORTH AND SOUTH

RELATIONSHIPS IN THE LIVES OF PEOPLE WITH LEARNING DIFFICULTIES

STORIES, VISIONS AND VALUES IN VOLUNTARY ORGANISATIONS

Metaphor and Dialectic in Managing Diversity

Christina Schwabenland
Reader in Public and Voluntary Sector Management, University of Bedfordshire, UK

First published 2012 by
PALGRAVE MACMILLAN

Palgrave Macmillan in the UK is an imprint of Macmillan Publishers Limited, registered in England, company number 785998, of Houndmills, Basingstoke, Hampshire RG21 6XS.

Palgrave Macmillan in the US is a division of St Martin's Press LLC, 175 Fifth Avenue, New York, NY 10010.

Palgrave Macmillan is the global academic imprint of the above companies and has companies and representatives throughout the world.

Palgrave® and Macmillan® are registered trademarks in the United States, the United Kingdom, Europe and other countries

ISBN 978-0-230-25255-4

This book is printed on paper suitable for recycling and made from fully managed and sustained forest sources. Logging, pulping and manufacturing processes are expected to conform to the environmental regulations of the country of origin.

A catalogue record for this book is available from the British Library.

Library of Congress Cataloging-in-Publication Data
Schwabenland, Christina.
  Metaphor and dialectic in managing diversity / Christina Schwabenland.
     p. cm.
  ISBN 978–0–230–25255–4
    1. Diversity in the workplace–Management. 2. Intercultural communication. I. Title.

HF5549.5.M5S39 2012
658.3008–dc23   2012012792

10   9   8   7   6   5   4   3   2   1
21 20 19 18 17 16 15 14 13 12

Printed and bound in Great Britain by
CPI Antony Rowe, Chippenham and Eastbourne

Contents

Acknowledgements

My gratitude is first of all to my students who generously allowed me to borrow their metaphors and who participated so wholeheartedly in the module I taught for many years on *Managing Diversity and Equality*. Many of these students were at the time, or have gone on to occupy positions where they are able to have a significant impact on diversity and equality policies. I am also very grateful to all the other participants in the various research projects I have referred to throughout the book, who have been very generous with their time and their thoughts.

Since 2006 I have been involved in researching diversity management in voluntary organisations with my colleague, Frances Tomlinson, who is currently based at London Metropolitan University. Working with Frances has been a very rewarding experience; she is a generous and supportive colleague and we have shared data, ideas, papers and inspiration! This book would not have taken the form it did without her contributions.

Digby Warren and colleagues from the Centre for the Enhancement of Learning and Teaching at London Metropolitan University provided the initial impetus for me to write up my experiments with pedagogy, and gave me tremendously helpful comments and feedback in the early stages.

Finally, love and appreciation to Doug Holton, my partner, and to Heloise and Abelard.

Some of the ideas presented in Chapters 3, 4, 6 and 7 have appeared in an earlier form in the following publications:

Schwabenland, C. (2011) 'Surprise and Awe: Learning from Indigenous Managers', *Journal of Management Education*, 35/1: 138–154

Schwabenland, C. (2009) 'An Exploration of the Use of Disruption as a Pedagogic Intervention', *Educational Action Research*, 17/2: 293–309

Schwabenland, C. (2008) 'Representations of the Ideal as Symbols of Subversion', in Kostera, M. (ed.) *Mythical Inspirations for Organizational Realities*, pp. 88–99, Basingstoke: Palgrave Macmillan

Schwabenland, C. (2006) 'The Influence of Cultural Heritage on Students' Willingness to Engage in Peer Assessment', *Investigations in University Teaching and Learning*, 3/2: 100–108

Schwabenland, C. (2006) 'Stories, Mythmaking and the Consolation of Success', in Satterthwaite, J., Martin, W. and Roberts, L. (eds) *Discourse, Resistance and Identity Formation*, pp. 59–75, Stoke on Trent: Trentham

Schwabenland, C. and Tomlinson, F. (2008) 'Managing Diversity or Diversifying Management?' *Critical Perspective on International Business*, 4/2–3: 320–333

Tomlinson, F. and Schwabenland, C. (2010) 'Reconciling Competing Discourses of Diversity? The UK Non-Profit Sector Between Social Justice and the Business Case', *Organization*, 17/1: 101–121

Permissions

Permissions have gratefully been received from the following:

Permission to cite Hugh MacDiarmid pp. 214 and 215 received from Carcanet Publishers 1992
Permission to cite Mahmoud Darwish pp. 27 and 291 from *The Butterfly's Burden* received from Bloodaxe Publishers 2007
Permission to cite Mahmoud Darwish pp. 26, 130, 137 and 156 from *A River Dies of Thirst*, Mahmoud Darwish, Saqi Books, London 2009
Permission to cite Gergan p. 107 as an epigraph on page 27 received from Sage Publications 1992

The author has made every effort to obtain permission for using material which is believed to be under copyright protection. We will be glad to hear from those holders of copyright who could not be appropriately acknowledged in this edition of the book because of circumstances beyond the author's control and will be pleased to set right in future editions of the book any mistakes or oversights that might have occurred in the current edition.

1
Re-writing Imagination into Management

Introduction

I think [managers] need the skills that allow them to work within a system but to deliver the results that they want, that the people they support, need. I think that's very, very challenging. I think the level of innovation, the level of imagination needed to work within what are increasingly tighter controls and restrictions, whilst delivering, I think is very challenging.

This book is about the role of imagination in management, and specifically, in managing diversity. The quotation I have chosen as my introduction comes from an interview I carried out with the chief executive of a large voluntary organisation in the UK that provides a wide range of services for people with disabilities. In it we discussed the issues and dilemmas he was experiencing in implementing diversity initiatives within the organisation. I chose this quotation because of his emphasis on imagination – something that is rarely discussed in the plethora of books and articles on diversity management. But imagination is at the heart of managing diversity, in particular, two forms of imaginative activity, metaphor and dialectic.

Managing diversity requires us to engage in the tension field between similarity and difference. Diversity management is about the processes involved in identifying what we have in common with each other, where we differ and what implications these similarities and differences have for achieving organisational goals. But the particular similarities and differences that diversity management concerns itself with are those of identity, the ways in which we create images of ourselves and others. Metaphor and dialectic, considered as modes of thinking, open up new possibilities for engaging creatively in this tension field.

Within contemporary management discourse 'managing diversity' has become the expression of choice to refer to a wide range of policies and practices designed to respond to the increasingly heterogeneous nature of the workplace. Usually regarded as having emerged from the United States as a successor to, or development from the discourse of equal opportunities (Kirton and Green 2005, Wrench 2005, Kandola and Fullerton 2003), the term is generally used to refer to the practices that have evolved in response to the need to accommodate a workforce in which the hegemonic image of the worker as white, male, young, able bodied and heterosexual has been challenged by the competing demands of women and people from groups and communities who may have experienced significant disadvantage in the workplace. Many of these demands have also been supported by an increasing body of legislation that requires employers to have good policies and practices in place to ensure that workers are not subject to unfair discrimination. Although much of this discourse tends to focus on differences within formally bounded geographic areas such as cities, regions or nations, as organisations are increasingly likely to work across national boundaries, diversity management is also being extended to encompass the cultural issues that arise in multinational teams.

In this book I am taking a rather different approach to those which are primarily concerned with policy and practice. I have chosen to concentrate on the individual and on the importance of the imagination for increasing agency. By emphasising the role of the imagination I am focussing my attention at the level of attitudes and beliefs rather than behaviours. The inter-relationship between belief and behaviour is complex, however much practice based work aims to inculcate a prescriptive collection of behaviours and techniques in the hope that following these will lead to a more accessible workplace culture in which individual differences are not only tolerated but welcomed. This approach is not necessarily wrong. Certainly, overtly discriminatory and oppressive behaviour should always be challenged. Learning and adopting new forms of behaviour can lead to changes in the way people think, and there is a wide ranging literature that explores how this occurs in organisations (although often, following Foucault's idea of disciplining regimes, in an undesirable way). However, this approach has been overemphasised at the loss of more nuanced attention to the importance of underlying beliefs and the influence that our imaginative constructs play in forming and shaping our responses to the environments and relationships in which we find ourselves. I am specifically interested in *how* social imagination constitutes social reality (Ricoeur 1986) and whether increasing our awareness of our imagination at work can lead to transformations in our thinking.

There are, however, limits to individual agency. I am also interested in how it is that many well-intentioned people, working within systems and practices that are intended to be non-discriminatory, nonetheless often find that having good intentions is clearly not enough. There are very unpleasant and bigoted people in this world but I think that they present a rather different set of problems. My focus is on the people who have, or certainly appear to have a sincere desire to work towards a more equal society in which people are not subject to discrimination because of systemic disadvantage and yet often find themselves reproducing those selfsame patterns of marginalisation and exclusion.

In this chapter I will sketch out some of the key debates and dilemmas surrounding the discourse and practice of diversity management. I aim to highlight some of the more problematic aspects of these debates, and in particular, the relative lack of demonstrable successes in order to make the case for the development of a different approach. I will then go on to give a brief introduction to my underlying proposition, namely that metaphor and dialectic, considered as ways of thinking, offer the means for a more active and self-reflexive engagement with our imagination at work. The subsequent section will locate this proposition within a relativist ontology and an approach to organisation studies that draws on social construction and complexity theories. The chapter concludes with a brief summary of the research projects that provide the empirical data on which the book is based.

Managing 'Diversity'? *'Managing'* Diversity?

It hardly needs saying that the term 'managing diversity' is imprecise, contested, and applied in different, and often conflicting, ways. In fact, it is hard to imagine another expression that arouses such a wide variety of opposing views and opinions. These range from the celebratory, in which diversity is presented as a paradigm shift that makes possible the achievement of organisational goals while simultaneously liberating people from long term, deeply rooted, systemic marginalisation (Kandola and Fullerton 2003, for example) to the profoundly critical in which diversity is regarded as a rhetorical device that allows and even contributes to the perpetuation of disadvantage and oppression (Wrench 2005, Lorbiecki and Jack 2000).

Within these opposing positions can be located a number of other critical debates. Prominent amongst these are the relationship between diversity and equality (and between equality of opportunity and equality of outcome), the relevance of the 'business case' for diversity and whether it overlaps or conflicts with the moral, or social justice case, and debates about whether an emphasis on diversity in a broad sense serves to mask the specificities of oppression as it is experienced by men and women, people from minority ethnic backgrounds, people with disabilities and so on.

Although diversity as a concept may have radical roots – for example Johns (2004) and Tomei (2003) see its beginnings in the social movements such as the civil rights movement, the women's movement and the gay liberation movement – for many other commentators diversity is more likely to be associated with a neo-liberal, managerially driven agenda, according to which the 'business case', rather than ethical or moral considerations, is the main driver for inclusive and non-discriminatory organisational policy and practice (Tomlinson and Schwabenland 2010). The main argument behind the 'business case' is that a workforce that is representative of a wide range of socio-demographic categories is advantageous as a means to obtain business advantage. Liff (1997) summarised the development of the diversity paradigm as a movement from an approach to diversity that seeks to dissolve difference (an assimilationist model) through accommodating, valuing and finally, utilising differences (for company objectives).

Whether or not there is an *inherent* tension between an approach based on utilitarian arguments – the business case – and an approach based on social justice and human rights is another critical point of debate in the diversity and equality field. However, presenting these two approaches as essentially oppositional becomes problematic when the 'business' of the organisation is itself concerned with achieving social justice as is the case with many organisations in the public sector (where much of the practice of managing diversity has originated), the voluntary sector (many voluntary or non-profit organisations can trace their origins to these same social movements) and in the growing area of social enterprise (Tomlinson and Schwabenland 2010). Furthermore, within the corporate sector the increasing awareness of its 'social' responsibilities suggests that even here these aspirations cannot always be separated.

The two words 'managing diversity' are so often used together that they seem to represent a single idea. But, as Liff (1997) shows, the tensions between different approaches to diversity highlight some of the underlying difficulties that may be obscured by this portmanteau expression. In the last few years a growing body of work on the intersections and conflicts between different aspects of identity has emerged. For example, black feminists and women from the global South argued that much of the work of white, Western writers ignored the multiplicity of experiences and manifestations of oppression (Foldy 2002, Narayan and Harding 2000, Cavanaugh 1997, Mohanty et al 1991). And the possible tensions between someone's religious affiliation, their sexual orientation and their experiences of disability may lead to conflicts and contradictions that are hard enough to resolve on an individual basis, let alone within an organisational setting. So 'diversity' is a single word that encompasses a multitude of different forms of identity and affiliation.

Furthermore, what do we actually mean by '*managing*' diversity? *Can* diversity be managed? 'Management' is a similarly inexact term. Czarniawska Joerges and Wolff draw a helpful distinction between the tasks of leadership, management and entrepreneurship. They write:

> ...leadership is seen as symbolic performance, expressing the hope of control over destiny, management as the activity of introducing order and co-ordinating flows of things and people towards collective action and entrepreneurship as the making of entire new worlds. (Czarniawska Joerges and Wolff 1991: 529)

Czarniawska Joerges and Wolff's definition of management chimes with that of the proponents of the business case for diversity who suggest that a diverse workforce is good for business *because* it will lead to 'enhanced innovation, creativity and problem solving, better customer services and improved quality' (Kandola and Fullerton 2003: 51). Diversity is primarily presented here as a resource to be *managed* in the sense described above of 'introducing order and co-ordinating flows'. The underlying assumption seems to be that diversity is not an inherent good but a potential resource. But this begs the question about the value of those aspects of workers' identities and histories that are not easily harnessed to organisational objectives. It also highlights the debate about the extent to which 'management', in its task of co-ordination, is necessarily synonymous with 'control'. Goldberg comments that 'corporate and *managed* multiculturalisms have proved themselves effective tools for managing and maintaining a *constriction* of diversity that otherwise might be unmanageable and overwhelming from the standpoint of bureaucratic and administrative technologies' (Goldberg 1994: 29 my emphasis). And indeed, writing from a critical perspective, Janssens and Zanoni (2004) suggest that the managerial discourse of diversity is *always* a discourse of control.

Arguably achieving some of the objectives of the business case, such as enhanced creativity and innovation, also calls for entrepreneurship, the 'making of new worlds'. Bringing together people with different backgrounds and perspectives is seen as conferring a business advantage *because* out of these encounters new ideas and possibilities may emerge. Although evidence to support this assertion may be thin on the ground (see, for example, the meta-analysis by Wise and Tschihart 2000) this idea does accord with much of the current thinking on creativity in organisations more generally.

I previously carried out a research project into creativity in voluntary organisations in which I explored the ways in which creativity was conceptualised and how people experienced the creative process. I interviewed senior managers working in organisations that were generally regarded as being particularly innovative, and asked them to describe how new ideas were developed. Creative ideas were consistently identified as 'resulting from a number of disparate things coming together, whether these "things" were people, teams or circumstances' (Schwabenland 2006a: 113). This example is only one of many that described the creative process in very similar terms:

> *We used to idea hop between each other, one of us would get an idea, we'd chat about it quickly with the others and the links would come.*
> (Voluntary sector chief executive cited in Schwabenland 2006a: 113)

Creative ideas did not emanate exclusively from specially identified 'creative' individuals or departments but through the process of bring people together and allowing ideas to emerge.

> *Sitting in a senior management team meeting was quite amazing because someone would come up with an idea over here, it would pinball around the table, five minutes later it would be turned into fact and then it would be presented to the outside world as a fait accompli.* (Voluntary sector manager cited in Schwabenland 2006a: 111)

These findings echo other studies of creativity in an organisational context, and do lend support for one of the pivotal arguments of the business case for diversity. They also demonstrate that management need not necessarily be synonymous with control. However, on a more cautionary note, when Mintzberg (1987) and King and Anderson (1995) explored the conditions in organisations that allow such creativity to thrive, they identified such factors as participatory leadership, opportunities for employees to exercise discretion and autonomy, a climate that is encouraging of creativity and tolerant of risk and failure, and a culture that is relatively free of rigid traditions and role demarcations. These are not generally qualities that characterise diversity initiatives. Certainly in the UK much of what is generally regarded as good diversity practice has been developed by the regulatory commissions established by statute to provide employers with practical assistance in implementing the various pieces of anti-discrimination legislation. In contrast to the conditions that encourage creativity and innovation, much of this practice, characterised by audits, measurement, monitoring, tool kits and the like, has become highly mechanistic.

Furthermore, it would be reasonable to expect that if the current pre-scriptions for good practice were effective we would have seen significant changes over a period of time, with companies that have good diversity practices showing increasing competitive advantage on the one hand, and a gradual disappearance of patterns of disadvantage on the other. But in many cases this is not what has happened. For example, the con-tinuing pay gap between men and women (17.1% as of 2008), the rela-tive disadvantages in the employment rates of people from different minority ethnic groups and the low rate of employment of people with disabilities (approximately 50% of people with disabilities were in employ-ment in 2007, with especially poor rates amongst people with mental health problems of whom only 21% were employed) are all things that might have been expected to disappear over time. After all, in the UK unequal pay and discrimination in employment on the basis of gender and race have been illegal for over thirty years, disability for over ten years and, of course more recent legislation has extended this protection to cover sexual orientation, religion and age.[1]

Even more evidence that challenges the effectiveness of traditional ideas of good practice comes from Race for Opportunity's[2] survey of employers most highly rated for their diversity initiatives in which the 2009 league table was led by two private sector firms, British Telecom and Pearson.[3] The performance of these firms may indeed be highly laudable, but what is more significant is the poorer relative perfor-mance of public sector organisations. This is especially concerning because since 2000, in the UK, the government's policy approach has been to shift its emphasis from that of preventing discrimination to actively promoting equality and the main instrument for effecting that change has been the establishment of a legally binding positive duty to promote equality which requires public organisations to publish equality action plans and impact assessments. As the government chose not to extend the positive duty to the private or voluntary sectors, partly as a result of lobbying from the Confederation of British Industry (CBI),[4] it would be reasonable to expect greater progress to come from the public sector.

The positive duty is a legally binding obligation that goes beyond the requirement that an organisation demonstrate that it is not discriminating against people from legally protected groups. Initially applied to race discrimination (from 2000) the positive duty is a direct response to the perceived failures of policy and practice that were highlighted in the Macpherson Report on the police handling of the investigation into the death of Stephen Lawrence and the concomitant emphasis on 'institutional racism' (Bhavnani 2001). The idea behind the positive duty is that preventing discrimination, while necessary, is not, in itself sufficient to create a more equal society. The positive duty represents a radical change in the way in which the role of legislation is conceptualised. It was extended to disability in 2005 and gender in 2007, and to the other areas covered by anti-discrimination legislation; religion, sexual orientation and age in 2010. But, as before, these positive duties to promote equality are only binding on the public sector and statistics published in 2005 by the National Council of Voluntary Organisations (NCVO) on the rates of employment of people from different ethnic groups in the private, public and voluntary sectors showed very little variation between the sectors (although the voluntary sector led in employment of women, both generally and in senior positions). These statistics, combined with the superior achievements of the two private sector firms identified in the Race for Opportunity's league table, would seem to represent a significant critique to the ways in which the positive duties are being implemented.

Fredman and Spencer propose that there should be a requirement on employers to assess their workplace in terms of four dimensions; equal life chance, equal dignity and worth, accommodation and affirmation and equal participation, and that the views of people who are most likely to experience discrimination are sought (Fredman and Spencer 2006: 5). They describe the positive duty as confused and suggest that there should be some flexibility in the specific measures that an organisation adopts, as these will differ in importance and relevance from organisation to organisation. However, many organisations have responded to the positive duties by developing a *less* flexible and *more* uniform approach to practice.

Cornelius comments on the discrepancy, in many organisations, between the views of management and of workers on their internal equality initiatives with workers generally being much less positive, in terms of what 'feels fair' (Cornelius 2002: 49). Cornelius, along with Fredman and Spencer are amongst a number of writers who have explored the applicability of the capabilities approach, pioneered by Amartya Sen and Martha Nussbaum, to the management of diversity and equality within organisations. The capabilities approach asks some very helpful questions, in particular, what people are able to be and do. 'Ability' in this sense is a development of the notion of freedom, since being free to do or be something without the capability to realise that opportunity is of limited value. Cornelius (2002) in her book on diversity management suggests that the capabilities approach has much to offer by focussing on the importance of agency. She points out that agency needs to be understood not only in individual terms but also with regard to the responsibility we all have to create an environment which is supportive to ourselves and others. McCarthy and Dimitriades write that:

> ...the challenge of this era of difference is the challenge of living in a world of incompleteness, discontinuity and multiplicity. It requires generating a mythology of social interaction that goes beyond the model of resentment that seems so securely in place in these times. (McCarthy and Dimitriades 2000: 202)

What are the capabilities needed to live in such a world and what might such a mythology be? If we accept that the business case for diversity is limited then diversity needs to be reframed within the discourse of social justice. This point needs to be clearly made because issues of justice and equality do not always feature highly within the discourse of the business case (see Kirton and Green 2005 and Lorbiecki and Jack 2000). And reasserting the importance of the social justice case requires us to engage in the complexity of overlapping and conflicting under-standings of identity that is inherent in a plural society. Generating such a mythology of social interaction requires us to engage our ima-gination in the task of creating a vision of what a more just, equitable and plural society might be like.

A society 'as eloquent as poetry'

The American political philosopher Martha Nussbaum writes that in order to live well in a pluralistic democracy we need to cultivate the capacity for 'critical examination of oneself and one's traditions', 'the ability to see [ourselves]...as human beings bound to all other human beings by ties of recognition and concern' and the '*imagination* that is cultivated through the arts' (Nussbaum 2007: 291–294 my emphasis).

The first of these, the capacity for critical self-reflection, is probably the least controversial. Activities designed to develop students' ability for engaging in critical reflection are built into most postgraduate courses in management education, and certainly in the various modules on *Managing Diversity and Equality* that I have taught for several years. Critical reflection has also, at least to some extent, formed an integral element of diversity and equal opportunities training programmes in all their different manifestations (see Bhavnani 2001 for an interesting discussion of the evolution of these different approaches).

The second of Nussbaum's criteria, seeing ourselves as inextricably bound to each other, is framed by her as a capacity but it is also, arguably, a statement of belief; a belief about the world and our place within it. Different philosophical approaches (and different approaches to teaching management) may promote this idea of relatedness to a greater or lesser extent, but it is particularly (and inescapably) relevant to the idea of diversity, especially her emphasis on the ties of *concern*. Michael Eric Dyson writes:

> When I get knowledge, I get desire. I get hungry for the same liberty I find in the books, the science I study, the music I hear. I want my society as eloquent as the poetry I memorise. I want my living conditions to match the beauty of the algebraic formula I work. I want my people as blissful and harmonious as the symphony I listen to. I may also want to stamp out the horrors I read about, put an end to the suffering I hear in the music of the desperate or use what I know to help the subjugated. I might get inspired or enraged, mad or distraught, stumped or determined to act. (Dyson 2004: xxiv)

Dyson clearly demonstrates how, for him at any rate, artistic experience is directly related to his concern for social justice. In the above quotation he interweaves artistic appreciation with a passionate emotional engagement with a vision of a society 'as eloquent as…poetry'. Hugh MacDiarmid, a Scottish poet, suggests (appropriately enough, in poetic form) that this might not be just any kind of poetry but that which seeks 'to do justice to the discrete as well as to the organically integrated aspects of society'.

> Poetry of such an integration as cannot be effected
> Until a new and conscious organisation of society

Generates a new view
Of the world as a whole
As the integration of all the rich parts
Uncovered by the separate disciplines.
That is the kind of poetry I want. (MacDiarmid 1992: 214, 215)

When MacDiarmid writes that we need a 'new view of the world' he is echoing Ricoeur's (1986) observation that social imagination is *constitutive* of social reality, that it is through our imagination that we bring such new realities into being. In McCarthy and Dimitriades' challenge for a conceptualisation of social reality that moves beyond resentment they are challenging us to create an imaginative model of such a society. Tsoukas suggests that organisation is 'not only a feature of the world...but also of our thinking *about* the world' (Tsoukas 2006: 231 emphasis on the original). Organisation theorists who work within a psychodynamic/ systemic tradition often use the phrase 'organisation-in-the-mind' (Lawrence 2000, Armstrong 1991, Reed 1978) because it is the imaginative construct we create and through which we mediate our understanding of the external world that is the organisation they analyse.

Without some idea of where we want to go, however inchoate or shapeless it may be, we are reduced to playing an essentially reactive role. I think this is what Ahmed means when she writes that 'feminism isn't only against, it is for' (Ahmed 2004: 178). And yet, I have been surprised at how rarely students taking my postgraduate module on *Managing Diversity and Equality* have given any thought to what kind of a society they want to create, what it would look like, feel like, how it might work. They may have highly tuned their critical skills towards identifying what doesn't work but they have little idea of what they would put in its place.

Furthermore, imagination promotes empathy. Nussbaum (2007) and Kohn (1990) emphasise empathy as one of the capacities needed to work towards social justice and greater equality and freedom for all in a complex and pluralistic society. Imagination makes empathy possible; imagination *is* empathy – 'the ability to think what it might be like to be in the shoes of a person different to oneself, to be an intelligent reader of that person's story and to understand the emotions and wishes and desires that someone so placed might have' (Nussbaum 2004: 4).

Kohn's conceptualisation of empathy is more refined: for him empathy is the ability to enter into the experience of the other, but in such a way that we do not become submerged into that other. This requires us to develop the capacity to perceive the other as self and the self as other.

These different perceptions need to be kept in tension so that in the awareness of the other as self, that is achieved through empathy, there is also an awareness of self as other, as the observing self (Kohn 1990). This tension can be understood as a tension between similarity, that which we share with the other, and difference, that which is separate.

Metaphor and diversity

Holding concepts of similarity and difference in tension is what we do when we think in metaphors. It is for this reason that I am proposing that developing our capacity for metaphorical thinking may provide a resource to help us in working with diversity. A metaphor proposes a relationship between two ideas or concepts, generally ideas that belong to different frames of reference. Through the initial perception of the differences between the two concepts we are led into a new understanding of that which is similar. When the poet writes 'my love is a rose' it is the initial impression of difference (people are not plants) that leads us to the similarity (there is something rose-like about the person the poet loves). To give an example that is more relevant to the workplace, several years ago I interviewed a voluntary sector chief executive who used the phrase 'stuffing envelopes' when she was describing her approach to leadership (Schwabenland 2006a: 146). She did not mean that this was literally how she spent her day, but that as a metaphor 'stuffing envelopes' expressed something about the way she understood her role. Stuffing envelopes is an activity that has particular resonance in the voluntary sector because an organisation often communicates its concerns and mobilises its supporters through mail shots (as, for example, the Amnesty International letter writing campaigns on behalf of political prisoners). The actual tasks of filling and addressing the envelopes are often done by volunteers (and the ethos of voluntarism is critical to the sector's sense of identity). Her metaphor, therefore, captures both the similarity and also the difference between her role and theirs. The metaphor serves to emphasise her identification with the sector's values. It communicates similarity (in that she probably still does, occasionally, help with the mail shots) and difference (she is the chief executive, not a volunteer). These two concepts of similarity and difference are held in tension in the metaphor, a tension that is irresolvable.

Ricoeur suggests that there can be at least three different tensions within a metaphor; the tension within the statement (between tenor and vehicle, focus and frame and principle and secondary subject), the tension between two (or more) interpretations (a literal interpretation and a non-literal interpretation 'whose sense emerges through non-sense') and 'the tension in the relational function of the copula between identity and difference in the interplay of resemblance' (Ricoeur 2007: 292). It is the third of these tensions that relates most directly to Kohn's proposition that empathy requires us to enter into the life of another but in such a way that we retain our awareness of our distance from that other. The copula is that which mediates the relation between similarity and difference and ensures that the irresolvability, or the paradox of literal and metaphorical truth, is maintained. We can also see that the other tensions Ricoeur describes are also very relevant to the practice of diversity. For example, the tension between tenor and vehicle could be seen to be at the heart of many of the debates about humour versus offence. The use of stereotypes and generalisations about people seems relevant to the second area of tension, that of the literal and the metaphorical interpretation.

Metaphorical imagination creates meaning through proposing and disrupting notions of similarity and difference but it is also characterised by irresolvability. A metaphor is not an allegory. Metaphorical thinking refuses closure.

Dialectic and diversity

Dialectic is also concerned with notions of similarity and difference but approaches them differently. Metaphor brings different elements together in order to emphasise their similarity. Dialectic positions these elements, or ideas in opposition in order to demonstrate their difference. The dynamic of metaphor lies in creating tension; the dynamic of dialectic lies in a continual movement to and from opposing polarities of unification and distanciation. The idea of dialectic is sometimes portrayed by the yin/yang symbol, and although the pictorial representation appears static, the idea behind the symbol is of a perpetual motion between the two elements.

The following quotation demonstrates how the idea of dialectic can be manifested in an organisational setting. It is taken from an interview I carried out with the Indian chief executive of an NGO that campaigns on women's issues. In the excerpt she is telling me how the organisation goes about researching and developing a policy position, in this case, about the impact of religion on the lives of women.

A discussion needed to be held. Then a study had to be conducted. So each [of the] *groups were asked to do a quick, spot survey and study how religion impacts on the lives of women. And then we see what the areas are where*

they have impacted.... So as we moved from one to another we were able to estab-
lish a common position. So this is necessary. Constantly necessary to arrive at the
root cause. (Indian NGO chief executive cited in Schwabenland 2006a: 172)

'Moving from one to another to establish a common position' is a description of a dialectical process. As with metaphor, the idea of dialectic, 'the contradiction and reconciliation of opposite standpoints...the unity of opposites' (Walsby 1965 cited in Milner 1989: 180) has a rich and varied heritage. In the Western philosophical tradition dialectic is usually described as originating in Grecian thought, primarily as a method of argumentation, out of which new knowledge emerges, rather as in the example above. Dialectic also appears in Eastern philosophy; dialectical dynamics underpin the Chinese concept of yin/yang, as mentioned before and the dance of Shiva, in Hindu cosmology. Shiva, in his representation as Nataraja is depicted surrounded by a circle of fire, within which he dances in an endless movement from creation to destruction to creation; order emerges out of chaos but then disintegrates back into chaos. The mathematician Ian Stewart, in a reference to Shiva's dance, writes that 'instead of two opposed polarities there is a continuous spectrum. As harmony and discord combine in musical beauty, so order and chaos combine in mathematical beauty' (Stewart 1997: 17). The quotation above demonstrates both of these different interpretations; dialectic as a method of argumentation and, through the use of the phrase 'constantly necessary', dialectic as perpetual movement.

Metaphor and dialectic as ways of thinking

It is clear that both metaphor and dialectic are ways of thinking that engage with notions of similarity and difference albeit in different ways. Metaphor works though association; Bruns (1992) describes this as poetic logic. Aristotle famously wrote that the most important requirement for a poet 'is to be good at using metaphor...for the successful use of metaphor is a matter of perceiving similarities' (Aristotle 1996: 37). The primary emphasis of metaphor is on similarity. Dialectic, on the other hand, works through the recognition of difference. Metaphorical thinking proceeds through association and correspondence; poetic logic resides in the appreciation of the similarity that binds two concepts together. Dialectical thinking, at least in the classical Greek understanding, proceeds through rational, philosophical logic. Dialectic is the principle that structures formal debates in which argument develops through a movement from thesis to anti-thesis and then either to synthesis, or to a moment in time where one side is regarded as having 'won' the argument.

Bohm (2008) however, argues for a different conceptualisation of dialectic which is more open ended and participative; he imagines it as creating a space where people come together so that new understandings can emerge. Bohm's dialectic is alchemical; the dynamic of dialectic is that of the crucible.

The following example better illustrates Bohm's alchemical interpretation of the dialectic process. Here, the Indian chief executive of a drama project working with marginalised communities is describing the way in which the company builds a piece of theatre out of the immediate concerns of people living in isolated and economically deprived areas. Initially the performers group will visit the area:

When they come back the whole performers group sit together. So then the people who have not gone [on tour] they start questioning. And the people who have gone, they start answering. And by that it's a kind of process of identifying the correct problems and the proposed kind of pattern of script. (Indian NGO chief executive cited in Schwabenland 2006a: 173)

This example is particularly interesting because it describes the creative process occurring within an organisational context as a dialectical one. The contribution of the two groups, each with different experiences and roles, is critical to the development of the play, and, illustrating Bohm's interpretation, the contributions of all the participants are valued.

Bruns writes that all interpretation is underpinned by what he terms 'the quarrel between poetry and philosophy' (Bruns 1992: 229). The dynamic, or necessity of movement in poetry is towards a logic of similarity that can be comprehended intuitively (Bruns also uses the word 'anarchically'). Philosophical logic proceeds consequentially – concepts are analysed and ordered methodically according to a pattern that is comprehended, or determined rationally. These two dynamics, in their more degenerate forms, already play a major role in theorising and sensemaking on issues of diversity and equality. Metaphors become essentialised as stereotypes. Oppositions become essentialised into binary conflicts. And, of course, the potential consequences cannot be underestimated – people kill on the basis of their conceptualisations of each other. 'Metaphorical choices are no laughing matter, especially in politics' writes Geary. He points out that while 'political crises are not resolved simply by choosing alternate metaphors' (Geary 2011: 127) there is nonetheless a world of difference in the possibilities that ensue from metaphors such as 'axis of evil' and 'extended hands', each used by (different) American presidents in foreign policy statements.

Organising in a world of incompleteness, discontinuity and multiplicity

In an article in *The Observer* (a UK weekly newspaper) Jason Burke attempted to analyse the processes that lead to the radicalisation of young Muslims. He observed a common theme in his interviews with men who had contemplated (and in some cases carried out) terrorist attacks, namely the difficulties they experienced in making sense of conflicting identities, captured by a quotation from one young man who: 'support[ed] England at football and Pakistan at cricket'. Burke writes:

> It is in that tension that everything is playing out...it is all about how 'the global plugs into the local', about the interaction between these identities. (Burke 2007: 16)

Burke emphasises the compelling attraction of the 'single narrative' that 'says that Muslims are under attack all over the world', 'the oil that allows the radicalisation machine's many cogs to turn' (Burke 2007: 17). Indeed, one of his respondents said that the only thing that stopped him in the moment when he was about to detonate a bomb was hearing the voice of someone he was about to kill, speaking with an accent similar to his own. That moment of recognition prevented him from being able to carry out the bombing because his perception of his potential victim as other than himself had been disrupted.

It is hard to find a more compelling argument in favour of the need to develop the capacity to think metaphorically and dialectically, to manage our awareness of similarity and difference in such a way that they do not become essentialised. These ideas are not new; the relevance of stereotyping and the ways in which we create our constructions of the other are common themes in the literature on diversity. What is less familiar in the literature (although not in organisations studies more generally) is the suggestion that managing diversity also requires us to engage with uncertainty, ambiguity and irresolvability.

McCarthy and Dimitriades write about the 'challenge of living in a world of incompleteness, discontinuity and multiplicity' (McCarthy and Dimitriades 2000: 202). Engaging with the diversity of humankind brings us into encounters with the many different ways people have for constructing meaning about themselves, about their social worlds and about their visions of the just society. We need to be open to the possibility that some of these different constructions may be at least of equal value to our own and even, perhaps, more compelling. If this is so, then we have to assume that there is no single perspective or take on the truth, or truths of appearances. Mehta writes that 'a study which seeks to comprehend from within the faith and traditions of other men [sic] must go much further than acquiring mere information about them. It must strive to comprehend the other in its otherness, let it speak to us in its difference from us and *allow it to lay hold of us in its claim to truth.*' (Mehta 1985: 117 my emphasis) He goes on to write:

> True dialogue is less a telling each other than a questioning of each other and it never leaves us where we were before, either in respect of our understanding of the other or of ourselves. (Mehta 1985: 122)

A relativist ontology underpins much of the theorising on organisations and organising that has been influenced by the poststructuralist, postmodern and social constructionist schools of thought. However, one of the consequences of allowing ourselves to consider the relative nature not only of other truth claims, but also of our own, is the possibility of experiencing discomforting feelings of disruption, confusion and anxiety. Finding ourselves somewhere other than 'where we were before' can be unnerving. The dangers that arise from this are many; one is the 'resentment' referred to by McCarthy and Dimitriades (2000), another is the risk of adopting what Mehta refers to as a strategy of 'defence through insulation rather than active grappling or dialogue' (Mehta 1985: 118). Metaphor and dialectic, although different in their modes of operation, may suggest alternative ways of grappling with difference that resist both of these dangers.

Mehta suggests that India and the West (he capitalises 'West') have adopted 'different approaches to difference'. He characterises the Indian approach as being one in which difference is either absorbed and assimilated, or rejected. In contrast, in the West we apply 'the intellectual activity of making distinctions, of dividing and separating' (Mehta 1985: 118) in order to define and re-define by relationship to that which is different.

The question that I aim to address in this book is how we can go about this 'active grappling' with the differing truth claims of our own and others. Within the frame of a relativist ontology, I take a social constructionist approach in which attention is given to the processes of sensemaking and the creating of meaning(s) as individuals take on roles and shape perspectives in an on-going dialogue between their sense of self and their understandings of others.

Recently there has been increasing interest in exploring whether or not complexity theory can provide useful insights into the dynamics of humanly created organisations. Some of this work may be of particular relevance to studying diversity management. According to Critchley,[5] the complexity approach suggests that 'organisations have no material-ity' but that they are 'social processes of communication and inter-action'. Complexity theory suggests that organisations are unpredictable and uncontrollable and that organisational change follows a non-linear trajectory (because cause and effect are simultaneous). However, patterns do *emerge.*

Complexity theory has emerged out of parallel work going on in the physical sciences exploring the phenomena of organising in nature and in which 'phenomena were no longer perceived as either ordered or disordered, either stable or unstable, either organised or disorganised, but could paradoxically be both *at the same time* (Shaw 2004: 20 emphasis in the original). Some examples include the flocking and migrating patterns of birds and the behaviours of colonies of ants and bees. Such self-organising patterns have been observed to emerge, 'at the edge of chaos...producing patterns that propagate, grow, split apart and recom-bine in complex ways, paradoxically producing order and disorder at the same time' (Shaw 2004: 67). The complexity approach is 'a different way of thinking that stays in the tension of paradox as the movement of the sense-making process itself' (Shaw 2004: 21). Although the analogy between people in organisations and flocking birds may not entirely hold, this approach to thinking from within the paradox bears a strong resem-blance to Bruns (1992) description of poetic logic as a more anarchic structuring of thought, and seems to resonate with the idea of managing diversity through the tension between similarity and difference.

Tsoukas suggests that the usefulness of complexity theory lies in its presenting us with 'metaphors that posit new connections, draw our attention to new phenomena and help us see what we could not see before' (Tsoukas 2006: 232). These new insights may be particularly relevant to diversity for three reasons. Firstly, as a theory of organisa-tional change, the complexity approach offers some useful perspectives into change management initiatives (and why they often fail) which are helpful in understanding the implementation of *diversity* policies and strategies in organisations.

Secondly, the complexity approach puts diversity at the centre of its theorising about organisational change. According to Stacey et al (2002) change occurs when patterns shift, and patterns shift when difference is introduced. Diversity is *intrinsic* to change. Critchley says that in his consultancy work he looks for possibilities of pattern disturbance through the *amplification of difference.* Consultants, he suggests, '*live on the edge of similarity and difference*' (Critchley ibid: my emphasis).

Thirdly, the complexity approach stresses the importance of relationships. Meaning is created in the interactions, or conversations between people and in this sense complexity theory has some overlap with social constructionist approaches. 'Conversations are patterns of gestures and responses and cultures are emerging patterns over time that have become repetitious' (Critchley ibid).

> The diversity arises in the scope for different interpretations open to people communicating with each other...it is in these ongoing differences of interpretation that individual and collective identities are continually recreated and transformed. (Stacey et al 2002: 189)

The complexity approach is not only relevant to diversity generally: through its emphasis on paradox, on the 'amplification of difference' as a means of facilitating change, and on the importance of 'relatedness', it suggests ways of thinking that share common ground with metaphor and dialectic in their approaches to working within the tension between similarity and difference. Tsoukas suggests that viewing organisations as complex systems requires '*explor[ing] complex ways of thinking* about organisations-as-complex-systems' (Tsoukas 2006: 231 my emphasis). Tsoukas develops his ideas about what such 'complex thinking' might consist of by drawing on Bruner's distinction of two different modes of thinking, the 'logico-scientific' and the 'narrative' 'each providing distinctive way of ordering experience, of constructing reality...the one lead[ing] to a search for universal truth conditions, the other for likely particular connections between two events' (Bruner cited by Tsoukas 2006: 232–233). Bruner's distinction between these different modes of thinking echoes Bruns' (1992) between philosophic and poetic logic.

Tsoukas further argues that complex thinking includes the capacity for holding together an awareness of contextuality, reflexivity, purpose, motive and temporality. He demonstrates how these elements come together in citing an example of Ricoeur's about the various things that are happening in the action of reciting of a psalm. In this action 'memory (past) and expectation (future) interact to influence attention and thereby producing the threefold present of our experience (the present of the past, the present of the present and the present of the future)' (Tsoukas 2006: 253). This example offers an interesting insight into the ways in which patterns and behaviours repeat themselves in organisations, even when, as in the case of diversity initiatives, there may be a conscious desire to alter them. But it also suggests the possibility of disrupting those processes.

Metaphor and dialectic are two such examples of complex thinking. These may be particularly relevant to exploring the dynamics of sense-making around diversity. At the level of the individual agency they suggest possibilities for engaging creatively with the ambiguity and uncertainty experienced whenever we are confronted with the other in ways that challenge our taken-for-granted assumptions about the world. At the organisational level they offer ways of understanding, and perhaps for transforming, the relationships between individual and the systems in which they find themselves. At the societal level they may provide us with useful tools in negotiating between different, and sometimes conflicting visions of the just society.

Conclusions

The increasing diversity of the workforce and its implications for management continue to be the focus of a great deal of interest. This is partly because of the importance and urgency of the issues that are incorporated within the term 'diversity' and also because of an increasing concern that many of the dilemmas of diversity management are not proving particularly amenable to easy solutions. There are, of course, many factors involved that are beyond the scope of individual managers to significantly effect. However, there is growing recognition that much of the current orthodoxy about good practice in this area is limited in its effectiveness. There seem to be some intractable conflicts and paradoxes that are not easily resolved. When individual managers are unable to think around them, these can lead to paralysis rather than change, resulting in the maintenance of the status quo.

In this chapter I have attempted to introduce the main themes I will be developing in greater detail throughout the book and also to make the case for the relevance of metaphor and dialectic, as 'complex modes of thinking about complex organisations' (Tsoukas 2006). Metaphor and dialectic offer ways of engaging with the tension between similarity and difference that underpins much of the way in which we experience many diversity issues, but in such a way that this tension can be thought about and engaged with, without the necessity of resolution. I have argued that there are two, important aspects of the diversity debate which have received little attention so far. One is the importance of the imagination as being foundational to thought (although a recent exception is Richard Bronk's book (2009) on the 'romantic economist'). The second area that has been neglected to date is a focus on attitudes and beliefs rather than behaviours. What this book does not do, therefore, is to offer specific advice on practice. It does not engage in debates about the nature of oppression in organisations or of the specifics of race, gender, disability discrimination and the other equality 'strands'. Nor does it look in detail at policy formation and implementation. The book aims instead to make a contribution to the structure/agency debate by focussing on the individual and on the possibilities that are open to them for change.

Throughout this book I have drawn on several research projects as illustrations of the themes developed in each chapter. The first of these projects is an action research based enquiry into my own teaching practice, evaluated partly through a reflexive diary and partly by students' reflective reports. The second project consisted of a series of focus groups, also carried out with students. The third is a study of equality and diversity practice within the UK voluntary sector, carried out by myself and a colleague, leading me to develop a small, pilot project exploring the work of voluntary organisations in India, Ireland and Israel/Palestine working across divided communities. The final project I draw on is a case study I carried out several years ago into an NGO in India. I want to conclude this chapter by providing a brief summary of each of these projects.

In 2004 I began teaching a postgraduate module on *Managing Diversity and Equality*. The module was originally aimed primarily at students taking degrees in human resource management and it was one of a portfolio of courses accredited by the UK based Chartered Institute of Personnel Development (CIPD). However, over the last five years the module has become increasingly popular with students from a much wider range of degree programmes, not only those based in the Business School, but also from sociology and humanities based programmes. A substantial number of students taking the module are employed in jobs with a significant amount of managerial responsibility, often in human resource management, but also in more generic management, or increasingly, in jobs that specialise in diversity and equality issues. I devised an action research project, enquiring into my own teaching practice on this module, and in particular, to evaluate the impact of a programme of exercises I had created in order to help students to develop their capacity for metaphorical thinking. (This programme of exercises is described in more detail in Chapter 4).

All the students are asked to write a 1,000 word reflective report at the end of the semester and these reports are enormously helpful in providing me with feedback about the module as well as offering the student a chance to embed their learning. Many of the observations I have used throughout this book come from these reports (cited, of course, only with the students' permission). I also carried out a number of follow up interviews about four months after students finished the module. I wanted to discover whether there was evidence that students had developed an increased awareness of how metaphors structure our thinking, and whether they had been able to draw on that awareness to help them in managing their relationships with the people with whom they were working. I was also interested in whether there was evidence that these transformations had been facilitated through increased imaginative awareness or through empathetic engagement in the lives and concerns of others. In analysing the interviews, I explored whether students showed an ability to 'think metaphorically' in terms of holding concepts of similarity and difference in tension, and also whether they demonstrated a facility with associational thinking. Crucially, I wanted to find out if these capacities are of use to them at work.

The second research project I am drawing on here is also based on my teaching practice and consists of a series of focus groups I carried out with students in the UK and in India. Three of these groups comprised students who were currently working as managers in the voluntary sector (either in a paid or voluntary capacity, as, for example, trustees, or students on placement) and studying on one of three courses in voluntary sector management, an MSc in Organisation and Community Development (with a specific focus on refugee run organisations), an MA in Voluntary Sector Studies and, in the Indian focus group, the community work specialisation of the MSc in Social Work. A fourth focus group consisted of international students taking a module on cross-cultural management, exploring their fears and fantasies about peer assessment, in particular concerns about whether students from different cultural backgrounds could assess each other's work.

The third research project is a study of equality and diversity practice within the UK voluntary sector carried out by a colleague and myself. We have conducted a series of interviews with diversity specialists, managers (including chief executives) and project workers from a wide range of organisations, the main criterion being that the managers regard their organisation as being involved in concerns of social justice. Some of these organisations are working directly with people who are the 'focus' of diversity initiatives: people with disabilities, people from minority ethnic groups, older people. Other organisations are working with people whose experiences may be no less marginalising – for example substance misuse, homelessness, difficulties coping with childcare and parenting – but whose experiences are often invisible within the diversity discourse.

We have had several main areas of interest in carrying out this research. One was to uncover how 'diverse' identities are constructed in relation to organisational goals and mission, and in relation to a range of stake-holders – not only paid employees, but organisational clients, members, volunteers, trustees and funders. We were particularly interested in how the 'business case' for diversity was constructed in organisations where the 'business' is social justice (Tomlinson and Schwabenland 2010).

From these exploratory interviews we developed two more recent pieces of work. The first used action learning with voluntary sector managers to provide an environment where people can learn from each other and work together on developing individual approaches to some of the more intractable dilemmas of engaging in diversity issues in the workplace. The second project that has grown out of our original work is a series of interviews in organisations working specifically across religious divides in geo-graphic areas where these different cultural and philosophical allegiances are seen as providing one part of the rationale for increasing violence and mistrust.

We Make the Road by Walking is the title of a book by Horton and Freire on education for social change (Horton and Freire 1990). Their title captures the sense that the researcher/teacher/manager is not in some way 'outside' of the organisation; theirs is a view of the creation of reality as on-going and participatory, in which the researcher and the researched create the research together through the questions they ask, the answers they give and the interpretations they make. The implication of this way of thinking is that the teacher/researcher does not wholly 'control' the situation, still less its impact on the research 'subjects' but rather takes a particular role in the joint participation in, and creation of that experi-ence. That particular role is, however, located within a discourse of power. The teacher/researcher/leader may be a co-participant but a participant who is regarded as a supposed expert in their field and who wields influ-ential power and perhaps, in the relationship with students, normative power as well. The teacher awards the grades. The manager may wield the power to bestow or withdraw employment. Nor can we ever really know what the impact of our involvement has been. Dyson's response to these concerns is to advocate for maintaining a position of 'structural humility':

...you're always surprised by people who claim you have influenced them because you can never accurately or adequately measure such a thing. We are prevented by circumstance and environment and context from knowing the true nature of our own influence, which is why we should remain structurally humble. Not falsely modest, but structurally humble...we never know when someone is watch-ing or listening. I've had people around the country, folks who've read my books, articles and essays, or hear my sermons, lectures or commentary...tell me that something I've said or done has changed their lives. That's a huge responsibility and we've got to accept it as part of our duties as public intellectuals... The best we can do is to represent the truth as honestly and as clearly as we understand it with all the skills at our disposal. (Dyson 2004: 16–17)

I hope that I have been able to demonstrate at least a measure of such humility.

I have organised the book into two sections; Part I explores metaphor and Part II focusses on dialectic. In each section there are three chapters; the first chapter develops the theoretical argument and the following two chapters focus on application. The 'application' chapters also follow a similar pattern; after an introduction the chapter's theme is developed in relation to the individual, the organisation and the wider society.

The concluding chapter includes a summary of the main findings presented in the earlier chapters. I will again turn to the dilemmas of working in conditions of complexity and ambiguity, to the notion of 'not-knowing' and the difficulties, but also the opportunities that this creates for managers.

Part I

Metaphor and Managing Diversity

2

'All beautiful poetry is an act of resistance'[1]: Introducing Metaphor

> Why do we find it so congenial to speak of organisations as structures but not as clouds, systems but not songs, weak or strong but not tender or passionate?
>
> (Gergan 1992: 107)

Introduction

This is the first of the three chapters that explore the relevance of metaphor and metaphorical thinking to managing diversity in organisations. In this chapter I describe the theoretical framework that underpins my proposition and in the two subsequent chapters I go on to look at how these can be developed in practice. My starting assumption is that the nature of organisations, and of the functions and activities within them, can be fruitfully explored by trying to understand the way in which people use language to interpret their experiences of organisational life. To answer Gergan, I am assuming that if we prefer to speak of organisations as structures, this is because we perceive a correspondence between our idea of a structure and our experience of organisations. However, our interpretations can only ever be partial, they cannot encompass the totality of possible meanings. If we were to re-imagine our organisations as clouds, we might discover other correspondences that might help us to understand our experiences in new ways.

It matters how we think about organisations because our thoughts help to determine how we behave, and our behaviour in turn contributes to the reality of life in organisations as it is experienced by ourselves and others. These processes are iterative, because thoughts influence actions and actions influence thoughts. Furthermore, our thoughts are not always (or often?) rationally determined. Emotional experience lies behind much of our thinking and that experience is given expression through images and symbols.

Metaphor is one such example of our symbolic imagination at work. In the last thirty years there has been an explosion of interest in metaphor, an interest that Punter notes, 'shows no sign of abating' (Punter 2009: 7). In 1980 Lakoff and Johnson published a very influential book called *Metaphors We Live By*, in which they suggested that metaphor is not just a 'rhetorical flourish' but that it is foundational to thought. Their proposition provided the impetus for significantly increased attention to the role of metaphorical thinking in a whole range of different applications, including in the fields of social policy and organisation studies, most notably Morgan's (1986) *Images of Organization*. Within this still growing body of work it is possible to distinguish two different, although complementary approaches: metaphor as a way of conceptualising organisations and metaphor as medium for managing organisational processes.

Schon's (1979) work on generative metaphors is an early contribution to the first of these approaches. He suggested that metaphors influence how we frame social and organisational problems and gave, as an example, two contrasting views of urban housing, based on two very different metaphors, which 'generated' very different solutions. In policy documents of the 1950s and early '60s poor, urban areas were described as 'blighted' and 'diseased'. These descriptions give way, in the late '60s and '70s, to descriptions of 'natural communities' 'struggling to help themselves'. Schon suggested that the earlier discourse stemmed from a metaphor of health (and its negative corollary, disease) while the latter derived from an organic metaphor. The metaphor of health 'generated' the solution of bulldozing the old tenement areas and constructing new, affordable housing with plenty of open spaces and fresh air. A decade on, the suggested solutions were of 'helping people to help themselves' and minimising disruption to existing, if fragile, networks. Schon argued that it is important to recognise the generative metaphor at work because while it is unconscious the proposed 'solution' seems obvious and unquestionable – yet his example shows how radically different were the solutions generated by different metaphors.

In 1986 Morgan applied Schon's idea of generative metaphors to organisations. In *Images of Organization* he argued that organisational theories are based on 'images', or metaphors of what organisations are. He wrote that 'theories and explanations of organisational life are based on metaphors that lead us to understand organisations in distinct yet partial ways...the use of metaphor implies a *way of thinking* and a *way of seeing* that pervade how we understand the world generally' (Morgan 1986: 12). Morgan demonstrated that many of our conventional ideas about organisations and management are based on such 'taken-for-granted images' as machines, organisms, brains, cultures, political systems, psychic prisons, flux and transformation and as instruments of domination. Organisations 'are' all and none of these; metaphors are partial yet illuminating devices for understanding particular aspects of organisational reality.

The other main approach to theorising on metaphor has been to use metaphor as a way of understanding, and facilitating the functions of leadership and management. Some examples include organisational development (Oswick and Grant 1996), effectiveness and leadership (Kay 1991), maintaining and stabilising expectations (Beavis and Ross Thomas 1996) and creativity (Schwabenland 2006a). Pondy (1983) highlighted the use of metaphor to facilitate organisational change through reinforcing traditional values. For example, using the metaphors that express the underlying values of the organisation to frame the future plans implies that these values will still be present in the unknown future. Mangham gave another example of metaphor facilitating change management when he suggested that the use of 'wild west' imagery to describe corporate take-overs might serve to elevate a financial transaction to the realms of heroism (Mangham 1986). Abravanel suggested that metaphors not only bridge past and future but that they also 'mediate contradictions between the components of organisational ideology' (Abravanel 1983: 274). He suggests that there is always a contradiction between the ideal, 'what should be done' and the practicable, 'what *can* be done'. The tension between these is managed through 'mediatory myths' – mythologised institutional rules, rationalised justifications and legitimising myths.

In these three chapters I aim to apply each of these approaches to metaphor to understanding firstly, how diversity in organisations is conceptualised (in the next chapter), and secondly, the utility of metaphor in challenging limiting preconceptions and stereotypes about ourselves and each other at work. In this chapter I begin by analysing how metaphor works. I will then go on to explore the heuristic function of metaphor, or metaphor as theory, and the aesthetic function, or metaphor as experience (Ricoeur 2007). I will also focus more specifically on the relevance of metaphor to diversity: in particular, current debates about beauty and diversity (drawing on Scarry 2006) and beauty and equality (drawing on Nussbaum 1995).

How does metaphor work?

Aristotle famously wrote that 'the greatest thing by far is to be a master [sic] of metaphor. It is the one thing that cannot be learnt from others; and it is also a sign of genius since a good metaphor implies an intuitive perception of the similarity in dissimilars' (Aristotle, in the *Poetics* cited by Ricoeur 2007: 227). What Aristotle actually meant by this has been the subject of debate for centuries (Ricoeur 2007, Heath 1996) and the nature of these debates to some extent reflect the various developments in the theory of metaphor more broadly. For example, the primacy that Aristotle gives to metaphor appeared radical when metaphor was primarily regarded as a form of rhetorical embellishment, a sort of baroque flourish to add flavour to description. But more recent developments, such as those of Ricoeur (2007) and the aforementioned Lakoff and Johnson (1980) have focussed on metaphor as epistemology, metaphor as one of the ways in which thinking proceeds. If language is a representation of reality rather than reality itself then all language can be regarded as metaphorical. From this perspective it is not the primacy that Aristotle accords to metaphor that is controversial, but his suggestion that the mastery of metaphor is a sign of genius, as we are *all* users of metaphor. But is Aristotle saying that we cannot all learn the use of metaphor, or is he suggesting that we can only reflexively learn to understand ourselves as makers of meaning; that such learning cannot be taught but can come only from inward exploration?

Aristotle also writes that metaphor involves 'intuitive perception of the similarity in dissimilars'. Here, he is suggesting that intuition provides us with a valuable means to knowledge, and furthermore, a knowledge that is not immediately obvious, but represents some deeper level of interpretation and understanding. In this sentence he presents us with the two aspects of metaphor that I want to develop in these three chapters; the heuristic, or sensemaking function of metaphor and the intuitive, or aesthetic function of metaphor. However, before exploring what functions metaphors carry out I want to look in more depth at how metaphor works.

Metaphor works by evoking the imagination. Metaphor works by highlighting certain aspects of shared experience while obscuring others. Metaphor both interprets *and* creates reality.

Pondy defines a *simple* metaphor as one in which 'the assertion, perhaps made indirectly or surreptitiously, that "A" is "B" where A and B belong manifestly to different categories' while an *extended* metaphor is 'two things or events identified over and over again in different ways or over time'. A myth is such an 'extended' metaphor because it represents 'a timeless pattern which explains the present and the past as well as the future...myth establishes an extended metaphorical relationship between events separated in time and space' (Pondy 1983: 159).

A metaphor then, is a proposition that there is a relationship between two ideas or concepts that are generally regarded belonging to different frames of reference. A metaphor can therefore be understood as a theory about that relationship and it includes a theory of similarity, that which is shared between the two concepts, and a theory of difference, that which is not shared. Metaphor 'makes us look at the world afresh but it often does so by challenging our notions of the similarity that exists between things; how alike they are; and in what ways, in fact, they are irreconcilably unlike' (Punter 2009: 10).

It is the irreconcilability, between that which is similar and that which is different, which creates a tension. Ricoeur identifies at least three different kinds of tensions within a metaphor. The first is the tension of rhetoric; between tenor and vehicle, focus and frame and principle and secondary subject. The next is the tension of interpretation; between two or more interpretations or between a literal interpretation and a metaphorical interpretation 'whose sense emerges through nonsense'. The third is tension of relatedness 'the tension in the relational function of the copula between identity and difference in the interplay of resemblance' (Ricoeur 2007: 292).

Ricoeur's first area of tension applies in those metaphors where there is a primary object whose meaning is being elucidated through the use of the descriptive, or secondary object. However, Punter notes that in many instances each of the two concepts in the metaphor work on each other, simultaneously influencing our understandings and interpretations of both. Kay (1991) suggests when a metaphor is used to express A in terms of B there may be at least four meanings being conveyed at the same time; that A is B, that A is not B, that there is a new understanding which is 'AB-ness' *and* that this new perception of AB-ness may open up new possibilities of meaning (this is Schon's identification of the *generative* capacity of metaphor). In this sense metaphors carry multiple meanings, and in so doing convey a sense of the provisional nature of reality.

Metaphors work through surprise; there has to be something about the juxtaposition of the two elements of the metaphor that makes us pause, that stops us in our tracks. For a metaphor to be productive, in the sense of producing new ways of thinking or new interpretations and understandings, the tension in the relationship between the two concepts and their fields of reference needs to be maintained. If the degree of difference between them is too great there is no new meaning created; if the distance is too small then we lose our awareness of the difference between the referential fields (Morgan 1980). Therefore, metaphors work through provoking a kind of disorientation, or cognitive dissonance (Jussim 1992, Lord 1992), a rupture in that which is taken for granted, through the juxtaposition, or insertion of the unexpected into the expected.

Deliberately provoking disorientation is, of course, a common strategy amongst humourists and also within the theatre, as, for example in the dramatic genre that Esslin (1961) described as the 'theatre of the absurd'. Absurdist playwrights such as Beckett, Albee, Pinter and Ionesco deliberately juxtapose the expected and the unexpected, such as the two characters in Beckett's *Endgame* who live in dustbins (Schwabenland 2009: 296).

I have also used metaphor as a means of provoking disorientation in teaching diversity management in order to challenge some of my students' use of traditional, and limiting stereotypes. In commenting on his experience of the module, one of my students wrote:

> ...*it* [the course] *makes the students think and reflect on issues discussed in class, ... This was <u>strange and weird</u> at first, especially when the topic is against one's ethics.* (student cited in Schwabenland 2009: 296 my emphasis)

This student's use of the phrase 'strange and weird' evokes his experience of disorientation, of a dissonance between his taken-for-granted assumptions about ethics and the ideas presented in the class. Perry (1999) suggested that the sense that a student makes of a disorientating encounter between themselves and the teacher 'will bear varying degrees of congruence and incongruence with the forms of expectancies the person brought with them to the experience' (Perry 1999: 46) and will determine whether the student will assimilate the new experience into an existing mental schema or create a new one. Just how great the incongruence is, writes Baxter-Magdola, 'depends partially on their original view of the world, partially on the other views they encounter and partially on the context in which the encounter takes place' (Baxter-Magdola 1992: 200). The uncomfortable feelings provoked by disorientation can cause one to retreat into oneself, rather than opening oneself up to new possibilities, however, Ahmed interestingly distinguishes between the experience of being 'being struck *by*' and 'being struck dumb' (Fisher cited by Ahmed 2004: 180 my emphasis). Ahmed relates shock to wonder and wonder, the 'strange and weird', as my student wrote, to learning that is embodied: 'the body opens as the world opens up before it...wonder is a passion that motivates the desire to keep looking' (Ahmed 2004: 180).

Likening metaphors to Escher paintings, Punter concludes that 'they can never reveal their own meanings because they are perennially on the point of turning into their own other' (Punter 2009: 82). The 'turn' into 'our own other' is located in the tension between the perception of self as other, which can be provoked by disrupting or dissonant experiences, and of other as self that Kohn (1990) describes as empathy, the ability to enter into the experience of the other but without becoming submerged into that other. The tension between these perceptions, the moment of the turn from self to other and other to self, is the copula of metaphor, the device that allows it to 'function in two referential fields at once' (Ricoeur 2007: 299).

Bruns (1992) writes that knowledge of the other is predicated on knowledge of self. Lakoff and Johnson (1980) also describe self understanding and mutual understanding as iterative processes, processes that are mediated by the metaphors we use to construct coherent narratives of our lives. Punter likens metaphors to dreams, in which we generate any number of strange and wonderful images that stand in a metaphorical relationship to some inner reality that is seeking expression. The similarity between metaphors and dream images leads him to suggest that we are not always in control of our metaphors. He writes:

> ...the subject who speaks is, in one sense, a puppet, at the mercy and under the authority of a different self within the self, an unconscious master [sic] who is speaking all the while, although we can perhaps attend to that other only in our dreams or on the analysts' couch. (Punter 2009: 77)

Here Punter also highlights another significant aspect of metaphor, namely that metaphors emerge out of our unconscious and are generally the product of associational patterns of thinking, which Bruns (1992) refers to as poetic logic. In the previous chapter I briefly alluded to the idea of an on-going 'quarrel between poetry and philosophy' which may have originated in a chapter in Plato's *Republic,* although it has also been suggested that Plato himself regarded it as a more ancient idea (Bruns 1992: 229, McInery undated). In a more contemporary interpretation Bronk, in his book on *The Romantic Economist,* criticises the 'continued widening of the dialectical schism between the rationalist and the romantic outlook' (Bronk 2009: 46). The distinction rests on the proposition that rational, or philosophical thinking proceeds via the 'primary laws of logic' (Milner 1989: 228) where 'one statement follows from the other...according to some principle of internal necessity' (Bruns 1992: 229). Romantic, or poetic logic, follows a more 'anarchic' trajectory (Bruns 1992) structured by association. Milner suggests that rational thinking works 'very well for managing the inanimate material environment' but is less helpful for understanding the inner world because it assumes that there is a rigid differentiation between subject and object. Poetic, or associational, logic can navigate this terrain more effectively since 'the point about a symbol is that is both itself and something else' (Milner 1989: 228).

Lehrer draws similar conclusions but from a very different starting point. In a review of current developments in the neurophysiology of insight, he suggests that there are links between the processes involved in insight and those of language comprehension 'such as the detection of literary themes and *the interpretations of metaphors*' (Lehrer 2008: 43 my emphasis). He notes that a leading cognitive neuroscientist, Mark Jung-Beerman:

> argues that these linguistic skills, like jokes, require the brain to make a series of distant and unprecedented connections. He cites studies showing that the cells in the right hemisphere are more 'broadly tuned' than cells in the left hemisphere, with longer branches and more dendritic spines. 'What this means is that neurons in the right hemisphere are collecting information from a larger area of cortical space'. (Jung-Beerman cited by Lehrer 2008: 43)

To summarise the argument so far: a metaphor represents a particular form of theorising about similarity and difference. The metaphor brings ideas or concepts together in such a way that there is a tension created between them that is irresolvable. The tension arises out of the juxtaposition of the usual and unusual in such a way that it promotes a certain feeling of surprise or shock that can disrupt taken for granted patterns of thinking. Metaphors, in common with dream imagery and poetic imagery emerge through association, a process that is less under conscious control than more rational forms of thinking but which draws on a wider range of experiences and impressions.

Having provided a brief overview about how metaphors work, in the following section I will go on to explore what metaphors do, drawing on a useful distinction that Petrie (1979) suggests between the heuristic and aesthetic functions of metaphor.

The heuristic function of metaphor: *Metaphor as theory*

Morgan (1986) argues that all theories are based on metaphors. All theories about organisations start from metaphors about what organisations are; 'metaphors that lead us to see and understand organisations in distinctive, yet partial ways...metaphor exerts a formative influence on science, on our language and on how we think' (Morgan 1986: 12–13). If we agree with Morgan, then our theories about how diversity should be managed within organisations must also be based on metaphors of what diversity is.

The proposition that metaphors are foundational to thought is based on the idea that 'experience is never directly of the world as it is but is always in part constituted by our modes of representation and understanding' (Petrie 1979: 440). In other words, we cannot make sense of anything without at least provisionally locating it into some frame of reference, or category that already exists within our imagination. Lakoff and Johnson point out that 'categorisation is primarily a means of comprehending the world' (Lakoff and Johnson 1980: 122). These frames of reference are themselves metaphors. In this sense, all thinking is metaphorical.

There are a number of implications that follow from this proposition. The first is that if metaphor 'works' by suggesting similarity between two frames of reference that have hitherto been regarded as dissimilar, there may be limitless numbers of such frameworks and a multiplicity of possible meanings. Therefore, any interpretation is limited and provisional.

For example, the chief executive cited in the previous chapter may indeed, at times, carry out her leadership role in a participatory way, as implied by her metaphor of stuffing envelopes. At other times she might be ruthless, autocratic, indecisive, vague, petty etc. This example serves to demonstrate the relevance of the theory of metaphor to diversity issues because it offers a way of understanding identity as itself a metaphor, one frame of reference amongst many which co-exist, overlap and conflict. Punter writes that metaphors 'are radically unstable; their meanings are always fluid, changing according to historical and cultural contexts, with the meanings trapped inside them constantly overflowing, refusing to be pinned down' (Punter 2009: 106).

Secondly, metaphor also alerts us to the provisional nature of interpretation precisely through the juxtaposition of the similar and dissimilar which forces us to take stock and 'see' that which we have hitherto taken for granted in a new light. Ricoeur suggests, in his words 'rather venturesomely' 'if metaphor belongs to an heuristic of thought, could we not imagine that the process that *disturbs and displaces* a certain logical order, a certain conceptual hierarchy, a certain classification scheme is the same as that from which all classification proceeds?' (Ricoeur 2007: 24 my emphasis).

Badrinath's (1996) analysis of the ways in which certain meanings come to inhere to particular categories challenges us to look more carefully at how these processes take place, and more specifically, how they can be inclusionary or exclusionary. He writes:

> Practically every branch of Western human knowledge is rooted in definitions. To define a thing is to set limits to it. One result of this process of definition is that whatever human material does not fit into those definitions is either denied, or somehow forced into those definitions. In Indian tradition the emphasis is not on definitions but on what is called *lakshana*. *Lakshana* are attributes. We need not the definition of truth but the *lakshana*, the attributes of truth. (Badrinath 1996: 158–159)

Lakoff and Johnson (1980) suggested that categories are not defined (or not *solely* defined) in terms of an agreed set of inherent properties but that those attributes that we add or subtract to the category (or what Ricoeur would term the 'frame of reference') are determined largely by our own experiences and further, primarily in terms of our interactions with others.

Lipner (1997) describes one of the ways in which meanings can become generalised so that what may have originated in the process of making sense of a specific experience may inhere to the wider framework of reference. He gives two examples; '"the cloth is burnt" when only a part of it is, and "the village is on fire" when only some of its huts are' (Lipner 1997: 305). This process of using a single, or partial example to stand for a larger group, called *synecdoche* is, of course, one of the dynamics at work in stereotyping whole groups of people according to the attributes of only a few (or even of one).

Shelley wrote that 'metaphorical language marks the before unapprehended relations of things and perpetuates their apprehension until words, which represent them, become, through time, signs for portions or classes of thoughts, instead of pictures of integral thoughts' (Shelley cited by Barfield 1999: 45). This pertains particularly to the perpetuating of stereotypes (such as woman as carer, or man as breadwinner) which are at their most potent when most taken for granted. The limitations of common metaphors for diversity more generally, such as mosaic (the idea that each separate piece is only valued if located in its rightful place) or the melting pot (that all differences must be submerged into one common identity) may be hidden not only in their day-to-day usage, but in their more foundational sensemaking functions unless they are made more explicit.

Therefore, it is the *awareness* of the provisional nature of metaphor, metaphor as signifier of *lakshana*, that is critical to working with diversity because it is only through that awareness that we can question the hitherto taken-for-granted, foundational metaphors that structure (and also limit) our thinking. An awareness of the limitation of metaphor in general forces us to acknowledge the limitations of all metaphors. Metaphor resists closure. And this is where metaphorical thinking has more radical potential because it is out of the awareness of the provisional nature of any one interpretation that there comes the possibility for transformation, for thinking anew.

Petrie (1979) began his analysis of this transformational aspect of metaphor by struggling with what initially appears to be an insoluble paradox: if experience can only be mediated through existing modes of representation and understanding, how can we learn something radically new that requires us to change these contexts of understanding? In other words, how do we create new frames of reference that allow us to make sense, rather than non-sense out of the metaphor? His suggestion is that metaphor enables us to cross 'the epistemological chasm between old knowledge and radically new knowledge by providing a *rational* bridge from the known to the radically unknown, from a given context of understanding to a changed context of understanding' (Petrie 1979: 440). Metaphor does this when it presents us with a theory that is simultaneously about similarity (the known context of understanding) and difference (a hitherto unknown context). And it facilitates this change of context, as noted before, through disruption (Schwabenland 2009), disturbance (Ricoeur 2007) and curiosity (Petrie 1979, Green 1979).

However, Sticht (1979) suggested that although metaphorical thought *may* lead to a radical shift in the conceptual schema this is not necessarily always the case. Metaphors also communicate meaning *within* a conceptual frame. For example, Sticht suggests that in the Bible, the purpose of the metaphor 'shepherd' for the Lord is to explain, rather than to disrupt.

> When teachers use metaphors as efficient tools of communication it is *not desirable* to produce excessive puzzlement in students. Rather the effective use of metaphor for effective communication requires the teachers to know that students possess the knowledge addressed in the metaphor. (Sticht 1979: 477 emphasis in the original)

Black (1979) draws a relevant distinction here between comparative and interactive metaphors in which comparative metaphors are those that exist within a similar mental schema, and may not necessarily promote radical learning, while interactive metaphors, or generative metaphors (Schon 1979) may *create* the similarity rather than express one that is already understood. Petrie also points out that a given metaphor might be comparative for the teacher but interactive for a student. The example he uses here is of a teacher using the metaphor of solar system to describe the atom, which, he argues, would be a comparative metaphor for the teacher who already understands an atom in this way, but interactive, or radical for the student because a new way of seeing has been generated (Petrie 1979: 443).

However, this distinction between metaphors that explain and those that promote transformations in conceptual schema is questionable. Although some metaphors may provoke more shock, or disruption than others, Sticht points out that 'the consideration of metaphor as a tool for thought...is concerned with the discovery of relationships between seemingly disparate domains and an exploration of the extent to which they can be related' (Sticht 1979: 479). Even in the Biblical example above, the metaphor of shepherd is not effective unless its explanatory power is based on generating some new insight. If the student's, or listener's pre-existing schema already contained an understanding of the divine as including shepherd-like qualities the metaphor would not produce any disruption at all.

Furthermore, Black suggests that the process of thinking metaphorically changes the understanding of *both* elements of the metaphor (suggesting that it is not only the understanding of the divine that is being altered by the metaphor of shepherd but also that of the shepherd by the metaphor of the divine). Black writes:

> ...the presence of the primary subject incites the hearer to select some of the secondary subject's properties...invites him [sic] to construct a parallel implication-complex that can fit the primary subject and...reciprocally induces change in the *secondary* subject (Black 1979: 29 my emphasis).

Even in the instances where the process of becoming aware allows foundational, or 'preconscious' (Schein 1991) metaphors to surface, although there may not be a change in the conceptual, sensemaking schema there must be a change in our relationship to it. Awareness renders the familiar strange.

For example, in a commentary about the module, one of my students wrote that the course:

>...entirely changed my view about disability. The reason behind this appeal is rooted back to my home country situation where disability is the synonym of negligence, exclusion from the society...from this course I have learned that people are not disabled but the view of society about disability makes disabled people disabled. The society needs to realise that disabled people can be converted to able people and be added to the mainstream of the society by removing the barriers which hinder them to access the society. (Cited in Schwabenland 2009: 302)

Here, the student has reframed her understanding of disability, the attributes that she would have previously included within this classification have been changed. The meanings of exclusion and negligence are no longer inherent in the category of disability. Sticht comments on the ways in which changing the meaning of metaphor changes ourselves:

>The meta-cognitive knowledge of how to manipulate ideas *explicitly* in metaphor so as to transform either one's own or another's knowledge into new knowledge makes metaphor a major tool for extending our capacities for analytical thought, while at the same time changing us as tool users. Though the types of changes produced by the use of metaphor as a tool for thought may not yet be fully understood, it can be argued by analogy that just as the repeated use of a hammer may strengthen the arm, the repeated use of metaphors may strengthen the powers of analysis and synthesis. Also, much as the telescope may produce knowledge that changes our basic assumptions about ourselves and the nature of our universe, the use of metaphors may...bring about basic changes in how we understand ourselves and the world around us. (Sticht 1979: 485 my emphasis)

To summarise: metaphors shape our thinking, they are foundational to thought. In this sense we cannot become metaphorical thinkers, we *are* metaphorical thinkers. The processes of theorising and sensemaking about our world are metaphorical. But developing our capacity to observe these processes as they occur helps us to increase our awareness of the provisional nature of our interpretations and the many possibilities of meaning. Metaphor is itself foundational to a relativist ontology of multiple theories and interpretations. The more we become aware of the ways in which we are creating our own meanings, and the more we begin to comprehend the ways in which these meanings can be empowering or constraining, the more opportunities we have to change them. And as we change our meanings we change ourselves. Ricoeur writes that 'there is no self understanding that is not mediated by signs, symbols and texts; in the last resort understanding coincides with the interpretation given to these mediatory terms' (Ricoeur 1991a: 15).

One potential area of difficulty however, is that we do not always *want* to have our assumptions disrupted. Esslin writes that the absurdist genre of theatre developed out of a 'tragic sense of loss at the disappearance of ultimate certainties' (Esslin 1961: 291). Perry, who was writing in an educational context, suggested that there is a *hierarchy* of developmental stages in which a student moves from certainty and the unquestioning acceptance of authority towards a more relativist positioning, implicit in the notion of growth through the levels. He located 'the loss of the Absolute' in the middle of his developmental stages in which the student moves beyond the assimilation of new information into their existing frameworks of reference and towards the creation of new, mental schema:

> ...the point of critical division between 'belief' and the possibility of 'faith'. Belief requires no investment by the person. To become faith it must first be doubted.... If one later commits oneself to a faith in an Absolute *there is a criterion which reveals that this Commitment has been made in the context of a relativistic world.* This criterion is one's attitude towards other people with a belief or a faith in a different Absolute. They cannot appear as alien, as other than human: one must, however paradoxically, respect them. In one sense they 'must' be wrong, but in another sense no more so than oneself. (Perry 1999: 146 emphasis in the original)

Perry himself accepted that there was a degree of cultural hegemony about his assumptions and for many of us the rupture with certainty and the emphasis on relativity may require too great an accommodation. In that case this may not be perceived as liberating but as enforced acculturation into those assumptions that are privileged within the environment in which the student/manager is operating (Schwabenland 2009: 299). Another of my students commented:

In Nigeria you are just supposed to read and say what you have read. If you put forward any ideas of your own you are criticised for being too arrogant.

Who are you to know more than the teacher? But here it is exactly the opposite. (cited in Schwabenland 2009: 298)

These processes of sensemaking are clearly of central importance to our understanding of diversity. If our understanding of the other is mediated through our understanding of ourselves and shaped through previous interactions we need to develop greater awareness and understanding of this process of metaphorical sensemaking. Otherwise there is little possibility of change. But change can be uncomfortable and disruption can be frightening. It is through its aesthetic function that metaphor can offer a way through these difficulties.

The aesthetic function of metaphor: *Metaphor as art*

Amongst the various ways in which the field of organisation studies has been enlarged and enriched over the last few years is through the application of insights from other disciplines, including that of aesthetics. Aesthetics offers us a way into elucidating aspects of human motivation and of the judgements that we make about organisational activity. Strati, in his book on *Organization and Aesthetics* (1999) charts some of the developments of this approach and, citing Rusted (1987), he distinguishes at least three different ways in which aesthetics can be helpful; firstly, in using analogies from the arts to develop greater understanding of organisational processes (Vaill's 1989 work on managing as a performing art is an early example); secondly, through applying aesthetics to explore the idea of beauty within organisations and thirdly, by looking at the ways in which ideas about the aesthetics of organising are negotiated in practice (Strati 1999: 6). Another application is to the study of creativity, and its cousins, innovation and entrepreneurship within organisational settings. Aesthetics also helps us to understand some of the cultural aspects of organising and in particular, the meanings attached to organisational artefacts (Schein 1991). As an example of this, Strati discusses the multiple meanings that come to accrue around the object of the chair in an organisational context.

If aesthetics has relevance to the understanding of organisational processes more generally, how does it help us in enhancing our understanding of the managing of diversity? I want to suggest that exploring the aesthetic function of metaphor can be helpful in two ways; firstly, through the ways in which the aesthetic appreciation of the metaphor can promote the experience of empathy and secondly, by establishing an aesthetics *of* diversity. While the cognitive function of metaphor creates the opportunity for changes in the conceptual frameworks used in sensemaking, the aesthetic function of metaphor can facilitate a shift in the *emotional* frameworks. Furthermore, a greater appreciation of the aesthetics of diversity, as they are negotiated in an organisational context, can help us to achieve greater understanding of the ways in which different meanings of diversity come to be created and maintained.

Aesthetics and emotional engagement

Good poetry speaks to our hearts as well as to our minds. Aesthetic imagination engages us emotionally. Petrie emphasises the capacity of metaphor to appeal to our emotions when he says that 'metaphor enables one to transfer learning from what is well known to what is less well-known in a *vivid* and memorable way' (Petrie 1979: 439 my emphasis). It was the immediacy of the emotional experience that led the poet Keats to conclude that 'what the imagination seizes as beauty must be truth' (Keats 1817, reprinted 2009: 489). Keats believed that philosophical logic 'imposes an artificial order and arrangement... which will not arrive at truth because it is consciously deliberative in its intent' (Bate 1939: 16) whereas imagination 'apprehends more thoroughly through minute associations...which the intuition will feel' and is to be 'trusted above reason because it is not an abstraction' (Keats cited by Bate 1939: 22–23). Owen Barfield writes similarly:

> When I try to describe in more detail than by the phrase 'aesthetic imagination' what experience it is to which, at some time or other I have been led...I feel myself obliged to define it as a 'felt change of consciousness'. (Barfield 1999: 20)

Nussbaum believes that it is through our empathetic imagination that we can 'understand the emotions and wishes and desires' (Nussbaum 2002: 299) of people in different positions to ourselves and 'which can make other people's lives more than distant abstractions' (Nussbaum 2004: 1). Keats called this experience the 'momentary identification of the imagination with its object' (Bate 1939: 25).

  D'Addelfio suggests that our capacity to experience empathy, which he calls 'intelligent feeling' (D'Addelfio 2006: 8) can be deliberately nurtured through narrative and poetry. He further suggests, as does Keats, that empathy 'turns' on recognition. Walker describes recognition as a capability; citing Charles Taylor she writes that 'processes of learning and identity formation are "intrinsically connected to the processes of recognition"' (Walker 2006: 73). Here again is the idea that knowledge of self and knowledge of other are intertwined. Illeris also suggests that recognition is an intrinsic element of reflexivity, the recognition of similarity that is 'mirrored in the self' (Illeris 2002: 95). D'Addelfio writes that; 'speaking about empathy as a pedagogical category...means speaking about the fundamental role of "recognition" – i.e. of being recognised by someone else – for the discovering, the gain and the growing of freedom' (D'Addelfio 2006: 11). But while Walker, Illeris and D'Addelfio all link empathy with recognition they seem to be deploying the concept in different ways; the recognition of the self in others and the recognition of the self *by* others: recognition as it is experienced by the *receiver.*

Walker and D'Addefino are writing in support of the capabilities approach which was developed originally by Amartya Sen and Martha Nussbaum out of a concern for social justice. Initially focussed on development economics (drawing on Sen's work on the importance of incorporating choice and ethics into indices of poverty and Nussbaum's concerns with women's empowerment), central to the capabilities approach is the identification of those that are needed to live well in a plural society. This approach is well suited to diversity for two reasons; firstly, it explicitly sets out to 'explore the relationships between equality, inclusion and human development' and to identify those capabilities which can 'overcome wider socio-economic and political constraints'.[2] Secondly, as has been mentioned before, the capabilities approach pays due regard to the importance of emotions, and in particular, to empathy. For example, Walker links recognition with three of Nussbaum's ten, central capabilities: those of practical reason (through the development of a person's 'own views about what would be for them a good life'), affiliation (through the importance of social learning and social networks) and the ability to discern, 'mobilized through imagination and emotions, and the 'values of empathy and mutual recognition, compassion and respect' (Walker 2006: 98–99).

However, recognition is necessarily limited; there is always a surplus of meaning, that which is *not* recognised. Subramanyan (1994) points out that 'all artists know that their perceptions of the world do not strictly conform to the camera image...these differences result from the limitations of the perceptual mechanism, cultural predispositions and personal choices... The same set of facts can produce many alternative configurations, each with its own aura of truth' (Subramanyan 1994: 6, 10).

> …when you suddenly come upon an unfamiliar object the lamp of perception flares: you pay closer attention to object illusion and your interpretive apparatus. You come home in the evening from your place of work – is that a furry floor-rug near the bookshelf? No, dear no! It is your dog sprawled out and snoozing. You feel relieved: but realise that a dog can look like a rug…. Now what is challenging in an art object is not its verisimilitude – i.e. the closeness of correspondence of two visual facts or images – but the elusive possibilities that float in the magnetic distance between. (Subramanyan 1994: 11)

This idea of a surplus of meaning reminds us again that the ways in which we interpret our perceptions can only ever be provisional and should not be fixed either in our own minds or in others. Furthermore, we also need to remember that empathy is not always an unlimited good. Walker cites Papastephanou's caution against an 'uncritical kind of empathy which…claims to "know" how it feels to be handicapped, or working class or black, or poor and so on' (Walker 2006: 71). It is the need to avoid that kind of uncritical empathy that Kohn (1990) suggested required the ability to enter into the experience of the other without becoming *submerged* into that other. Nussbaum also notes that we should always 'bring ourselves and our own judgement to the encounter with another' (Nussbaum 2002: 299). The tension that metaphor creates between experiencing the other as self and self as other resides in the 'magnetic distance between' these perceptions.

Ricoeur writes that *'distanciation…*is contemporaneous with the experience of belonging that is opened or recovered by poetic discourse' (Ricoeur 2007: 370 emphasis in the original):

> What is given to thought in this way by the 'tensional' truth of poetry is the most primordial, most hidden dialectic – the dialectic that reigns between the experience of belonging as a whole and the power of distanciation that opens up the space of speculative thought (Ricoeur 2007: 371).

It is through poetry that the aesthetic function of metaphor is realised, and through poetry we are able to enter into the emotional life of another while maintaining an awareness of our distance from it. Ricoeur is proposing that the capacity to think metaphorically is not only of critical importance if we are to live well in a diverse society; he is also suggesting that a diverse society is essential if we are to 'think' well. The aesthetic function of metaphor in promoting the emotional experience of empathy with another person whilst also allowing us to maintain a sense of distance is clearly relevant to diversity in that it gives us an emotional insight into the other as well as a cognitive insight. But is it possible to go beyond this to conceptualise an aesthetics *of* diversity?

The aesthetics *of* diversity

Strati's (1999) book on the aesthetics of organising devotes a whole chapter to a discussion of the beautiful in an organisational context. He gives several examples from his interviews in which people describe their organisation as beautiful. He also noted that such instances occurred infrequently although it is impossible to tell whether this is because people are more likely to think of their organisations as ugly, or because we are not accustomed to consciously deploying aesthetic judgements in conceptualising organisations. There is some research that suggests that people do invoke artistic analogies at work such as Vaill's (1989) work on management as an art form and my own work on creativity in voluntary organisations in the UK. Some examples of phrases that my interviewees used that directly drew on analogies with the arts were phrases such as 'drawing strategy' and 'dancing a meeting'. One very interesting example concerned an organisational re-structuring:

> *So having freed up the organisation...without tight controls allowed something to emerge that has a sunshine about it, you know, a sort of Bonnard type image which wouldn't have happened if we had been more dour about it.* (Voluntary sector chief executive cited in Schwabenland 2006a: 113)

In all of my examples and also in the two that Strati cites, the managers were the founders of their organisations and so for them, the representation of the organisation as a work of art is perhaps not so surprising. But Strati also observed that his respondents applied the analogy in very different ways. One respondent's conception of beauty was derived from the Pythagorean ideal of harmony while the second respondent talked about how it was the qualities of the organisation that aroused in him an experience of beauty; joy, loyalty and a need to be cherished.

How do these different understandings of beauty in an organisational context apply to diversity? In Barfield's essays on 'poetic diction' he suggests that there is an 'aesthetic value of the unfamiliar'. The example he gives is that of learning a foreign language where:

> ...aesthetic pleasure arises from the contemplation of quite ordinary expressions couched in a foreign idiom. It is important, then, to note that this is not, in so far as it is aesthetic, the pleasure of comparing different ways of saying the same thing, but the pleasure of realising the *slightly different thing that is said*... The element of strangeness in beauty...arises from contact with a different kind of *consciousness* from our own, different yet not so remote that we cannot partly share it...strangeness, in fact, arouses wonder when we do not understand, aesthetic imagination when we do' (Barfield 1999: 197–198 emphasis in the original).

Barfield's description of aesthetic pleasure also comes from the *experience* of beauty, as did the second of Strati's respondents, rather than from an organisational embodiment of beauty.

In her book on India Nussbaum writes of the 'teeming and beautiful chaos of an Indian city' (Nussbaum 2007: 334). In this example she seems to be suggesting that there is an intrinsic beauty in diversity. However, when she quotes from Walt Whitman's poem about the United States she is making a further link between notions of beauty and *equality*:

> Here the flowing trains, here the crowds, equality, diversity the soul loves.[3]

Shelley, in his essay *A Defence of Poetry*, famously called poets the 'unacknowledged legislators of the world' (Shelley cited in Reiman and Powers 1977: 508), and so did Whiman in the following lines:

> For the great Idea, the idea of perfect and free individuals,
> For that the bard walks in advance, leader of leaders.
>
> For the great Idea,
> That, O my brethren, that is the mission of poets.[4]

The notion of poet as 'prophet and social activist' is also one that Blake would recognise. Writing in *The Guardian*, Eagleton suggests that 'politics today is largely a question of management and administration. Blake, by contrast, viewed the political as inseparable from art, ethics, sexuality and the imagination'.[5] Seamus Heaney, Mahmoud Darwish and Adrienne Rich are more recent examples of poets who have explored the connections between poetry and social change. In his essay *The Redress of Poetry* Heaney writes that poetry 'offers a response to reality which has a liberating and verifying effect on the individual spirit' (Heaney 1996: 2), for the poet 'the movement [within the writing process] is from delight to wisdom' (Heaney 1996: 5).

The political philosopher Elaine Scarry also argues that beauty can promote justice, that 'beauty is a call on us to create something better' (Scarry 1999[6]). Her argument is interesting and also provocative. Firstly, she suggests that the apprehension of beauty is not only 'life-restoring' for the beholder but that the object or person perceived as beautiful is enriched by that perception. Beauty is 'a compact, or contract between the beautiful being (a person or thing) and the perceiver...each "welcomes" the other' (Scarry 2006: 90).

Secondly, she explores the etymological connections between the notions of fairness as beauty[7] and fairness as justice, which turn on the concept of symmetry. She proposes that 'beautiful things give rise to the notion of distribution...to fairness not just in the sense of loveliness of aspect but in the sense of a symmetry of everyone's relation to each other' (Scarry 2006: 95).[8]

Thirdly, she suggests that beauty promotes peaceful and equitable relations amongst people, through the desire to protect that which is regarded as beautiful.

> ...it's not just that beauty is neutral with respect to justice. Beauty is, actually, very much leading us to justice. So by this account, it would be my vision of things that we are able to create a world in which caring about beauty also leads to a diminution of injury...the word injury and the word injustice are the same word (Scarry 1999: reference op cit).

Scarry's argument suggests that beauty is relevant to the quest for a more just and equal society. But it is in her exploration of how the appreciation of beauty becomes more than an abstraction that there is an overlap with the idea of metaphor. She argues that 'when we see something beautiful we undergo a radical decentring' (Scarry 2006: 111). She cites Simone Weill in proposing that beauty 'requires us to give up our imaginary position as the centre' (Scarry 2006: 111), a process that Iris Murdoch described as 'unselfing'. Murdoch also suggested that 'the appreciation of beauty' is 'an entry into the good life since it *is* the checking of selfishness in the interests of seeing the real' (Murdoch 1970: 65). Scarry describes this 'as though one has ceased to become the hero or heroine of one's own story' (Scarry 2006: 113). In this experience of 'unselfing' one has begun to be able to perceive the self as other and the other as self.

Scarry's argument is appealing in many ways. But there are two possible difficulties with it. The first is that when Scarry links beauty, symmetry and justice she is drawing on a very specific idea of the beautiful, and here she is echoing Strati's first respondent whose conception of beauty was equated with order and harmony. But can we talk about beauty in such universalistic terms or do different cultures create different notions of what constitutes the beautiful? Is Scarry's proposition not at odds with the very idea of diversity? It is interesting that Scarry describes beauty in terms of fairness, order, and symmetry while Nussbaum suggests that chaos and disorder may also be beautiful.

A second problem is that although it may be that the appreciation of beauty *can* lead to a desire for justice it is not necessarily the case that it always does. There are too many examples of cruel and ruthless dictators who were great connoisseurs of the arts – Hitler's appreciation of Wagner, Shahjehan's (alleged) order that the builders of the Taj Mahal be blinded so that they could not appreciate its (symmetrical) beauty are only two such examples.

However, perhaps what we can take from these arguments is firstly, that while beauty, diversity and equality may not *always* be linked they *sometimes* are. Can we then determine what factors may influence that process? Secondly, even if beauty may not always lead to equality there is an aesthetic dimension to diversity and to diversity management that warrants further investigation. If cultures influence the aesthetic judgements the individuals within them make, then it may be fruitful to attend to the processes by which these judgements are negotiated, as well as to the content of these meanings as they inhere to particular organisational artefacts and symbolic devices such as the practices and rituals that surround the implementation of diversity policies.

Conclusions

'A good metaphor' writes Geary, 'like a bolt of lightening, provides a sudden flash of insight, a glimpse of illuminated ground on which experiments can be made. Things look strange when lit by lightening, but it is that very strangeness that enables us to see them differently' (Geary 2011: 207). Morgan writes that effective leaders and managers 'have a capacity to remain open and flexible, suspending immediate judgements whenever possible, until a more comprehensive view of the situation emerges' (Morgan 1986: 13). In this chapter I have argued that metaphor promotes just this flexibility. Metaphor does this by reminding us that our judgements are always provisional. Just as there is no limit to the metaphorical possibilities for framing a situation, so there is also no limit to the number of possible interpretations.

I have also sketched out some of the ways in which metaphor is *specifically* relevant to the managing of diversity. Managing diversity is itself a metaphorical process insofar as it requires us to engage in the tension field between similarity and difference. The specificities those similarities and differences are illuminated by the metaphor and can then, as Geary notes, 'be experimented with', accepted or discarded. Metaphor brings us into an encounter with ourselves as an other and with the other as ourselves. Furthermore, as metaphorical thinking proceeds through association, it widens the range of possible interpretations that are available to us. This is the cognitive, or heuristic function of metaphor.

But metaphor also has an aesthetic function. Abbs suggests that the aesthetic 'is a mode of intelligence working not through concepts but through precepts, the structural elements of sensory experience and that the arts are the symbolic forms for its disciplined elaboration and development' (Abbs 1996: 47). Abbs believes that we are aesthetic beings long before becoming rational beings – our earliest impressions and sensemaking activities are mediated through sensation. Metaphor, in its aesthetic capacity draws us from sensation to sensibility. Furthermore, by provoking an experience of empathy metaphor 'unselfs' us, reducing the distance between self and other.

I have also described some of the arguments that are made for the attribution of a connection between poetry and social justice (and I will return to these in more detail in the concluding chapter). These arguments also draw on both the cognitive capacity of metaphor (in its evocation of an association between beauty and fairness) and the aesthetic function (through the emotional, and transcendental experience of beauty).

Abbs cites comments that Joseph Conrad made in a preface to a collection of short stories:

> My task which I am trying to achieve is, by the power of the written word, to make you hear, to make you feel, to make you see. That – and no more, and it is everything. If I succeed, you shall find there according to your deserts; encouragement, consolation, fear, charm – all you

demand – and, perhaps, also that glimpse of truth for which you have forgotten to ask. (Conrad cited in Abbs 1996: 50)

Conrad's truth is Keats' truth, the truth that is apprehended through beauty.

I hope that I have succeeded in making a strong case for the importance of metaphorical imagination in helping us to live well (by which I mean living justly) in a diverse society. But are there hidden dangers lurking in metaphors? If metaphors are powerful that power is not always necessarily benign. All metaphors are limited, that is the limitation of metaphor. Although metaphor *can* alert us to the provisional nature of sensemaking it can also *obscure* that awareness. Metaphor can produce a 'one-sided insight. In highlighting certain interpretations it tends to force others into a background role' (Morgan 1986: 13). Geary (2011) notes that shortly after taking office the Obama administration decided to stop using the metaphors of a 'war on terror' and a 'war on drugs' because evoking battle imagery was seen as counterproductive.

Taras (2007) points out that in their heuristic function metaphors can not only promote new insights through shifts in conceptual frames, they can also constrict thinking by creating 'a cognitive straitjacket' (Taras 2007: 56). Metaphors can be 'misleading' and their influence can be 'perverse'. This is obviously of relevance to the perpetuation of negative stereotypes about groups of people, one of the most ubiquitous ways in which discrimination proceeds.

Petrie (1979) worries that metaphor encourages 'sloppy' thought rather than analytical rigour. However, if we regard a metaphor as the product of associational thinking this argument falls. A metaphor suggests that two entities or ideas have certain similarities while also retaining other, distinctive features. The various stages of argumentation that set out the nature of these similarities and why the speaker believes they exist, may generally be implicit rather than explicit, but are nonetheless inherent in the metaphor. Otherwise the metaphor would have no meaning. What is distinctive, however, is the way in which the theory is created. Metaphorical theory does not follow a linear trajectory; it is associative, multi-dimensional, sometimes chaotic. This is what Bruns refers to in describing poetic logic as 'anarchic' and 'subversive' (Bruns 1992: 229). And as a metaphorical theory is always a provisional theory the door is always open for alternative conceptualisations to be made.

Sticht identifies another danger, particularly in the context of education or training. Metaphors 'like other more or less "context-bound" figures of speech run the risk of leading to misunderstanding, because a large number of readers [sic] may not share the required experiences for receiving the large chunks of information to be transferred by the metaphor' (Sticht 1979: 478). This is an important point, especially for a teacher or trainer working in a multi-cultural setting. Taras also suggests that metaphors can perpetuate binary thinking resulting in narrowing, rather than widening conceptual frameworks 'excludin[ing] the possibility of a middle ground by setting lines of boundaries' (Taras 2007: 56). Punter goes even further in pointing out that there are power relationships embedded in the choices and interpretations of metaphor. He gives as an example the African writer Chinua Achebe's novel *Things Fall Apart*. The novel's title is a reference to a quotation form a poem by Yeats: 'things fall apart; the centre cannot hold' (Yeats 1965 cited in Punter 2009: 117). But Achebe's intention is to re-present the metaphor of the 'centre' within a postcolonial perspective, in which it is 'perceived, if not as a malignant force, then at the very least as responsible for the very social, political and cultural problems now being encountered in Africa' (Punter 2009: 117). (Dipesh Chakrabarty, of course, makes a similar point when he uses the metaphor of the 'province' in his book *Provincializing Europe* to disrupt Eurocentric notions of 'centre'.)

These two examples demonstrate clearly that the similarities and differences that different people perceive within the same metaphor, may themselves differ significantly. The metaphor of the 'centre' means very different things to Yeats and Achebe. Geary cites an experiment conducted in the 1980s when a fictitious person, one 'Donald Leavis' was invented and presented to participants as 'the George Wallace of Northern Ireland'. The participants all concluded that Donald Leavis was a conservative politician with bigoted views. They were much less likely to suggest that Leavis might have been disabled or had been married several times, although both of these characteristics were also true of George Wallace (Geary 2011: 147). They made choices as to which similarities and differences were salient to them – different participants might have made different choices.

A final challenge is that if all language is metaphor (Punter 2009) then in some ways it is a non-sequitur to say that metaphorical thinking is critical to working with diversity – there is no alternative to metaphorical thinking, we cannot make a decision to stop thinking metaphorically. But it is the development of *awareness* of ourselves as metaphorical thinkers that remains critically relevant, because it is only when we become aware of our metaphors that they can be interrogated. It is out of our apprehension of them as provisional sensemaking devices that new possibilities emerge.

Our awareness of the fluidity of interpretation also needs to be applied to the distinction between the heuristic and aesthetic function of metaphor. Poetry, as described by Barfield, Scarry and Murdoch, has a heuristic function but it fulfils it sensually, by evoking delight. If one of the values of metaphorical thinking is that it defies closure and resists either/or duality then thinking about metaphorical thinking should not fall into the same trap. However, with that cautionary note, I will continue to make use of this distinction, as a sensemaking device, in the next two chapters, in order to explore some of the practical applications of these functions of metaphor to managing diversity. In the next chapter I will develop the notion of metaphor as theory to demonstrate how attempts to encourage critical reflection on the metaphors that structure our thinking about diversity in organisations can allow previously unquestioned and taken-for-granted assumptions to be explored. In the subsequent chapter I will discuss ways in which the aesthetic function of metaphor can lead to transformations in those very preconceptions about ourselves and others.

3
Fireworks and Football Crowds: Metaphor as Theory

Diversity is like a patchwork quilt which is made up of many intricate stitches, fabrics and shapes that end up forming the quilt. You need the individual parts but you also need the imagination, the thinking process of how you are going to do it and the skill. You need to think about how the individual pieces fit together, you need to look at the different colours, tones and textures; you have to imagine what it might look like in different ways, you may need to play around with the pieces before settling on what you think you want to do. However, you leave yourself some room just because you know that while you are doing the patchwork [you] might find something else that might be better. Hence, you have some flexibility....[1]

Introduction

McIntosh (2010) suggests metaphors communicate in at least three, distinct ways: firstly, metaphors can express ideas which are hard to convey using more literal language, secondly, to present complex information compactly in a way that 'captures the richness' succinctly, and thirdly, to 'transmit some sense of the vividness of an experience' (McIntosh 2010: 119–120). The metaphor of the patchwork quilt, as described by my student above, demonstrates all three. The metaphor itself is not an unusual one. In 1997 Prasad and Mills commented on the way in which diversity was 'celebrated' in textbooks on human resource management and organisational behaviour 'with the help of evocative metaphors such as the melting pot, the patchwork quilt, the multi-coloured or cultural mosaic and the rainbow' (Prasad and Mills 1997: 4). But the detail provided in this example and the portrayal of the imaginative processes of the quilt maker's art function as a rich, complex and very vivid description of managing diversity.

The purpose of this chapter is to explore the heuristic function of metaphor, metaphor as theory. The chapter is primarily illustrated with examples of metaphors that management students have used, such as the patchwork quilt above, to capture a sense of what diversity means to them and to analyse some of the assumptions that underpin these meanings. Much of the data that I use, throughout this chapter and the next, comes from notes I have taken about a series of exercises I developed to encourage students' capacity for metaphorical thinking. Others come from students' comments, both during the exercises and in reflective reports that they wrote at the end of the semester.

To develop our understanding about the ways in which metaphors structure our thinking and expose, or surface underlying preconceptions about people, practice and organisations, I am drawing on Schon's early work (1979) on 'generative' metaphors and on the application of metaphor to theorising about organisational processes initiated by Morgan (1986) and developed by many others since (McIntosh 2010, Kostera 2008, Tsoukas 2006, Grant et al 1998, Mangham and Overington 1987). My aim is to use metaphor as a means of uncovering, or bringing to light, some of the theories-in-use my students held about the meaning of diversity more generally, and of diversity management in particular. In so doing I am using metaphor as a methodology as well as a heuristic; metaphor is both the means in which I encourage students to give symbolic form to their perhaps hitherto unrecognised, or unknown conceptualisations of diversity, and metaphor is *also* the symbolic expression itself which is then open to multiple interpretations, both by my students and myself. The process of identifying these structuring metaphors is that of praxis, in which the action of thinking, and the theory that both creates and is created by that action are brought together into consciousness.

When I first came across the work of Argyris and Schon (1978) I was particularly fascinated by their distinction between espoused theories and theories-in-use. Espoused theories are those that managers use to describe their practice while theories-in-use are those that influence what managers *actually* do, and are founded on beliefs, which may reside at a largely unconscious level. Lawrence describes such unconscious beliefs as the 'unthought known' (Lawrence 2000: 11).

Ricoeur writes that 'what is at stake in a metaphorical utterance…is the appearance of kinship where ordinary vision does not perceive any relationship…it is a calculated error which brings together things that do not go together and by means of this apparent misunderstanding it causes a new *hitherto unnoticed* relation of meaning to spring up between the terms that previous systems of classification had ignored or not allowed (Ricoeur 2007: 51 my emphasis). It is Ricoeur's suggestion that metaphors allow for the emergence of the 'hitherto unnoticed' that makes the link between metaphor and Argyris and Schon's concept of the 'theory-in-use'.

Gibbs suggests that metaphors function as heuristics at 'all levels of understanding (comprehension, recognition, interpretation and appreciation)'. The study of metaphor must include 'not only how metaphor creates new modes of conceptual understanding but also how it exploits pre-existing metaphorical ways of understanding experiences that are a fundamental part of the poetic mind' (Gibbs 1994: 264).

But can these 'unthought knowns', or 're-existing metaphorical' dispositions actually be regarded as theories? Cazal and Inns (1998) present a number of critiques to the idea of metaphor as theory. They point out, quite rightly, that the metaphors that Morgan (1986) identified as the structuring assumptions about the nature of organisations lead to any number of different theoretical developments; for example, Morgan suggests that the organisation-as-organism meta-metaphor underpins such different developments as population ecology and human relations, and they conclude that metaphors may *promote* theorising but do not do that work themselves. Cazal and Inns prefer to attribute the lesser powers of representation and conceptualisation to metaphor. They write that 'such a weak conception of theory is obvious with the puzzle metaphor used by Morgan: in this instance knowledge and even theory would simply be the juxtaposition of various components' (Cazal and Inns 1998: 182). But their argument seems to me to be missing the point. It is in that very act of juxtaposing ideas that a (perhaps very small and embryonic) theory is generated. The 'theory' represented in the metaphor of organisation-as-organism is that there are aspects of similarity as well as difference that can be discerned when comparing organisations to organisms. That those aspects can, in turn, generate a wide range of new theories, some conflicting, does not invalidate the originating metaphor as itself, a theory. It does, however, raise the issue of how metaphors are to be interpreted. If interpretation is regarded metaphorically as association, it must follow the logic of the poetic mind.

In this chapter I am concerned with surfacing my students' 'pre-existing' understandings of diversity as they are expressed metaphorically. In analysing these metaphors there are, therefore, a number of different perspectives and levels of communication to be considered.

Firstly, there are the interpretations and associations that students made to their own metaphors. The quotation that I used at the beginning of this chapter in which one student likened diversity to a patchwork quilt is one of these. Some of these interpretations I recorded in note form during the discussions in the seminars, others came from students' reflective reports and as such, could be regarded as the products of reflection on reflection.

Secondly, there were interpretations that emerged in discussion, as one person's metaphor sparked off another's and as students responded to each other. These are more collective interpretations, the beginnings of the creating of a cultural repository for the group. Thirdly there are my own associations and interpretations, mainly developed in writing, after the seminars.

In the following three sections I will describe some of the provisional and multi-faceted (Kay 1991) meanings, or theories about diversity that emerge from these students' metaphors. Some of the metaphors describe the students' growing awareness about the ways in which metaphors structure their own thinking, and these, along with a brief presentation of the metaphors that students used to conceptualise the relationship between the individual and the organisation, are the focus of the next section. Following that I go on to analyse metaphors about *managing* diversity. In the subsequent section I present metaphors that offer conceptualisations of the relationship between the individual and the wider society. Many of these metaphors represent understanding of diversity as relatively unproblematic but in others a 'shadow side' of diversity management is more strongly discernable. Where the students themselves offered interpretations of these metaphors I have indicated this; the other interpretations are mine.

Metaphors of the relationship between the individual and the group

> *Each of these* [sessions] *started with an exercise which, whilst being enjoyable also challenged my beliefs and personally held stereotypes.*

The exercises referred to in this quotation were designed primarily to engage students' 'active imagination'. This is a term coined by Jung (cited by McIntosh 2010) to describe a process of engaging with our subconscious thinking, primarily through developing our awareness of the thoughts that are there and that are often only available to us in symbolic form. Samuels describes this process as a 'temporary suspension of ego control, a "dropping down" into the unconscious and a careful notation of what one finds, whether by reflection or by some kind of artistic expression' (Samuels 2008: 6). Once the discovered thought has been given form it is then available for reflection. In this section I want to describe each of these stages in more detail and then follow that discussion with a presentation of some specific metaphorical representations of the relationship between the individual and the group.

The first step in engaging the active imagination is to find a way to circumvent, or step aside from the ego, in order to allow the awareness of a different way of thinking to emerge. This requires us to temporarily suspend judgement. McIntosh (2010) notes that the ego may put up some resistance to being sidelined. Marion Milner, the psychoanalyst and diarist, wrote an account of her experiments in following the journey of her own thoughts. She cited Stebbing:

> ...the opposite of thinking clearly is being muddled. To be conscious of being muddled is a horrible experience. To avoid it we may even be tempted to shut our minds and swallow a belief, ready made, from some expert authority. (Stebbing cited by Milner 1986: 232)

However, the resistance and the muddle are necessary corollaries of allowing ourselves to be open to new ways of thinking. Milner again: 'it will mean walking in a fog for a bit but it's the only way which is not a presumption, forcing the self into a theory' (Milner 1999: 87). One of my students wrote:

However much I had thought that I wanted to avoid stereotypical thinking at all costs – discussions and the teaching material used got the underlying assumptions out in the open nevertheless.

The next step in the process is sometimes described as 'letting things happen' (Stevens in McIntosh 2010: 74). Milner likens this experience to that of a farmer, waiting for the 'first shoots to reach the daylight' (Milner 1989: 163) and Keats described it as 'negative capability' 'when man [sic] is capable of being in uncertainties, mysteries, doubts, without any irritable reaching after fact & reason'.[2] Milner writes of 'an internal gesture of submission' (Milner 1986: 207), 'a feeling of great stillness and austerity' where her mind no longer was 'grabbing after pleasures like a burrowing mole as [in] blind reverie' instead 'it hung suspended and watchful like a hovering kestral' (Milner 1986: 50).

I was able to scratch below the surface and pay attention to what and how statements are being relayed. Not to mention whose views are pushed under the carpet but how easily it [the media] can change how people think.

The third stage of engaging the active imagination requires reflection. Milner firmly believed that 'when you give your mind the reins and let it rove freely there is no such thing as irrelevance, so far as the problems of the mind are concerned what ever thought that pops up is in some way important, however far fetched it may appear' (Milner 1986: xxi). However, she was sometimes intrigued and bemused as to why some things aroused in her 'deep echoes of importance' while others 'did not mean anything to me at all' (Milner 1986: 48).

Mezirow writes that it is the 'critical reflection on their experiences, which in turn leads to a perspective transformation' (Mezirow 1991: 167 cited by Imel 1998: no page). However, Illeris makes a distinction between reflection and reflexivity, commenting that reflection, in the sense of 'after thought' does not necessarily disrupt our underlying cognitive structures. It is through reflexivity, he suggests, that there is more potential for transformation,; in which 'an experience or comprehension of something is mirrored in the self of the learner...its significance for the self is in focus and the experience is evaluated with personal identity as a yardstick' (Illeris 2002: 46).

> ...what is special about reflexivity is that it involves the organisation of the self...[which] must today be first and foremost be understood in relation to the general societal conditions that mean that the individual constantly has to choose his or her way... (Illeris 2002: 95)

One of my students wrote:

...with these exercises I understood that sometimes people in general, including me, are used to see things in a single manner when the reality is that situations are more complex and have more rough edges than they seem.

The final stage in the process of engaging with the active imagination often involves the expression of the newly recognised thought in symbolic form. Boyce-Tillman writes that 'all descriptions of creativity... include a measure of chaos or darkness – a time when the whole appears to fragment before it re-establishes itself again in a different configuration' (Boyce-Tillman 2007: 89). Reed similarly suggests that creativity is located in a psycho-dynamic process which requires periods of regression and fragmentation but which in turn lead the individual to seek for new symbols for the identification of meaning. At the identification stage the fragmented thoughts are brought together at the deep level of 'conscious or unconscious thought, or dreams' (Reed 1995: 12). The quotation cited below, taken from one student's reflective report, is an unusually vivid description of this process:

Then there were the metaphors. Christina challenged the class to think of metaphors for diversity. My mind which had been repressed in Organisation Prison was now free to wander through the endless images that flashed through my consciousness. Such wonders as the DNA double helix and its potential to create infinite diversity through its infinite permutations sprang to mind. All the rivers of earth and all the rivers on not-yet-discovered planets and moons joined together and flowed into gigantic oceans that spread across space and time providing sustenance to sustain diverse forms in all corners of the universe. But then the universe collapsed back into singularity. The explosion of diversity that had been born from the 'big bang' had disappeared. There was nothing left.

Gibbs writes that metaphor is 'not [a] linguistic distortion of literal mental thought' but instead constitutes a schema in which 'people conceptualise their experience and the external world' (Gibbs 1994: 1).

In the exercises that I developed with my students I encouraged them to give shape to these imaginative expressions through the form of metaphor. Alvesson writes that a constructive use of metaphor is 'to examine the more basic assumptions of a particular conceptualisation of a phenomenon and bring these more clearly to the surface' (Alvesson 1993: 117). Once the 'unthought known' (Lawrence 2000: 11) becomes accessible in its metaphoric form it then becomes available for interpretation.

This course has made me realise how some of my own prejudices and preconceptions about the people around me are socially constructed and has encouraged me to think independently and form my own opinions.

These examples illustrate some of my students' observations about the processes of engaging with the active imagination. In the following and subsequent sections I now want to move on to present some of the specific metaphors they used in their conceptualisations of diversity. I have organised these into a number of fairly loose categories.

Firstly, all of the metaphors express some thing of the tension between the individual and the group. Some of the metaphors focus on aspects of identity while others emphasise the relationships between individuals, and between individuals and the group. In some the metaphors describe the connections between people; others evoke the experience of separation.

The metaphors of diversity as a fruit salad or a stir-fry were often presented as representations of the differences between individuals within a group. Interestingly, there was rarely any consideration of the container, the fruit bowl or the frying pan. Instead, the discussions concentrated on the ways in which the differences between each ingredient are clearly visible, they have not been blended together, as, say, in a smoothie. The bowl of fruit, one student said, contains fruit that comes from all over the world, and is full of vitamins and goodness. Although the differences between the fruit and vegetables were important, the relationships between them were presented as being unproblematic.

A variant on this theme was the bouquet of flowers, also a recurring metaphor. The predominant interpretation that was given was that each flower is beautiful on its own, but even more so when they are all brought together in the bouquet. In this metaphor the differences in the individual identities are still paramount but bringing them together produces something new.

Other metaphors emphasise the similarities between individuals. Still on the theme of food, one example was a box of All Sorts, sweets made from liquorish in which the shapes and the colours are different but the taste is the same in every piece. Even greater emphasis on similarity was suggested by the tube of smarties or M&Ms, in which the external shapes are the same, the centres are all chocolate; only the outside colours are different. However, another student said that flowers all come from seeds which look alike but produce very different looking flowers.

There were also metaphors in which individual identity is clearly visible, as in the fruit salad, but the emphasis is more on the group. One such example is that of beads in a necklace where there are different shapes and kinds of stones. Another example given by one student was a shop where there was something for everyone. Another student suggested the traditional symbol of the Olympic games; five differently coloured circles interlinked. This metaphor seems to suggest a similar interpretation to the smarties – each ring is the same size, only the colours are different. But the emphasis the student gave to the Olympic symbol was more on the inter-connections between the circles whereas the spaces between the individual smarties are less clearly defined and always changing. Similarly, when a Chinese student suggested the metaphor of the yin/yang symbol, in her interpretation she talked about the fit between the two oppositions rather than their differences.

Finally, there were a number of metaphors suggested in which individual differences are almost subsumed into a collectivity. In metaphors such as a car, or the body, individual identities are still perceptible but the different parts or organs are all needed for the whole to work; in fact it cannot work in isolation (unlike the different pieces of fruit in the fruit salad). In the piano keyboard *'the black and white keys need each other'*. But in metaphors such as a river flowing into the ocean, a curry where all the different spices combine to create a new flavour, the individual has almost completely disappeared. Interestingly, one student said that you can always add more spices to the curry, there isn't a limit to the number of flavours that can be combined. Another said that the ocean contains lots of things not yet discovered.

Taken as a group these metaphors depict a wide range of aspects of the relationship between the individual and the group. Many of them present this relationship in quite idealised terms. They represent the utopian form of the business case for diversity in which the difficulties and tensions are minimised, to the extent of being airbrushed out of the discourse.

Metaphors of *managing* diversity

The metaphors that I have presented so far emerged in a variety of contexts throughout the semester. In this section I want to focus on metaphors that students used when they were specifically asked to reflect on *managing* diversity within an organisational context. The majority of these metaphors were generated at the beginning and end of the module. The students were asked to work in pairs or small groups, with colleagues of their own choosing.[3] I would ask them to come up with one or two metaphors that capture some sense of what diversity management means to them. I would note down the metaphors from the first week and then refer to them again at the end to stimulate a discussion about whether or not these metaphorical conceptualisations of diversity management had changed during the course of the semester.

Some students are initially unfamiliar with the notion of a metaphor and so to start them off I would usually describe some of the most common metaphors for diversity, such as the melting pot and the mosaic. I show them the covers of two very familiar books about diversity; the 2005 edition of the Kirton and Green textbook *The Dynamics of Managing*

Diversity which is illustrated with a picture of an open tube of smarties (the aforementioned little chocolates with different coloured coatings) with some of the sweets falling out onto a table, and the book by Kandola and Fullerton (2003) which uses the mosaic as its subtitle: *Diversity in Action: Managing the Mosaic.*[4] I then point out that each metaphor conveys a different understanding of diversity, and that there are also different levels of possible interpretations that can be made. For example, the tube of smarties might be understood as suggesting that although we are all different on the outside (the different colours) we are all the same underneath (and this always stimulates a good debate). The tube holding the smarties is rigid with fixed and unyielding boundaries.

In the discussions about these metaphors I also suggest that the tube that holds the smarties and the structure of the picture of the mosaic can be regarded as images of organisations. The essence of the 'business case' for diversity is that having good diversity policies and practices is 'good for business', that the differences that people bring with them into the organisation represent an asset that it can utilise to improve its overall functioning (Tomlinson and Schwabenland 2010, Schwabenland and Tomlinson 2008, Kandola and Fullerton 2003). But the metaphor of the mosaic suggests that only certain kinds of differences or attributes are welcomed. What happens to the pieces of coloured glass or stone that do not have a place in the overall picture that is being formed, the pieces that are the 'wrong' shape or colour? Swann (2010) comments that 'the mosaic reproduces a view of dominant white culture as the grout and individuals and their cultures as static, singular and self-contained... difference is acknowledged and celebrated but on narrow terms' (Swann 2010: 82).

I have sometimes then shown them pictures of traditional mosaics (Figure 3.1) and also mosaics by the Catalonian architect Gaudi (Figure 3.2). The Gaudi mosaics have more fluid boundaries and the underlying structure is less rigid. The grout is still white but the structure seems able to accommodate a greater variety of shapes, colours and textures.

The melting pot is another interesting and complex metaphor because although it has been very commonly used in America, it has been criticised by activist groups for its emphasis on assimilation. Consideration of the melting pot metaphor can stimulate a discussion on different interpretations of multiculturalism and questions about the contrasting policies and practices in the UK, the US and Frances; three countries that have developed quite distinct understandings.

Figure 3.1

Figure 3.2

These opening comments about metaphors are intended firstly, to demonstrate that there are no 'right' or 'wrong' metaphors, that all are interesting and potentially revelatory of multiple meanings. Secondly, exploring the notions of assimilation that are suggested by the melting pot and of conformity to the business case suggested by the tube of smarties and the more traditional structures of the mosaic, demonstrates that some of these interpretations may suggest more contradictory and unwelcome aspects of diversity management, a 'shadow' side. By raising this possibility at the outset my aim is to make it more possible for some of these less positive attributes to be explored.

Taken as a group, the students' metaphors seemed to reflect three different aspects of diversity in organisations. The first grouping of metaphors present quite static images and in that sense are similar to those of the melting pot and the mosaic. For example, one student said that diversity was like a pint of Guinness: white at the top. Similarly, another student represented diversity as a chocolate layer cake topped by vanilla icing. These metaphors are more complex than the ones I presented earlier and demonstrate a move away from the 'ideas about happy diversity' (Ahmed et al 2006 cited by Swann 2010: 82). (However other students disagreed with him, suggesting marble cakes and plates of cupcakes, each with different colours of icing.)

Another grouping concerned metaphors that focussed primarily on the activities and processes of managing diversity within organisations. Managing diversity is like using language, one student said; we all need to communicate but we can do it differently. The making of the patchwork quilt, the metaphor I used to introduce this chapter was suggested by a student who said that she had been reminded of the American film about the making of the quilts. Women make quilts; quilts are generational with a new piece being added when a new baby comes. The women tell stories as they are making the quilt and the quilt tells the story of the family and the community. So this student's quilt was a communal project, a group made her quilt, and its design and underlying structure may be shaped and changed over time. Her evocation of the relationship between the individual and the group represented in the processes of quilt-making is more complex than in many of the metaphors cited above, but it is still relatively unproblematic, a 'celebration of harmonious existence' (Prasad and Mills 1997: 4).

A more cautionary note is struck in another metaphor, that of diversity management as a jazz performance in which different things are going on, there is a measure of improvisation, but there may also be some discordant themes. The student who proposed this metaphor said that the musicians can choose to work through these discordant themes or start again. For some people jazz is beautiful but for others the discord is unpleasant.

The examples that I quote below come from exercises that draw on stories as myths, or 'extended metaphors'. Pondy suggests that stories can 'stand in a metaphoric relationship to real events' where the metaphoric relationship 'explains the present and the past as well as the future' (Pondy 1983: 159). As so much of the literature on managing diversity emphasises the importance of *valuing* difference (Kandola and Fullerton 2003, Liff 1997) I have experimented with asking the students to think back over their working experience and identify an incident or a time when they felt respected and valued. I then ask them to reflect on what was going on at the time and what made it such a good experience (Schwabenland 2008).

It is not unusual for the students to struggle to identify a good example. Sometimes they need quite a bit of prompting. However, what is striking is that when they do recount their stories there is an enormous amount of similarity in them. In the majority of examples the experiences of being respected and trusted, recognised and valued and allowed to use their own initiative feature highly. For instance, in one story a student said that her manager asked for her assistance in finding out why staff had expressed unhappiness in a staff satisfaction survey. Another recounted her pleasure at receiving an e-mail from her manager thanking her for welcoming a new group of interns. Similarly, a student working in a human resource department described being asked for advice by her manager, who had received a horrible e-mail and had drafted an angry reply. The student recommended that she 'sit on it' for the night. Her manager took her advice and the next morning, on re-reading her draft, decided not to send it and thanked my student for counselling caution. A fourth example is that of a student whose manager had asked for her advice on a particular problem. When the student suggested a solution she was given the responsibility for implementing it and when her idea proved successful her manager was impressed.

A myth functions metaphorically by juxtaposing the past and the present in order to show both how the present resembles the past and also how it differs from it. These stories could be said to function as myths in representing an understanding of what it means to be valued in an organisational setting. It is, however, very concerning that the students' said that such examples were rare. This raises the question of why it is that the experience of working in organisations can be so unrewarding, even for such employees as these, who are sufficiently motivated to be taking up postgraduate study, often at their own expense (Schwabenland 2008).

The following quotation is quite long and comes from a student's reflective report but it is worth citing in such length because of the way the student intertwines her metaphors for diversity with her metaphors of her own processes of learning as she reflected back over the eleven weeks of the module:

...relating the meaning of metaphor to diversification it came in my idea of a bouquet of flowers which has different types of flowers in it that originates and grew from different places and has different colours and sizes and mixing them together to create a bouquet. However, this bouquet would need water and air not to get wilted. It's like an organisation that has diverse people working in it but it needs a management or a human resource department to get its people organised and avoid losing them. More precisely, if there is inadequate professionalism in the human resource of an organisation it usually results in high staff turnover. In my own reflective way of thinking, as I applied this example to myself, is that diversity for me could be the different experiences I had in my life. Whether they are good or bad, however I learned from those experiences and the different trials that I am facing and the different goals or dreams that I have for my future. When I have mixed them all it could mean that my whole life is a bouquet of flowers, but the one that helps me to grow up as a person and enables me to achieve my goals in life is my own determination to go one step ahead and follow my dreams and which provides me water and air not to get wilted.

If I were a literary critic I might suggest that this student is mixing her metaphors a bit, but the processes of sensemaking that are revealed in this quotation are interesting and complex. The student moves from an initial identification of a metaphor for diversity to exploring its implications as an analogy for diversity management within organisations. But then her thinking moves on and diversity itself becomes a metaphor for making sense of her own life, as it has unfolded to date and she returns to her original metaphor, the bouquet of flowers, but with greater insight into the '*determination...which provides me with water and air not to get wilted*'. This paragraph nicely illustrates her experiencing of the iterative hermeneutic circle of explanation and understanding, as Ricoeur describes:

Explanation is a necessary step for understanding. We always explain in order to better understand. A text must be explained in its internal structure before being understood in its relation to the interest it arouses and to which it responds.... But the reverse is just as true. If understanding passes through explanation, explanation is completed in understanding. (Ricoeur 1992: 43)

My student's reference to the flower's reliance on water and air is illustrative of the third grouping of the different themes that resonated in the metaphors of diversity management, the relationship between the organisation and its environment. In one session there was a long discussion about a tree outside the window. Sometimes we could see the branches underneath the leaves and sometimes not. Some branches were in the light and some in the shade; some were thriving and some withering. One student wondered if there was enough sap to feed all the leaves. The tree needs a conducive environment to thrive – but the healthier it is the more it is likely to deprive smaller plants of direct access to the sun. Or is it shading them from the harmful rays of the sun that might cause the smaller plants to wither and die? These interpretations emerged in discussion during the class with different students contributing and building on the interpretations of others. This metaphor provoked a rich discussion about the nature of power relationships in organisations.

The metaphor of the tree focusses our attention on the environment and the elements within it that can make it wither or flourish. A similar theme is reflected in the metaphor of the cloud:

Clouds are visible and light waves affect their appearance. For clouds to form they need droplets of moisture or crystals. Clouds are fragile and ever changing and moving. [Diversity is] a visible mass of words, progress and practice that hang together, similar to those of raindrops that have come together to form clouds.

This is a nice reply to Gergan's question (cited at the beginning of the previous chapter) as to whether we should think of organisations as clouds! Another student said that diversity was like a flame. Within the flame you can see lots of different colours in it but it needs oxygen to thrive. These metaphors of trees, clouds and flames emerged in the same session and highlight symbiotic relationship between the organisation and its environment.

Metaphors of a diverse society

> The meaning of a society itself determines what is real. Thus the problems of a society depend upon how people in that society define themselves. (Turner 1992: 53)

The final group of metaphors I want to discuss in this chapter are those in which the images of diversity seemed to have relevance beyond the organisation. These are the metaphors that capture some sense of our experiences of living in a multicultural society. Anderson (1991) points out that communities are constructed in the imagination. It would be impossible for us to ever 'know' a community in any other way, as there are always more people included within these frames of reference than we would ever be able to meet face to face. Ricoeur (1974) also states that it is the social imaginary that constitutes social reality. Anderson writes 'communities are to be distinguished, not by their falsity/genuineness but by the style in which they are imagined (Anderson 1991: 6).

And, according to Charles Taylor, in his work on *Modern Social Imaginaries*, it is precisely through images, stories and legends that people 'imagine their social existence, how they fit together with others, how things go on between them and their fellows [sic] the expectations that are normally met and the deeper normative notions and images that underlie these expectations' (Taylor 2005: 23).

Diversity is like an orchestra – you have different people playing together, the parts and whole, all making beautiful sounds.

Cohen suggests that it is not only at the individual level that we use cognitive maps to make sense of our experiences but that collectivities do so as well (Cohen 1993: 101). The excerpt below is particularly interesting because as this student recalls her experiences of the two exercises on metaphor she starts with a such a collectively generated metaphor, the rainbow. But she then moves on to a different metaphor that she is able to more fully interpret.

At the first lecture of this course the lecturer asked the students what is diversity? My answer for this question is similar to others…[diversity is a] rainbow, because it shows seven different colours along together when it appears in the sky, and to be honest, I had no better idea [how] to create something that I am unsure about. And later, the last lecture that when the lecturer asked us again for this question then I realised that my answer is quite different from the prior one and I can explain it better than before. My answer [changed] from rainbow, it became a mixed fruit cake which I used to bake…the explanation of this [is that] as a cake being cooked always takes time, like people need sometimes to accept or learn different things, i.e. cultures, values and beliefs. The oven is the environment that is for heating the cake; the cake pan is the Government which is to form the cake and also prevent from damage [during] a long period [of] cooking time. Then the plain flour is society or organisation, the main body of cake, the mixed fruits are presented as the diversity of individuals, the sugar and butter can be the legislations which make cake taste better, make peoples' lives better.

Taylor suggests that the 'images that underlie the expectations' constitute an idea of a moral order, an idea that 'can be ultimate...or for the here and now...either hermeneutic or prescriptive' (Taylor 2005: 7). The example above illustrates this very well. As this student explores and explains the possibilities within her own metaphor, she interweaves images of the individual, organisation and the wider society. She moves from metaphor to analogy and then, in her concluding point, *makes peoples' lives better,* beyond an interpretive understanding of diversity to more prescriptive one. Her exploration of her metaphors allows her to 'surface' her underlying assumptions about the role of government within a just society.

The metaphors in the next examples demonstrate how the community of students can create its own understandings of a prescriptive moral order. The exercise that generated these examples drew on a slightly different use of metaphor, that of the role model as icon. In a session where we were to discuss the management implications of the 1975 (UK) Sex Discrimination Act, I would ask students to think about women whom they found inspiring, whether these were women they knew personally or more public figures. The majority of examples tended to be family members such as their grandmothers, mothers, aunts and wives. Some of the qualities about these women that they find inspiring are captured in such phrases as: *She goes all out for you...She didn't take any bullshit...She worked through hard times...She puts other people first...She was always kind, sharing, even when we had very little.* And, in a slightly different vein: *She came from a poor family, with no access to university, had seven children but still got a degree and PhD in fine art.*

There were also more public figures suggested and frequently recurring examples included Mother Theresa for 'her charity work and her loving nature' and Oprah Winfrey who 'makes it OK to be human and to talk about taboo issues, talking about rape, talking about her life, her story' (Schwabenland 2008: 96).

The qualities that underpin the students' choices of role models can be regarded as representing some elements of an underpinning moral prescription. In the discussion that follows we sometimes explore whether the values that the students have identified as important to them are those that are valorised in organisations, and the difficulties that both women and men may face in bringing these qualities into the work context, particularly those in management positions.

Reed (1995) suggests that groups, communities and organisations participate in the process of creating cultural symbols. The exercise described above is one such example of collective symbolic work. Once metaphors, whether as speech acts or as text, depart from the author they become part of the wider, cultural society in which they have been released. Their interpretations no longer simply 'belong' to the author. At this point the interpretations of others attain their own particular kind of validity.

> They contribute to the creative work of the self and the community, or a work of art or scientific discovery which is realised at a later stage... This is the stage of culture formation where community members evolve rituals to create tribal identification, exemplified for example in the primitive ritual behaviour on the terraces of football stadia. (Reed 1995: 12)

The metaphor of the rainbow, initially chosen by the student in the long excerpt I cited above, was one of the most commonly suggested metaphors for diversity, and as such, is an example of the shared understanding that Taylor (2005) suggests differentiates the social from the individual imaginary. The popularity of the rainbow is not surprising; many campaigning groups have adopted this metaphor and so it has a well recognised place in our collective repository of cultural artefacts. However, the rainbow provoked a variety of different interpretations. Cohen writes that communities may 'share the symbol but they do not necessarily share its meaning' especially 'those meanings [that] are the most elusive, the hardest to pin down' (Cohen 1993: 15). For some students, as in the one cited above, the metaphor was an image of diversity in which the shape and size of the colours were the same, but the different colours were each clearly perceptible, and the entity that was created by bringing the different colours together was more beautiful that any would be on its own. This interpretation seemed to reflect the relatively unproblematic understandings of diversity.

However, another student said that it would be impossible to perceive the beauty and variety of the colours in the rainbow without the contrasts between the different colours; it was these contrasts that created the beauty; this student's image of diversity is very different to that conveyed by the melting pot. And another student said that diversity is not only the rainbow but also the light that comes before it – the rainbow is refracted light that constitutes all colours; light is clear but what you see, the colours, are refracted light, unity and diversity together.

The emphasis on the environment needed for diversity to thrive was evoked by another student who pointed out that rainbows only exist where there is both sun and rain; the conducive environment here contains both the nurturing elements but also the shadow – in fact, the shadow in this example is represented as essential to the fulfilment of diversity's potential.

However, other evocations of the shadow side of diversity were less comfortable. Early on in my experience of teaching this module one student told me that she had been unsure about whether to chose to take it – for her the module was an elective, and when she had been deliberating over the possible choices, another student had said to her 'oh you don't want to do diversity, it's all just pink and fluffy'. My immediate response was; 'diversity's not pink and fluffy, it's red and bloody!'.

I have used this example on many occasions to initiate discussions about the shadow side of diversity. Kociatkiewicz and Kostera suggest 'not only individuals but also organisations create a shadow' (Kociatkiewicz and Kostera 2010: 258). The shadow is a Jungian archetype 'of self rejection, an assemblage of unwanted and destructive elements'. The shadow comprises those aspects of self and of organisation that are unwanted, unspeakable, uncontrollable, frightening, 'the denied and rejected elements of one's personality' (Kociatkiewicz and Kostera 2010: 259). The shadow is with us at all times, 'a dark companion that dogs our steps' (Stevens 1994: 64).

Jung suggested that the shadow, although a part of the self, was nonetheless often conceived of as the opposite, the other, the enemy. Stevens writes that 'in dreams the shadow tends to appear as a sinister, or threatening figure, possessing the same sex as the dreamer and is not infrequently *a member of a different nation, colour or race*' (Stevens 1994: 64 my emphasis). The shadow must inevitably play an important role in how our understandings of self and other are manifested and managed in organisations. Not only are elements of our unwanted selves likely to comprise elements of the formulation of insider and outsider identities in organisations, but the unacknowledged shadow sides of organisational attempts to control undesired behaviours can 'surface as powerful and usually uncontrollable impulses' (Kociatkiewicz and Kostera 2010: 259). The following example seem to capture this tension between the controllable and the uncontrollable:

During the last few weeks of the module my description of diversity changed from carnival to fireworks. Diversity for me is now not only about creating a healthy environment for everyone but a mixture of tension and content. To me fireworks have many colours although initially contained. Once they are lit they create a beautiful array of lights with incredible noise that can be deafening and irritating to some but enjoyable to others. If properly managed fireworks can be a pleasant sight and experience. If not managed properly however they can lead to an atrocious end.

Another metaphor that conveys some of this sense of the uncontrollable was that of *a chemical reaction – steam, possibility of explosion, you have to be aware of what's there, different elements which can combine to make something new or can explode.*

How else did the shadow manifest itself in the students' metaphors of diversity? One way was through the invocation of chaos. One student said that diversity was a crowd of football fans, *'people in a football stadium, all seeing the game from different perspectives'* and another wrote that diversity was a crossroads jammed with people all going in different directions. Some students likened diversity to the sea; its power was 'scary'. These metaphors contain an undercurrent of chaos and disorder; the noisy football fans, the confusion of traffic, the frightening power of the sea in a storm; *'oceans can cause floods and global warming'.* A sense of danger underpins these notions of diversity. Another student mentioned the London Underground Metro system: *when it works it is because of the contribution of different lines and speeds, otherwise there is chaos and meltdown.*

A different aspect of the shadow was demonstrated in the loss of identity, often manifested in the recurrent metaphor of the chameleon. One student said that the chameleon was like hidden discrimination, hidden and invisible identity. Another said that because the chameleon is able to change colour and fit into different environments, its identity is fluid and not fixed. For some students this quality was frightening but it was not always necessarily so (it reminded them of a quotation I had shown them from the *Guardian* journalist Gary Younge, who said at a conference that although he was a Black Briton, when he was in Shropshire he felt more Black, and when he was in Hackney he felt more British[5]).

Loss of identity was also highlighted in the following example:

In the last lecture we were asked to think of metaphors we would use to portray diversity… I decided on 'snowfall' and this is why. From a distance we recognise another human being, our bodies and the way we function is recognisable. On first appearance snowflakes also look similar… However, take a close look at the snowflake or talk to the individual…and you find out there is great detail and complexity in their structures... Each snowflake has a different structure, like everyone has a unique personality. As snow falls each flake is identifiable and separate but as it layers on the ground the individuals merge to create a single form. This made me think of organisations and how each group of people creates its own sub-culture but the organisation can also be viewed as a solid whole.

I presented this example at a conference and afterwards, in the discussion, one member of the audience said that for her the snow-storm was a very conservative metaphor, a metaphor of assimilation. She said that she saw the snowstorm as symbolising one of the accusations that is often made of the notion of diversity management, that although the rhetoric is of valuing difference it is underpinned by a discourse of conformity (Schwabenland and Tomlinson 2008, Lorbiecki and Jack 2000). She also observed that snow is a very white (although interestingly, the student whose metaphor it is, is Black).

Snow is a powerful metaphor evoking multiple meanings. In *Moby Dick* Melville's character Ahab writes:

> It was the whiteness of the whale that above all things appalled me...is it that by its indefiniteness it shadows forth the heartless voids and immensities of the universe...or is it that as in essence whiteness is not so much a colour as the visible absence of colour, and at the same time the concrete of all colours: is it for these reasons that there is such a dumb blankness, full of meaning, in a wide landscape of snows? (Melville cited in Turchi 2004: 27)

Reading this metaphor from another perspective evokes images from the science of complexity, which explores the ways in which individual particles combine and recombine endlessly in myriad complex and unpredictable, but mathematically precise ways. When viewed on a computer screen, this phenomenon, in which chaos and order are intertwined and enfolded within each other can appear awesomely beautiful, but the lived experience of an infinitely co-creating chaos and order may be more unsettling.

In many of these metaphors there are strong forces depicted as out of control. In contrast, were some of the metaphors of games such as snooker in which all balls are needed to play the game but *'someone is controlling the balls'* or football and cricket in which everyone plays a different role but is directed from the sidelines. The following metaphor is similarly ambiguous and to me, conveys a strong element of irony and scepticism about diversity management:

To me diversity management appears like a President or leader, promising to heal and reconcile all the elements of society.

However, butterflies come from the cocoons made by 'hungry cater-pillars'. As a counterpoint to these interpretations that stress the shadow side of diversity management was one student's metaphor of diversity as *summer in Canada because of clarity of light that reflects God's vision.* Another referred to diversity management as *the golden thread that runs through the business plan.* Finally, one student described the rainbow as 'God's promise', represented by the pot of gold at its end.

Conclusions

In this chapter I have attempted to demonstrate the use of metaphor, both as a means to engage the active imagination and also as one form of symbolic representation of what Mehta described as 'the basic, pre-theoretical affective dispositions [which] govern our primary attune-ments and are the basis on which we go on to build our theoretical constructs' (Mehta cited in Shah 1997: 4). These metaphors are revela-tory of the underlying assumptions that structure the frames of refer-ence from which we create our understandings of diversity. Using metaphor as a vehicle for gaining understanding has been a fruitful endeavour as evidenced by the richness and varieties of meanings that have been produced. One student wrote:

The metaphorical exercises at the beginning of the lectures were amazing. It has had a profound effect on the way I look at things. The way of looking at subjects (whether controversial, sensitive or difficult) from a symbolic per-spective that was not confrontational I felt was very powerful in its subtlety. The different mediums such as poetry, music and quizzes show the complex-ities of forms and ideas that make up the quest for philosophical thinking around diversity and equality and, policy and practice. I will definitely use this in training and presentations whenever I am able to.

Ricoeur (1991b: 316) suggests that a metaphor is a 'poem in miniature'.[6] Metaphors reveal their meaning through the tension that is created by the juxtaposition of two ideas, or concepts (such as diversity and rainbow, or diversity and the snowstorm). Metaphors result from associative thinking; the two elements in the metaphor are related to each other through poetic logic. The meanings that are suggested through this poetic relationship are multiple, overlapping, sometimes contradictory. Diversity both 'is' and 'is not' all of these.

A metaphor may be a poem, but is it also a theory? As mentioned already in the introduction to this chapter, Geary (2011) and Morgan (1986) would say that it is, but Taylor (2005) and Cazal and Inns (1998) all have significant reservations. Taylor regards the social imaginary as distinct from social theory in at least three different ways; firstly, that the imaginary is expressed in symbolic terms rather than theoretical terms; secondly, that the social imaginary is shared by a wider group of people than those involved in theory making and thirdly, that the social imaginary 'is a common understanding that makes possible common practices and a widely shared sense of legitimacy' (Taylor 2005: 23). Cazal and Inns' arguments share a discomfort with the more fuzzy nature of metaphor. They write: 'we agree that metaphors provide new insights [but] we deny that they produce any new knowledge...or directly generate, any new theory' (Cazal and Inns 1998: 182). But surely new insights *do* provide the basis for theory building? A metaphor 'is' a theory in the sense that it 'is' a poem (and in the sense that diversity 'is' a rainbow). All metaphors are limited, as are metaphors of metaphors. To say that a metaphor is a theory or a poem is to say that these concepts share similarities and differences. It is in the investigation of the nature of those similarities that new insights may emerge.

If the utility of the metaphor of metaphor as theory is in the potential for new insights, what theories about diversity are suggested by these students' metaphors? Some of them are representations of an idealised understanding of diversity where individual identity and organisational are both clearly visible (the fruit salad) with each enriching the other in a delicate balance. Being a member of a collective, in this reading, does not involve any sacrifice of individual needs or identities. However there are other metaphors in which the balance is more precarious and where either individual identity (the bouquet of flowers) or group identity (the orchestra) dominates. In the metaphors of the snowstorm and the river the individual identity has been completely submerged in the collectivity.

Other metaphors such as the piano keys and the yin/yang symbol focus on how the relationship between the individual and group is created and what binds them together. These metaphors suggest the importance of role and boundary. Inherent in some of these metaphors are dynamics of exclusion and well as inclusion (there is a strict ratio and placement of black keys to white keys on the piano; only five rings make up the Olympic symbol). This underlying structure of an insider/outsider boundary comes to the fore in the metaphor of snooker balls in which there is a clear pattern of exclusion as well as inclusion and also, as with the piano, a player who determines their role and function at any one time.

All of these metaphors also suggest particular understandings of the organisation. The organisations suggested by the piano or the five rings of the Olympic symbol are fixed and static – very different from those suggested by the metaphors of the kaleidoscope and the river, in which the organisation is fluid, ever changing, organisation as organising; order and chaos creating and recreating each other.

Many metaphors reveal a degree of scepticism about the rhetoric of diversity (the conformity implied by the snowstorm, the sense of inclusion but also of exile suggested by the African farm) and an awareness of the shadow side of diversity, the possibility of chaos and violence. But, as noted above, they can be read in more than one way. There are also suggestions of a more transcendent understanding of diversity. These different possibilities are best captured in the different interpretations of the rainbow: the intrinsic importance of contrast to the perception of beauty, but a contrast that is illusory and created through refracted light.

What are the implications for management that are suggested by these metaphors? The metaphors of the tree and the flame emphasised the factors needed to create a conducive environment. They also suggest that diversity is fragile, that it needs careful and delicate nurturing. The extended metaphors of events in which people felt valued at work provide more detail as to what that nurturing might consist of: respect, trust, appreciation, validation. And the characteristics of archetypal women who had inspired students included warmth, encouragement, sacrifice and a belief in individual potential.

> All symbolism, considered from the point of view of its dynamics, constitutes a vast expression of the imaginary at its cultural level. (Ricoeur 1992: 39)

Lakoff and Johnson (1980) point out that metaphors not only express meaning but create it. Our metaphors create our organisations, as Morgan (1986) suggested. Several of the examples I have quoted from students' reflective reports referred back not only to the metaphors they identified in the first week, but also to metaphors that other students had suggested. In many cases they related them to experiences they had had of learning in the module, demonstrating how the metaphors themselves had become embedded in their own sensemaking processes. These metaphors became shared heuristics, 'owned' by the class as a whole, a shared cultural repertory of symbols. One student wrote that *'this course was very free flowing, allowing one's creative thinking abilities to take full force'*. The metaphor of the river seems to lie behind her words.

The metaphors suggested here illustrate Ricoeur's 'tensional' truth of poetry (Ricoeur 2007: 371). This tensional truth is that of the relationship between self and other (Kohn 1990) the irony implicit in the analogy of the president, the chaos of the crowd. Milner (1989, 1999) describes the process of actively engaging the imagination as an *encounter with another*. She observed that 'my mind had a host of thoughts I never knew about' (Milner 1999: 88).

The poet, Mahmoud Darwish, writes:

> We need to return to being two
> To embrace each other more. There's no name for us
> When the stranger stumbles upon himself in the stranger! (Darwish 2007: 27)

In the following example one student demonstrates a new awareness of the ways in which her own behaviour unintentionally reinforced and maintained herself within her own comfort zone.

I had prepared a presentation with a group of people involving black and white students. From the group as a whole I mainly engaged with white colleagues from Eastern European backgrounds, as I have spent some time living in several countries there and felt closer to the 'cultural background'. Is the idea of diversity more idealistic than the reality?

This chapter has concentrated on the insights into diversity and diversity management generated through a consideration of the metaphor of metaphor as theory. In the next chapter I want to go on to consider how the metaphor of metaphor as art also has transformative potential.

4
Listening to Evelyn Glennie: Metaphor as Art

I realised the importance of exploring your imagination whilst under-standing and learning new topics.

Introduction

In this chapter I want to describe some of the ways in which managers, and management educators can engage the aesthetic power of metaphor to transform their perspectives and challenge negative and unhelpful stereotypes. The power of metaphor to shape the way we feel about ourselves and each other has been powerfully demonstrated by Asch's experiment (cited in Geary 2011) in which he gave two groups of people a list of attributes of an individual, identical save only for the word 'warm' in one list and 'cold' in the other. The group who had 'warm' in their list formed a better opinion of the individual than the other group. This is not entirely surprising as cold personalities are generally less well regarded than 'warm' ones. However, even more interestingly, Geary describes a development of Asch's experiment in which the groups again received identical list of attributes – but each of the participants in one group had been given a warm cup of coffee to drink just before starting the experiment while the other group were given a cold drink. Again, the drinkers of the warm cup of coffee formed significantly more positive judgements.

Geary suggests that this outcome could be the result of *synesthesia* 'the ability to perceive stimulus in one sense organ through a different sensory system' (Geary 2011: 77). Synesthesia is behind the ability that some people have to hear colour or feel sound. He suggests that 'if synesthesia is the result of cross-connectivity among the brain's sensory regions, the same connectivity could explain why so many metaphors take the commonly shared world of physical sensation as their source and the private, abstract world of ideas, feelings, thoughts and emotions as their target' (Geary 2011: 82).

Understanding how our minds create associations that influence the assumptions we make about ourselves and each other is immensely important. These associations, or stereotypes, can be tremendously powerful, especially when they occur, as they usually do, at an unconscious level. Butler, in her essays on 'frames' of war, argues that 'the "frames" that work to differentiate the lives we can apprehend from those that we cannot…not only organise visual experience but also generate specific ontologies of the subject…such that our very capacity to discern and name the "being" of the subject is based on norms that facilitate that recognition' (Butler 2009: 3–4). She argues that 'if certain lives do not qualify as lives or are, from the start, not conceivable as lives within certain epistemological frames, these lives are never lived, or lost in the full sense' (Butler 2009: 1). Butler's subject is that of war and violent conflict but the violence done on a day-to-day basis to young people as consequence of low expectations of black students, or students with disabilities can be no less damaging.

Collins (2009) and Dalal (2006) have analysed how certain symbolic associations come to inhere to the terms 'black' and 'white'. Collins describes her reactions when one of her students wrote:

> 'Black, black! Look at all the terms that go along with Black. They're all bad or ugly'. She then compiled a long list of all the negative uses of the term – black sheep, black magic, and a few that I had not considered. This student basically unpacked denigrating racial language and images that had been used to justify racism. (Collins 2009: 115)

Dalal suggests that at the mythological level in which one word comes to stand for another (the example he uses is 'rose' and 'passion') 'we have little choice in the associations that are already injected into words. We are born into a language world where the word "rose" *automatically* and apparently *naturally* not only makes us think of a particular sort of flower but also conjures up an association with passion and romance' (Dalal 2006: 138 emphasis in the original). Dalal goes on to demonstrate how a 'slippage' between the concepts of 'blackness' and 'darkness' have become elided and further associated with notions of good and evil. He acknowledges that there are some culturally 'positive' associations to blackness (such as being 'in the black', having a 'black belt' in martial arts) and some negative associations of whiteness (such as white elephants and whitewashing) however by far the majority of referents in English literature to blackness are negative and whiteness positive. Dalal writes that 'on examining the data three things emerge. Firstly, that things that have no colour get named black. Second, things get made black retrospectively. And third, things that are already black become increasingly negative over time' (Dalal 2006: 157).

Mezirow writes that 'perspective transformation is the process of becoming critically aware of how and why our assumptions have come to constrain the way we perceive, understand, and feel about our world; changing these structures of habitual expectation to make possible a more inclusive, discriminating, and integrating perspective; and, finally, making choices or otherwise acting upon these new understandings' (Mezirow 1991: 167 cited in Imel 1998: no page).

Bion claimed that 'all human thought and endeavour, whatever the field, originates in the transformation of emotional experience' (Bion cited in Armstrong 1989). Armstrong goes on to say that when he looks at a painting he does not have the *same* emotional experience of the painter:

> Rather I have an emotional experience myself and that may lead me to say, 'I never understood that before; how one object reflects and takes up the presence of another'. At one extreme this experience in front of a great work of art may lead me to change my life. I do not just understand or know something new, I become something new. (Armstrong 1989: 6)

The proposition I am exploring in this chapter is that such transformations can only occur when there is some realisation that has been effected through emotional engagement, and specifically that form of emotional engagement which is manifested as empathy. Although there are many ways in which our emotions may be so engaged, it is specifically the role of metaphor in its aesthetic function, that of metaphor as poetry, to do so. Heaney writes:

> Poetry is more a threshold than a path, one constantly approached and constantly departed from, at which reader and writer undergo in their different ways the experience of being at the same time summoned and released. (Heaney 1989: 108)

Many of the examples I am using in this chapter come from the programme of exercises I designed to develop students' capacities for metaphorical thinking and to encourage empathy. In the previous chapter I described three of the exercises; the opening and closing exercises where I ask them to conceptualise diversity through metaphor, the exercise on inspirational women as role models and the one that generates stories of times when students felt valued at work. The programme of exercises moves from validating the importance of students' own experience through to questioning their own assumptions. All of the exercises build on imaginative forms of language and communication and, as described in Chapter 3; they aim to engage the active imagination. The structure of the individual sessions reflects Edgar's four stages of imagework: 1) a descriptive stage, 2) an analysis of the personal meaning of symbols and images, 3) an analysis of the models used to inform students' imagery and 4) a 'comparative stage where respondents share and compare their imagework with the rest of the group' (Edgar 2004 as summarised by McIntosh 2007: 5). By including a group discussion in each exercise, these metaphorical heuristics are exposed to analysis and critical reflection. This is an essential part of the programme because the power of metaphors to limit and restrict our thinking can only be addressed through such interrogation.

In the next three sections of this chapter I will present some of the comments that students made as to how the aesthetic and emotional impact of these exercises helped them in confronting and transforming stereotypical assumptions about themselves, about working together in organisations, and within the wider society.

Challenging stereotypes at the individual level

I loved the ice-breaker introductions such as poems, legislation question-naires, evaluating your immediate environment and your identity in relation to your surroundings... Personally the skills discussed in this course have opened my eyes to see my working environment with more criticism.

In this chapter, as in the previous one, I am drawing on students' reflective reports to demonstrate the power of metaphor. In the previous chapter I discussed the ways in which metaphors can be helpful in 'surfacing' unconscious assumptions, or 'theories-in-use' (Argyris and Schon 1978). As long as these underlying assumptions remain unconscious their influence cannot be questioned or challenged. However, when they are captured and named then the on-going processes of sensemaking are disrupted. When this occurs through the aesthetic power of metaphor this disruption may promote the 'felt change of consciousness' (Barfield

1999: 20) that I alluded to in the second chapter. Schellekens writes that 'art can enable us to develop the kind of sensitivity that is central to moral understanding' (Schellekens 2007: 59). In the excerpt cited above the student writes of the 'love' that 'opened her eyes'.

Our group assignment made me realise that I don't always have to be the leader and that being a piece of a jigsaw is fine.

Although the aim of the course is to equip students with enhanced ability to engage with issues at work, some of the most inspirational examples of transformational learning are those that describe significant personal growth. Here is one of the most moving:

As the lectures pushed forward through a combination of clouds of personal confusion...a faint light appeared. It was a neon sign, still obscured, but I could discern that it was trying to explain why I was sitting in that classroom...gradually the mists began to clear. The neon sign became more visible, like a beacon, and I didn't feel so lost and confused in the class... The neon sign was now flashing an alert against the pressures of a society that tries to reduce identity to a unitary concept. I was beginning to under-stand why I had experienced so much animosity as a black, gay man. I was understanding the anger within me. And it made me feel better... What had been an ethereal passion was becoming a tangible force that had the power to open doors to more effective action...the reason for my desire to push was now dawning on me. I was beginning to understand my passion and this was providing strength. And strength mixed with passion is a formidable force.

This example is interesting on many levels. The metaphor of the faint light that becomes a neon sign and then a beacon is used to capture something of the emotional experience of learning – but the sign is presented as having a volition separate to the student; it was trying to explain...and as such, is an interesting manifestation of Milner's (1989) description of the 'other' within ourselves whose voice we can only hear when we put aside the conscious thoughts of the ego. Darwish asks:

Does the word guide the speaker or the speaker the word? The second line [of a poem] is not a gift, rather it is constructed by a skilful taming of the unseen... If you find your way to the second line in the laby-rinth of the possible then you will know the easy route to an appoint-ment with the impossible. (Darwish 2009: 137)

'An appointment with the impossible' is a rather wonderful way of describing transformational learning. Another student also wrote about the impact of the module on his acceptance of his sexual orientation:

I have always been confused about my sexuality. I was in denial since I was not sure about society acceptance and for fear that I will put myself at a disadvantage at employment I always kept it to myself. This module has made me fully understand the Discrimination Act 2003 [Employment Equalities Act (Sexual Orientation)] *that protect gay lesbian and bisexual people. I now know that employers are required to protect employees against bullying and harassment in the workplace. And protect against the violation of individual dignity…*

The example below also concerns an important transformation in the student's personal relationships:

Understanding the DDA [Disability Discrimination Act] *has also changed areas in my personal life in relation to how I interact with my wife who has dyslexia. Prior to this I was very dismissive of her disability… I have changed and am always available to help her in the areas of life she finds difficult.*

Imel writes:

> Perspective transformation explains how the meaning structures that adults have acquired over a lifetime become transformed. These meaning structures are frames of reference that are based on the totality of individuals' cultural and contextual experiences and that influence how they behave and interpret events…[and] will influence how she [sic] chooses to vote or how she reacts to women who suffer physical abuse, for example. (Imel 1998: no page)

In one exercise students are asked to 'play' with stereotypes by taking words that usually convey a negative association (such as 'all Americans are rude') and finding a different set of associations that are more positive (she was in *rude* health). These associations or frames of reference are highly culturally contingent, as is demonstrated in the following example:

I also found it interesting to hear others in the class say that their mums were role models because they stood up to their dads when they tried to make them wash up etc…in my house we always take it in turn, my brother and

I do chores equally...so I was shocked to find out that people still let boys do nothing.

In this quotation the students specifically links her learning to the experience of disruption (demonstrated by the word 'shocked') that has occurred as a result of coming into contact with students from different cultures. In one of the exercises on age discrimination I ask students to tell me about all the things they are looking forward to about growing old. Students also generally respond to this question with a similar shock; is there anything good about growing old? Realising this reaction can lead to an exposure of some of our limiting beliefs about age and also explore different cultural conceptualisations about life cycles and even about death and rebirth.

Darwish writes that 'identity is the distorted image in the mirror that we must break the moment we grow fond of it' (Darwish 2009: 156). Even the labels that we choose for ourselves are distortions. Our attempts to understand our own identity necessarily involve us in creating some separation, or boundary marking between that which I am and that which I am not. These boundaries are endlessly fluid and changing. 'To ask for a map is to say, "tell me a story"' (Turchi 2004: 11). Butler (2009) and Dalal (2006) note that the very permeability of these boundaries can be perceived as an existential threat, the threat of invasion and destruction. From this analysis challenge becomes a very risky proposition because if my understanding of you is likely to be altered, so is my understanding of myself.

In one exercise I employ Turchi's metaphor of the map as story and ask students to use spatial metaphors to conceptualising relationships of power. Students draw a map in which they 'locate' themselves in relation to individuals and institutions, some of which are likely to play a powerful role in their lives. Then they are asked to experiment with moving their own location in the map, thereby changing the spatial relationships. The idea for this exercise came from analysing some interviews I carried out many years ago with people working in voluntary organisations that aimed to empower people from marginalised communities. I was very struck by the frequency with which they employed spatial metaphors to describe their work. Communities were 'outsiders', 'living at the margins', at the 'bottom of the pile'. I was also inspired by experiencing the different sense of agency that comes from taking a phrase such as 'the workload is on top of me' and changing it to 'I am on top of the work'.

McIntosh, in an article entitled 'Poetics and Space' writes about the use of 'human geography' to promote reflective learning, exploring 'the linkages between the nature of the literal working spaces that we inhabit and the ways in which concepts of these spaces can be explored internally as reflection through imagery, either visual or literary' (McIntosh 2008: 77). Hage writes that the 'tolerated "Other"' is present within our world view, but 'only insofar as we accept them...[they] are never just present, they are *positioned*' (Hage 1994: 28 my emphasis). This exercise creates the possibility of exposing these positionings.

Some students find this exercise very trivial. However, for others the effect can be quite profound. The moment of discomfort usually comes when I ask students to move themselves around the paper, thus changing their spatial relationships to the other people and institutions they have written down. Occasionally students simply refuse to do it.

...we were required to draw a circle and put ourselves in the middle of the point and put the most important or close people [and then the] less important at some distance... In fact, this is very familiar to me as I work with people who have a learning disability and we have to do a personal plan for them which also includes this picture plan. So I enjoyed it a lot, but when the lecturer asked us to remove ourselves to a different place...[it was] hard to choose a place for myself. In my mind I did not want to be moved away from where I was. The more I moved from the central point the more I felt uncomfortable...

She goes on:

This is another task for me to learn how to improve my personal relationship with others who I may never want to be close or care about. The reasons for this are not because they are not important to me or they are always far away from me. In contrast, it may be the other way around. I was actually thinking of getting close to them and see how it can make any difference. So at present I am not only caring about loved ones but also need to consider others in the workplace and even the Government.

Although this exercise was designed primarily to explore the nature of the power relationships that are significant in students' lives both in a personal and professional context, and the extent to which the possibility of taking up of agency is influenced by our beliefs, when the students referred to their experiences of this exercise the learning they described tended to be more of a reflection on the nature of these relationships, as in the example above, rather than on the possibilities for challenging positions of marginalisation. However, the two examples cited below do touch on the issue of empowerment:

...the 'place yourself' exercise stood out the most. It was the realisation of where I really see myself in the world and who I deem to have power 'over' me. What was most interesting to see was how I could have placed myself anywhere on the page but chose to be in the centre. I saw myself as a 'sun' and those closest to me are fortunate to bask in my rays of warmth and compassion.

And empowerment is even more central in this example:

This week's starting exercise is currently taped to my bedroom door. Placing myself in the middle of a blank page, then slowly surrounding that tiny stick person by other important stick people, and some less important, and words of worries and stresses that a person is likely to encounter in their daily lives, then moving 'me' around the page to see how these other elements affect me when I am further or closer to them. Something 'clicked'. I am a worrier by nature... I wasn't cured by this exercise but I felt relief. Relief from a piece of notebook paper with poorly drawn stick figures on it. I often feel stuck in situations, be it at home, school or work, where I know I won't be able to change things immediately and as a result allow myself to feel trapped and helpless. I wouldn't go so far as to call it an epiphany, but it was a moment when I realised that essentially, I can take myself out of the game if I want and put myself back in. I am the boss of my life.

McIntosh writes that 'we exist in a world of images, visual, memory, metaphorical and language enhanced. Yet we often sleepwalk through the day unaware of the impact that these images could have on our practice if we stopped and took stock of them or shared them with others' (McIntosh 2008: 77). These examples demonstrate this impact at a personal level; in the next section I want to move on to explore the impact such experiences can have at an organisational level.

Challenging stereotypes at the organisational level

...the exercises at the beginning of each session, I enjoyed the fact that each exercise was different and enabled the students to understand diversity from all angles and not to be judgemental.

In this section I want to present some examples of instances in which managers and management students have been able to transform the hitherto unconscious associations they were making that could have limiting and detrimental consequences for colleagues at work. The 'work' of stereotyping proceeds through association. Stereotypes *are* metaphors; metaphors functioning as synecdoche, as in the example I gave in Chapter 2 where the part stands for the whole (as in 'the village is on fire' when only a few buildings are burning). The processes of making associations and then fixing them as synecdoche, for the most time occur unconsciously.

The American poet Robert Frost, in a lecture entitled *Education by Poetry* asserts that

> ...unless you are at home in the metaphor, unless you have had your proper poetical education in the metaphor, you are not safe anywhere. Because you are not at ease with figurative values; you don't know the metaphor in its strength and weakness. You don't know how far you may expect to ride it and when it may break down with you. You are not safe with science; you are not safe in history. (Frost 1931: 5)

The excerpt below is taken from the transcript of an interview with a grant officer from a charitable trust.

> *I think that the, there is a tendency to think that because it is a BME[1] group we can't expect them to uphold our notions of good practice because we have to expect them to behave and operate differently. And because there can be so much nepotism, because there can be so, this issue that you were talking about, 'because you're a volunteer you automatically get the job', and we, within the voluntary sector I think that there's a tendency to say 'well, we need to accept that BME groups will very often reflect the societies from which the majority of the members of that group will come.* (Manager of a grants programme cited in Schwabenland and Tomlinson 2008: 326)

This example is interesting for a number of reasons. The speaker here is undoubtedly well-intentioned; the organisation she works for provides funding to support organisations run by refugees, asylum seekers and people from minority ethnic groups. However, the quotation demonstrates how associational thinking creates stereotypes that can be limiting as well as liberating. Her 'use of the words "we" and "our" carry the clear implication that "our" standards are superior – and this is reinforced by her moving from the reference to nepotism to the suggestion that BME groups are likely to reflect the cultures that people come from' (Schwabenland and Tomlinson 2008: 326). This creates an association between the reference to corruption and the reference to the societies from which the people who work in the BME sector are likely to come. The effect of this elision is to suggest that these cultures are inherently corrupt, and therefore inferior. Here we see a frame of reference being created in the mind which might not only effect the funding decisions that are made but also the ways in which the organisations in receipt of funding are monitored and regulated.

This is a good example of the potential consequences that can flow from limiting associations about individuals and groups. The programme of exercises is designed to help students to identify and resist just such processes of creating and maintaining unhelpful and even detrimental associations. In order to find out whether the effects of the exercises had carried over into students' working lives, I carried out a series of follow-up interviews, generally between four and six months after they had completed the *Managing Diversity and Equality* module. I selected students to interview who were currently employed in a job that carried some management responsibility in order to find out whether they thought that taking the module had had an impact on their practice; whether they felt that they had challenged, or re-evaluated any of their own preconceptions about people, particularly people from groups who experience discrimination and whether they were able to draw on what I am describing as metaphorical patterns of thinking to solve work based problems. In the interviews I looked for evidence of associational patterns of thinking and their application to work situations, use of empathy and finally an enhanced capacity for challenging preconceptions.

Evidence of associative thinking

Within an organisational context, the capacity to expose, challenge and create alternative meanings rests, at least to some extent, on the ability to re-imagine the inter-relationships between the different people and activities that contribute to the organisation and its operations. It is this capacity that may be facilitated by associational thinking, as demonstrated in the following example:

I hope to have stopped considering the issue of diversity solely in terms of how it affects my actions in an HR environment, as I now appreciate that it is relevant in a much broader range of situations both personally and professionally. This realisation will shape my behaviour towards issues surrounding diversity.

Associational thinking clearly has potential beyond that of managing diversity and in the following examples students demonstrate their ability to develop a wider perspective and make connections. In the first two examples the students are describing the ways in which they are linking their student experience to their work:

I found myself linking modules up as I've been studying, 'oh, that links with that'...and I've also been able to apply it in my work which is an absolute luxury.

And:

...in some sense it wouldn't really matter what the course was, it's just nice to be learning. And to, sort of think bigger than just your particular workplace...there's a whole world out there and a bigger picture.

In the next example the student, who works in an HR department, describes her efforts to translate this learning to a specific problem, that of supporting managers who are involved in a restructuring. This quotation is interesting in its deliberate evocation of creative thinking and linking it to 'a bigger picture' and 'see[ing] different perspectives':

[I'm] *trying to think of a way that will make them...think about their teams more creatively and how they get their roles done and how they achieve their objectives. ...cause are they very, very focussed and therefore not seeing a bigger picture... [I'm] trying to get that manager to see it from a different perspective.*

These examples all demonstrate the use of associational logic and its application to problem solving at work. Developing the capacity to draw from a wider range of ideas and sources in making connections is one way in which perspectives can be altered and enlarged. However, for challenging preconceptions at a deeper level, some element of emotional engagement is required. One student began his reflective report with a reference to an 'old African saying':

...'one who has not been to another person's farm will always think that his own father's farm is the biggest in the village'. This African adage speaks a lot about my experience in my study of HRM in which a module titled Managing Diversity and Equality is one of the core subjects.

On one level this metaphor can be read as a statement about the student's enlarged awareness of different perspectives and contexts. But it is done through the evocation of home and might even be interpreted as conveying something of a sense of loss and exile from the certainties of childhood.

Evidence of increased capacity for empathy

Nussbaum (2007), D'Addelfio (2006) and Kohn (1990) all stress the importance of empathy in challenging limiting stereotypes. Simon Baron-Cohen is a psychologist who has pioneered developments in the understanding of autism. His interest in empathy has evolved from his desire to understand more about 'the factors causing people to treat others as if they are mere objects' (Baron-Cohen 2011: 37). He suggests that much of the behaviour that comes to be labelled as 'evil' originates in an absence of empathy. He writes that 'empathy is the most valuable resource in the world...[and yet] it is puzzling that in the school curriculum empathy features hardly at all' (Baron-Cohen 2011: 41). Although it is a small part of the overall curriculum on managing diversity my programme of exercises does represent one such attempt to promote empathy. Therefore, I was particularly interested in finding out whether my students had been able to develop a more empathetic approach to work. Each of the examples I give below has a direct bearing on the implementation of diversity initiatives. The first concerns the use and mis-use of humour – humour is, of course, a complex issue but it has immediate relevance to diversity not only because of the pain that inappropriate 'jokes' can cause, but also because a high proportion of cases taken to employment tribunals under the anti-discrimination legislation concern verbal harassment, justified in the name of humour. For example, the first person to take a case to an industrial tribunal under the 2003 Employment Equalities Act (sexual orientation) was awarded £35,000 because of his experience of being 'subjected to a campaign of ["humorous"] jokes and name calling.[2] In contrast, one of my students said that:

One thing I learned was that I had thought it was good to challenge stereotyping through jokes. And I used to sort of joke with my gay friends, and after the course I thought I shouldn't do that at work, because what might be a joke to me...could be upsetting colleagues and friends.

In her essays on 'excitable speech' (1997) Butler demonstrates the difficulties and complexities inherent in negotiating the terrain between 'the performativity that is hate speech and the performativity that is the linguistic condition of citizenship' (Butler 1997: 81). And yet, on a day-to-day basis, all of us, workers and managers, need to be alert to the potential for hurt that accompanies certain ways of using language. In a particularly powerful example demonstrating increased empathy, the following student told me how she had found the courage to take action against a member of staff who was making sexist and homophobic jokes and causing offence to other staff:

...the jokes that he made about people, you know, ringing up other members of staff...horrendous homophobic jokes he was telling... And you know I was sort of, I was the whistle blower on this and again, a direct result of doing Managing Diversity. Cause usually you sit there and you think, 'well you know, a bit of fun, whatever'. And then you just think 'hang on a moment. Is this the sort of person we want representing our organisation?'.

Empathy offers a useful way of navigating this terrain that can be easily accessed and utilised in work situations as is also demonstrated in the following example:

...rather than just whizzing out a Christmas card, [I found myself] actually thinking about it and thinking what's relevant, and having a chat with people from different religions, 'how would you feel if you received this?'

The third of these examples comes from a student who works in the human resources department of a large, multinational retail company, who said she had been:

...really reiterating to all of the people I've been involved in around maternity issues about how we need to consider these people really fairly...

Interestingly, the company where she works primarily produces women's clothing and the majority of both staff and customers are women. And yet, she has had to advocate for more empathy in the way it responds to pregnant women and women with problems finding appropriate childcare.

In the following example, the student only mentions the workplace, but one can hope that this change in perspective carries over into his personal relationships!

I have also changed my views towards women, in my country of origin, Nigeria, men have significant power and women tend to be submissive towards men. Being mainly women [on the course] *I experienced being a minority. I have learned that women are on an equal if not better footing than men. I believe this experience will influence the way I interview and recruit staff.*

Evidence of increased capacity to challenge preconceptions and practice

The following two examples demonstrate students bring together these two capacities, associational thinking and promoting empathy in order to challenge preconceptions that create limiting practices. In the first example it is the student who is doing the challenging, challenging preconceptions about young people who come from deprived communities is an integral part of his job. When I interviewed him he gave several examples of ways in which the module has helped him in his work.

I work with the corporate social responsibilities teams to recruit companies to work in the community, to support young people, mainly from secondary schools, to raise aspirations…in recruiting the companies we don't go in and say 'look these people are really poor', we say 'you can develop your staff by bringing your staff to come and work in the schools'… So you can use diversity to talk about the course to avoid victimising [young people], *say like, sometimes there are organisations that say 'look we want to give something back' – it sounds really patronising. What are you giving back? So to make them aware that it's not about giving back, it's about you putting your roots deeper and integrating yourself into the community and helping others to integrate…*

In the next example it is the student herself who is being challenged. Her example demonstrates that she welcomes the challenge and is comfortable with it.

…we've had arguments about temps…where we sat there and questioned 'should a temp be allowed to work at home?' And we thought…well, the argument against was 'well they're a temp'. Now how is that a good argument? And it's not a good argument really. So now the temp works from home. All it was, was data entry and they can do that at home on a computer. So sitting there and challenging preconceptions is, umm yeah, it's really good fun, actually…[my manager] *certainly challenges me…because I was the one sitting there and saying 'the temp should work in the office'. And then to sit there and think, 'well actually, do they?'.*

The following example shows how one student was able to connect the metaphor exercise with her work situation:

Diversity was described by some of the students at the beginning of the course as a layer cake, a Rubik cube, rainbow, mosaic etc. At the end of the course our description of diversity changed to that of a fruitcake, and the Rubik cube took on a different meaning depending on how you look at it and from which angle. The last session allowed me, and I hope my fellow students, to think, understand and contemplate the implication of diversity and its impact on us as individuals and on our work in general. Diversity to me is not a Rubik cube and a Rubik cube is not a management strategy but the two have to be brought together somehow by employers. For diversity and equality to work it must be everybody's responsibility: the state, the employer, employee and the community at large.

In this excerpt there is a progression described, illustrating many of the themes that I have touched upon to date; the use of metaphor to clarify the student's understanding of diversity, the ways in which these understandings are refined and challenged through interaction with other students, the ways they evolve over time, and finally, an observation about the inter-relationship of individual, organisation and society.

Challenging stereotypes at the societal level

Barenboim writes:

> If you wish to learn how to live in a democratic society then you would do well to play in an orchestra. For when you do so, you learn when to lead and when to follow. You leave space for others and at the same time you have no inhibitions about claiming a place for yourself. (Barenboim in Barenboim and Said 2004: 173)

In the final week of the module I often show the students a short extract from a documentary about the West Eastern Diwan orchestra, established by Edward Said and Daniel Barenboim, to bring together young Israeli and Arab musicians. The extract I play includes a scene of Barenboim conducing and performing Mozart's *Concerto for Three Pianos*. Barenboim is seated at the middle piano with an Arab and Israeli pianist on either side. The impact of this brief video clip can be experienced at a number of levels. There is the story of the founding of the orchestra, the visual impact of seeing the three pianists playing together and the aural impact of the music itself (although, of course, there will be students who don't particularly like Mozart).

This is one of three exercises that draw on classical art to expose students to its aesthetic power. One week I play them a short piece of percussion music played by Evelyn Glennie, an internationally renowned percussionist who has been profoundly deaf since the age of twelve (a fact which I don't reveal until after they have been listening to the music for some minutes). In another week when the topic is the legislation banning discrimination on the basis of sexual orientation I give the students a selection of extracts of poems and plays written by gay or lesbian authors, from Sappho to Oscar Wilde, but the selections have been anonymised. The students are asked to say where and when they thought they were written, although the purpose of the exercise is more to encourage them to experience the aesthetic power of the writing than to identify them correctly. Students often attribute the extract from *De Profundis,* written by Oscar Wilde to Nelson Mandela, as it is a powerful evocation of the experience of being imprisoned for who you are. When I say that although it is a good guess, to the best of my knowledge, Nelson Mandela is not gay, my response sometimes provokes a moment of disorientation because although the topic of the week's seminar is clearly known to all the students, they often lose sight of it while they are immersed in the poetry, I have found that some also seem to lose sight, at least for a brief moment, of the preconceptions they may have about the (im)morality of different expressions of sexuality.

In each of these exercises it is the experience of the artistic form, listening to the music and reading the poetry that is important – doing the task is really a surrogate for experiencing the art. When the students are told that the musicians have disabilities, that the poets are gay or lesbian, the impact of that information may itself challenge their assumptions about disability or sexuality. However, while each of these exercises is based on aesthetic experience, Barfield's 'felt change of consciousness' (Barfield 1999: 20), the notion of disability that is being disrupted by listening to the music is that of ability while the experience of reading poems written by gay and lesbian poets is slightly different. Here, the intention is to draw the reader into the experience of love, pain, loss and, in *De Profundis,* of being imprisoned and denied freedom. The music disrupts cognitive notions of who can do what, the poetry aims to promote empathy.

Listening to Evelyn Glennie

The exercise that is most often referred to in students' reflective reports is listening to Evelyn Glennie. Many credit it with transforming their preconceptions of disability and making them more aware of the dangers of making unquestioned assumptions. In the examples cited below the students describe a process of becoming conscious of the associations they were making to the music and how these associations were challenged.

This highlighted my naïve assumptions and made me question why I was so surprised at this. It proved a significant point that someone who had a disability was able to do some thing better than most people due to the very thing that labelled them as disabled.

…a personal favourite was the lecture on Disability and Organisation which began with some music. The music was highly skilled with complex off beat 3/4 drum patterns. Initially thought it was a newly found musical prodigy from the San Francisco jazz scene… Proving that assumption is not a good management strategy, the teacher informed us that it was a woman with a hearing impediment.

I remember the classroom filled with percussion and drumming when we arrived for the session in disability and deaf equality and thought immediately of some strange African tribal music. But no, the musician was actually a Deaf woman. While I work with a range of people from Black, Asian and minority ethnic backgrounds, drumming and percussion instantly triggered in my head pictures of half naked black people playing bongos and I didn't even think that was a bit odd!

In the following examples it is the emotional impact of Glennie's musician-ship that made the greatest impression:

When I heard that the music was created by a female artist who was also deaf I was utterly surprised. It seemed hard to believe that someone who was deaf could produce such magnificent sound without actually hearing it herself. This revelation made me realise that I should not take things at face value.

…listening to the instrumentals played by an artist I learned was deaf, the sound and composition of the music was just beyond words. The music was captivating and just flawless but what left me totally in awe was the fact

that the composer could not hear the sound or music... This gave me a new perception and understanding of disability...

And finally:

...now I think of disability in a different way... The pity I have felt in the past has been changed with respect and admiration.

It is important to point out that Evelyn Glennie herself might take a dim view of this exercise. She has written that 'it is the musician's job to paint a picture which communicates to the audience the scene the composer is trying to describe. ... If the audience is instead only wondering how a deaf musician can play percussion, then I have failed as a musician' (Glennie 1993 on-line). However, arguably, it is precisely because she has *succeeded* as a musician that the impact of the discovery of her deafness is so profound.

All of the examples I have given so far concern individuals, students or managers, recounting their own personal experiences of challenging, or being challenged. However, many organisations regard the task of challenging stereotypes and transforming preconceptions as part of their overall purpose. Below is an example taken from an interview with an Indian manager of using theatre and art to change the 'social images of women':

...the social image has been created, in our society, about women as a sacrificing woman or a crooked woman. There is no woman who can fight for the rights of themselves...and have a say in the decision making process. So that is why we started with a small project, a one year project, to identify interested women who want to write plays and who want to direct plays, who want to have their own poster exhibitions. (Voluntary sector chief executive cited in Schwabenland 2006a: 82)

One of the most common areas of activity for campaigning or advocacy organisations is that of challenging the prevailing, and usually negative images of their membership group that have the effect of limiting their opportunities. Below are several more recent examples of the kinds of activities these organisations are involved in. In the first example below a project manager working for an organisation that supports ex-offenders gives an interesting account of the way in which the organisation challenges the negative associations that people with an offending background often encounter:

I think what's positive about [the organisation] is that...in terms of employ-ment opportunities...your offending background does not bar you from a job as a project worker within [the organisation]*...again* [an offending back-ground] *may enable them to support their client better...it makes kind of like a role model, a standard to our clients and also in terms of how you respect your own clients because you're working a lot with colleagues and they have offending backgrounds so I think that...eradicates the stereotype really that I think we all have you know regardless of whether – you know what's said on paper – we all have stereotypes but it really does challenge them I think an organisation like* [the organisation] *does challenge the stereotype – and offenders come in all shapes and sizes!* (Senior project worker cited in Tomlinson and Schwabenland 2010: 112)

This is an interesting example of challenging stereotypes through the deliberate creation of role models. By employing ex-offenders as project workers the organisation is not only challenging the notion that offenders are not employable, it is also using that experience as an asset – an ex-offender can offer a kind of role model that people without that background could not.

The next example demonstrates the use of film as well as theatre to chal-lenge limiting assumptions, in this case about traveller communities.

We had a project, the Gypsy's Wish which was set up with travellers, the local Romany theatre... They produced a 17 minute film based on the experience of travellers...looking at some of the barriers they face, whether it's at school, outside the school...and then we showed it as part of the conference... I figured some of the voluntary organisations have probably never engaged with travellers before – there's this vision of them being 'well, they're X, they're Y, they're Z, there's all these assumptions...so it gave them a chance to actually ask them...and it was one of the feedbacks that got the highest – on the conference was the fact being that they could actually go up to them and found out some-thing they didn't' know about the travelling community before.

At the heart of this campaigning work is the desire to expose and chal-lenge those associations which are detrimental to our understandings of ourselves and each other and then to replace them with associations that carry less pejorative meanings. Organisations use a variety of methods in pursuing these aims – here I have chosen only those that have used aesthetic; theatre and film, and, in the example of the employment of ex-offenders, the metaphorical concept of role model.

Voluntary organisations established to advocate and campaign on behalf of discriminated groups often chose to challenge the particular labels of the day, especially those that are seen as carrying negative connotations. People First, a national user run organisation produced tee-shirts for sale with the phrase 'labels are for jars, not people'. People with learning disabilities dislike being regarded as retarded partly because of the accrued associations with school ground bullying and name calling but also because the label suggests an unchanging and limiting condition, while a 'difficulty' is something that may be overcome, or at least surmounted to some extent.

Associations such as 'slow' for people with disabilities, 'weak' for women, 'intolerant and inflexible' for older people all have their own etymological histories. Dalal suggests that 'the illusion of difference is based on the repression of similarity...the illusion of similarity is based on the repression of difference' (Dalal 2006: 178). An important question then becomes what aspects of identity a particular label exposes and what aspects are rendered invisible. Those repressed aspects of identity may emerge and demand recognition – or they may not. The current trend to find labels that convey a sense of dignity and the potential for self-actualisation may transform the lives of people who have been excluded and marginalised; it may also work to obscure the very real difficulties of struggling with one's own sense of helplessness and need.

Conclusions

> I walked, as a foreign tourist does...
> a camera with me and my guide a little book
> containing poems that describe this place
> by a few foreign poets,
> I feel as if I were the speaker in them
> And had it not been for the difference in rhyme
> I would have said; I am another. (Darwish 2007: 291)

Fady Joudah, one of Mahmoud Darwish's translators, describes Darwish's work as 'facing...a quintessential predicament for the poet; how to carry the "I" of the "we" without betraying one perception for the other' (Joudah 2007: xiii). This is the role of metaphor, to balance the 'I' and the 'not I' and to help us to see ourselves and our worlds anew. And it is this capacity that Kohn (1990) says is needed to live well in a plural society; the capacity to understand and experience how others understand and experience life, while simultaneously remaining at a distance from that understanding and experience.

The assumptions we make between different markers of identity and the characteristics we associate with those markers can have enormous, and often profoundly detrimental consequences. These processes of association proceed, to a large extent, unconsciously, and therefore, possibilities for transformational learning lie in becoming more aware of how we function as the creators of our own metaphors, and this awareness brings with it the possibilities of renegotiating our relationships with ourselves and others. This is the heuristic function of metaphor, and in the previous chapter I showed how a conscious use of metaphor can help to bring these associations to the surface. Once we are aware of the associations we are making we can chose whether or not we wish to continue to see them as valid. This is primarily a cognitive function.

> One could track the meaning of 'love' as a human experience through the changing arrays of metaphors in which it has been addressed. Metaphors change, and with them will change the quality and character of that which they express. Any contemporary usage then, is just that; it is the way in which we are accustomed to express the emotion now. (Mangham and Overington 1987: 14)

But is it through the aesthetic function of metaphor that real transformation can occur. Ricoeur writes that 'poetry and myth are not just nostalgia for some forgotten world. They constitute a disclosure of unprecedented worlds, an opening on to other possible worlds' (Ricoeur 1992: 54). As Lakoff and Johnson point out, '*no metaphor can ever be comprehended or even adequately represented independently of its experiential basis*' (Lakoff and Johnson 1980: 19 my italics). Keats believed that it was this intuitive capacity that rendered poetic truth more valid than philosophic truth, because the very act of creating a logical pattern through which to view the world consisted of creating an abstraction from the experience of the world that could only be felt intuitively. Furthermore, the capacity for being open to new insights arises from an ability not only to experience this intuition empathetically through the 'momentary identification of the Imagination with its object' (Keats cited in Bate 1939: 25), but to do so in a way that keeps one's own ego on the sidelines. It is through empathy that we momentarily allow ourselves to forget ourselves. This is the third stage of the process of engaging with our active imagination, described in the previous chapter.

In these two chapters I have attempted to describe some of the processes by which such transformational learning may be encouraged. Metaphors (and metaphors as stereotypes), function by highlighting some associational meanings and obscuring others. I have suggested that these ongoing processes of sensemaking can be disrupted, so that the chiara obscura patterns these frames of reference create can be evaluated anew. Some of the examples I have presented describe significant transformations in understanding. These examples have been exciting to write about and even more exciting to witness. They demonstrate the enormous capacity of the human spirit for change and growth.

Turchi writes that 'associative leaps through space need to be created. We need to understand what makes electricity arc through the air...the rewards include the powerful bolt of understanding a leap can create, an understanding that reaches the reader beyond words, beyond rational explanation, and so is more intensely felt' (Turchi 2004: 55). And in this chapter I have demonstrated that such experiences can facilitate transformations that have real consequences for people at work. The examples provided by my students have included people becoming more at ease with their sexuality, gender or disability. At an organisational level, the follow up interviews I carried out provided many instances where students had effected changes that really matter to the people they work with; the temp who was allowed to work from home, the man who was disciplined for sexist and homophobic 'jokes', the women receiving more generous maternity provision. Beyond the organisation, the changes that people recounted in their understanding of disability and of the attitudinal barriers that women face, may affect them throughout their lives. Small changes, perhaps. But Judith Butler argues that changes in the frames of reference that structure the ways in which we apprehend ourselves and each other can determine who is allowed to live or die. She writes:

> When those frames that govern the relative and differential recognizability of lives come apart...it is possible to apprehend something about who or what is living but has not been generally 'recognized' as life... And so, we have to ask what would it take not only to apprehend the precarious character of lives lost in war but have that apprehension coincide with an ethical and political opposition to the losses war entails... How is affect provided by this structure of the frame? (Butler 2009: 13)

It is important to remember that not *all* emotional reactions are equally 'truthful' in the sense that Keats suggests. The disruption of one's previous preconceptions *may* lead one to wonder and empathy but perhaps also to horror and revulsion, and to retrenchment (Nussbaum 2004). The experience *can* be enormously exciting, *really good fun, actually,* as one of my students wrote, but it is not always welcome and the following two quotations are important because they demonstrate this:

I didn't particularly like exploring...topics which were close to my own personal experience like race. It was very difficult to remain objective when such experiences may have angered you in the past.

...the course has aroused hurtful feelings about how I feel society has been unfair to the ethnic community... I have come to understand that everyone is indeed not the enemy but many are actually ignorant of the facts.

Perry similarly quoted from two of his students who also demonstrated that this questioning of assumptions is not always a painless process.

> It has involved the tearing away of a lot of beliefs in what has been imposed by convention and I think it does come down to you tearing away your faith... (cited in Perry 1999: 129)

These fears are not unreasonable. All growth involves some loss, the loss of who you were before, your old certainties, your comforts and reassurances, it is a form of leaving home. Bauman notes that culture can become 'a synonym for a besieged fortress' and cautions us to remember 'the close relationship between the degree of security on the one hand...and a willingness to participate in the search for a common humanity' (Bauman 2003: 141). There is an ethical dilemma here which is summed up well by Adam Phillips, writing in the context of attempts by the then UK government to pass legislation against the incitement to religious hatred:

> My guess is that everybody's going to have areas where they're going to be extremely resistant to debate, or debate will literally be redundant for them. And these might actually be the most powerful, dangerous and energy filled areas of their lives. (Phillips and Appignanesi 2005: 166).

He cautions that 'free speech is not only about saying the unacceptable thing to another person...it may also be about saying the thing that is surprisingly unacceptable *to oneself*' (Phillips and Appignanesi 2005: 162 my emphasis). Prasad and Mills (1997) note the often 'celebratory' rhetoric that surrounds much of the discourse on diversity may serve to mask the more complex, conflictual, and perhaps, echoing Phillips, the unacceptable aspects of engaging with diversity.

However, engaging with the diversity of identities that we and our colleagues at work adopt for ourselves and/or are given to us by others, is hardly something about which we have much choice. So the question then becomes one of how best to do it. These chapters have attempted to suggest some possibilities. Curzon-Hobson's (2002) suggests that an element of trust in the relationship between the teacher and the student is essential to critical pedagogy. But trust is complicated; it cannot be one way – the teacher too has to feel a degree of trust in her relationship with her students. She too has to be prepared to have her own preconceptions disrupted. Curzon-Hobson argues that both student and teacher 'aid in re-imagining the potentiality of the other' (Curzon-Hobson 2002: 271). However, the relationship between a teacher and students is not always so mutually beneficial, nor is it always, or even often analogous to the relationships between managers and workers.

What other implications do these observations suggest for the managing of diversity at work? I have suggested that the ability to challenge limiting stereotypes and disrupt the processes that create and maintain them is influenced by the capacity to think 'metaphorically' which is to think associatively and empathetically. This is Nussbaum's prescription to us to see ourselves as 'human beings bound to all other human beings by ties of recognition and concern' (Nussbaum 2007: 291). This associational and relational aspect of sensemaking is antithetical to much of the current management orthodoxy that seeks to separate people, tasks and operations from each other and also from the ethical concerns that underpin the very purpose of coming together in an organisation. Helping ourselves and others to 'see' the connections and the relatedness between people and between functions may, literally, save lives.

These three chapters have focussed on metaphor as a way of thinking and its relevance to the tasks of managing diversity. The next three chapters explore a different approach to thinking within the tension field of similarity and difference, that of dialectic, and similarly, trace its usefulness in the management context.

Part II

Dialectic and Managing Diversity

5
'Exchanges with strangers and things alien'[1]: Introducing Dialectic

Introduction

> Who can discern his own eyes' share of light
> When it is this light which gives each man his sight...
>
> You know of light thanks to its opposite
> Things show their opposite through lack of it. (Rumi 2004: Lines 683–684 and 1142–1143)

Metaphor and dialectic are ways of thinking that structure our relations with ourselves and each other. But while metaphor brings together ideas or concepts that are usually thought of as different in order to highlight their similarity, dialectic involves differentiation; identifying those characteristics that constitute difference.

Metaphor and dialectic structure the *products* of thinking, our thoughts. However, metaphor creates a tension between similarity and difference that is inherently irresolvable. Metaphor can be characterised as representing a model of 'neither/nor' thinking. For example when we say that 'my love is a rose' this statement is clearly *neither* true *nor* false. My lover is not going to transmogrify into a plant, but to say that he is not a rose renders the metaphor meaningless. The meaning of the metaphor is created in the tension itself.

Dialectic works differently. Dialectic is restless. While the tension between similarity and difference expressed in a metaphor is irresolvable, dialectic seeks resolution. One such form of resolution can be expressed as an 'either/or' model of thinking. Margaret Thatcher famously labelled people she felt she could work with as 'one of us' – implying that the others were not. You are in or out – no room for standing in the doorway. Either/or thinking is sometimes also described as binary thinking and it is enormously influential in creating notions of insider/outsider dynamics; the dynamics that create insider groups simultaneously create outsiders (Gergan and Gergan 2004).

Dialectic also asks us to consider what happens when differences meet. If we apply the metaphor of a magnet we see that opposites will either repel each other, resulting in creating further distance between them, or will attract so that they become fused into a whole. Although it is the opposites that repel, within each opposition is an element of similarity that attracts. Turn the magnets over and the force that pulls them together is very strong. Nested within the concept of opposition and separation is attraction and fusion. Fusion creates a new entity that can be characterised as a product of 'both/and' thinking – but unlike the productive capacity of metaphor, where differences and similarities are held in tension, the productive capacity of dialectic leads to hybridity – or to assimilation.

However, more often those characteristics that differentiate one thing from another are not so acute. They may be differences of nuance or emphasis or degree. When these differences are brought together the consequences may be less dramatic and more ambiguous. The bringing together of less strongly differentiated elements can result in conflict or creativity; paradox or stasis. When we apply this to diversity we can locate these different possibilities as points on a continuum from segregation to integration/hybridity to assimilation.

Although dialectic is a dynamic that seeks resolution there are different views about whether such resolution is ultimately possible. Within many Eastern philosophical traditions (and also in the more recent advances in chaos/complexity theories) we find the idea that dialectical movement is constant; that substances (which may be ideas and even cultures and civilisations) are endlessly combining, separating, recombining in iterative cycles of creation and destruction. In contrast, the Marxist approach to dialectics suggests that the oppositional interests of capital and labour will eventually cause the creation of a new social order that may be less inherently conflictual. While society is structured by conflicting ideas and interests these will clash, although the results of these encounters cannot be accurately predicted as they depend on the balance of forces. Nevertheless, although the outcome is not necessarily predetermined, in Marxist thought the potential of a new order that does *not* have conflict inherent in its being remains at least a theoretical possibility whereas in Eastern traditions the physical cycles of creation and destruction can only be transcended through translation to a metaphysical plane.

Why is an understanding of the dynamics of dialectic so crucial to managing diversity? Firstly, discrimination is itself a dialectical activity in which differentiating characteristics are attributed to another and in such a way that attitudes, actions, systems are created that disadvantage that other.

Secondly, dialectic is a dynamic of conflict. Gergan and Gergan write that 'successful organising establishes the ground for disorganisation. To elaborate: consider Bakhtin's (1981) important distinction between dialogue that functions centripetally (bringing language into a centralised form of organisation) as opposed to centrifugally (disrupting or disorganising centralised forms of understanding)' (Gergan and Gergan 2004: 51). The conflicts between individuals and groups whose interests are not the same generate dialectic responses in which some kind of change will occur.

Therefore, dialectic is at the heart of social and organisational change. If we are to understand social change, if we are to intervene to challenge systemic disadvantage then we must participate in a dialectical process. In the next section I will explore how dialectic works, the relationship between dialectic and dialogue, and some of the important differences in approaches; in particular the contrasting understandings of dialectic that appear in Eastern and Western philosophy. I will then go on to concentrate on the two, alternative centrifugal and centripetal dynamics of dialectic that Bakhtin identified, and I will briefly describe some of the ways in which these different dynamics structure forms of organisation and organisational practices, including those of the management of diversity.

How does dialectic work?

The dynamics of dialectic are determined by difference. Metaphor brings dissimilar ideas together in order to reveal their similarity; dialectic discerns differentiation by defining boundaries, contradictions and polarities. These movements are determined by centrifugal logics (which pull towards polarities) and centripetal logics (which pull towards synthesis and resolution).

Walsby describes dialectic as 'the contradiction and reconciliation of opposite standpoints, especially in the development of a person's thought; an idea, much older than the word, of the unity of opposites, not only in men's [sic] minds, but in the world' Harold Walsby 1965, cited in Milner 1989: 180). Dialectic is an abstraction, a way of characterising the underlying dynamics that determine how thinking proceeds. Attention to dialectic focusses our concentration on the relationship between entities, the movements between them and what happens at the boundaries.

Dialectic is profoundly influential as a pattern for structuring our thinking. However, as the quotation above demonstrates, different approaches emphasise different aspects of dialectic. As Walsby describes, dialectics can emphasise *contradiction* in which ideas are represented in opposition to each other. Dialectic dynamics can also propel conflicting ideas towards *reconciliation*. Dialectics can create a unity from the emergence of something new that has been forged out of the meeting of opposites. Dialectical dynamics can therefore be centrifugal, in which the separation of elements leads to their isolation and distinction, or centripetal, in which different ideas and elements are propelled towards fusion. Dialectical dynamics can be either finite, seeking resolution or infinite in which countervailing forces create iterative, oscillating cycles of movement. And they can be both finite and infinite at the same time; 'the centripetal force simultaneously functions centrifugally' (Gergan and Gergan 2004: 52).

Some writers suggest that all knowledge creation proceeds dialectically. For example, Cunliffe and Easterby-Smith suggest that 'learning is an embodied, dialogical activity intimately tied to how we feel, what we say and how we respond to others' (Cunliffe and Easterby-Smith cited in Reynolds and Vince 2004: 447). Bakhtin's concept of the self is 'an embodied entity...which is constituted in and through its dialogical relations with others and with the world at large' (Shotter and Billig in their commentary on Bakhtin 1998: 6). Similarly, Appiah writes that the self is dialogically constituted 'not only because it is in dialogue with other people's understanding of who I am that I develop my own identity...but also because my identity is crucially constituted through concepts and practices made available to me by religion, society and school and state' (Appiah 1994: 154).

Cunliffe and Easterby-Smith, Bakhtin and Appiah, in the examples cited above, use the word 'dialogic' rather than 'dialectic'. Even a fairly cursory survey of literature reveals that different authors use these two words in very different ways. In some cases the terms appear to be virtually interchangeable. For example, Morgan's characterisation of *dialectic* as 'the mutual interpenetration of opposites' (Morgan 1986: 258) seems not unlike Lyotard's description of *dialogue* as 'two parties coming to an agreement about the nature of the referent' (Lyotard 1988: xi cited in Letiche and Essers 2004: 76). And Gadamer writes that Schleiermacher differentiated between different kinds of dialogue including what he terms 'dialogue proper' which is concerned with the search for meaning *and is the original form of dialectics* (Gadamer 1993: 188 my emphasis).

However, other writers see dialogue and dialectic as fundamentally different. Probably the strongest distinction is drawn by Bakhtin, who regards dialectic as an abstract concept and dialogue as an activity achieved in social space. He writes:

> ...take a dialogue and remove the voices (the partitioning of voices), remove the intonations (emotional and individualising ones), carve out abstract concepts and judgements from living words and responses, cram everything together into one abstract consciousness – and that's how you get dialectics. (Bakhtin 1986: 147 cited in Jung 1998: 99)

Not only is dialectic an abstraction, according to Bakhtin's commentator Jung, Bakhtin equates dialectics with identity and modernity, and dia-logics with difference and postmodernity. The distinction he is making is that dialectic is a dynamic between two positions while dialogue has the capacity to be multi-vocal. Grant et al (1998) link these positions with developments in organisational theory, contrasting the 'monological...an attempt to 'construct a singular, coherent discourse or narrative' with the dialogical approach that 'explicitly acknowledges that "organisation" is comprised of a multiplicity of discourses' (Grant et al 1998: 7).

Bohm (2008) rarely mentions dialectic in his work on dialogue. How-ever, he does draw a distinction between discussion and dialogue. Bohm's discussion (which, he points out, shares its etymology with 'concussion' and 'percussion') 'emphasises the idea of analysis, where there may be many points of view and where everyone is presenting a different one – analysing and breaking up' (Bohm 2008: 7) and dialogue in which meanings are created in between and through the words people use. In describing the dynamics of dialogue he notes that when one person responds to another:

> ...the first person sees a *difference* between what he [sic] meant to say and what the other person understood. On considering this difference he may then be able to see something new, which is relevant to his own views and to those of the other person.... Thus, in a dialogue, each person does not attempt to *make common* certain ideas or items of information that are known to him. Rather, it may be said that the two people are making something *in common*, i.e. creating something new together. (Bohm 2008: 3 emphasis in the original)

Grant's and Bohm's conceptualisation of dialogue moves beyond that of oppositional perspectives to embrace many different ways of thinking.

Bohm suggests that the challenge in dialogue is that of 'allowing multiple points of view to be' (Bohm cited by Nichols 2008: ix). Here the distinction being made is not about the number of voices, or viewpoints, but about the nature of their resolution.

Gergan and Gergan's (2004) survey of different interpretations of dialogue highlighted a third debate; whether the resolution of a dialogue is the creation of something new, as Bohm suggests, or merely a 'reciprocal exchange of meaning' (Gruding 1966, cited in Gergan and Gergan 2004). This reflects the debate on metaphor (Sticht 1979, Petrie 1979, Black 1979) that I described in the second chapter and the question about whether a metaphor always leads to a transformation of conceptual schema.

Gergan and Gergan conclude that 'generative dialogue depends on the continuous generation of differences. The meaning making process is rendered robust by virtue of distinctive voices' (Gergan and Gergan 2004: 47). Again, there are echoes here of the debate on generative metaphors (Schon 1979, Black 1979, Petrie 1979).

Gergan and Gergan identified several features of dialogue: that dialogue originates in the public sphere, that dialogue is a form of co-ordinated action, that dialogue is historically and culturally situated and that dialogue may serve many purposes including both position and negation. They also suggest that 'dialogue [is] discursive co-ordination in the service of social needs' (Gergan and Gergan 2004: 42–44). In Ricoeur's work on utopias and ideologies he writes that 'the very conjunction of these two, opposite sides, or complementary functions [of ideology and utopia] typifies what could be called a social and cultural imagination' (Ricoeur 1986: 1). Ricoeur suggests that it is the movement between opposing polarities of thought that allows the imagination the space to create alternatives. Reedy also writes that 'the articulation of the good life involves both implicit and explicit critique of the prevailing social arrangements' (Reedy 2002: 170). When we are presented with images that are incongruous with our notion of lived experience this incongruity opens up/constitutes a new way of seeing.

These debates as to whether there is a difference between dialectic and dialogue seem to rest on three factors; firstly, whether thinking is necessarily abstract or can be regarded as a form of action; secondly, whether this action takes place only between two voices or can incorporate multiple voices and perspectives and thirdly, whether the interaction between these different perspectives necessarily generates new perspectives or 'merely' increased understanding. The latter debate echoes similar discussions on the heuristic functions of metaphor. The view that

I have chosen to take here is that the dynamics of dialogue are dialectical, that dialogue, whether between two or more voices, is *accomplished* through dialectics.

Dialectics in West and East

To add to the confusion, the etymology of 'dialectic' derives from the Greek verb for conversation (Flew 1979). Although there are many different traditions and understandings of dialectic they all have at their heart, the notion of the pursuit of knowledge as a shared endeavour, and one in which propositions are examined in relation to other propositions. Dialectic structures the dynamics through which the search for knowledge and truth (both contested terms) proceeds through identifying the relationships between differences.

Within the Western philosophic tradition dialectic is generally regarded as originating, in the form that we now it, in ancient Greece. Dialectic underpinned the dialogues of Socrates that were written down after his death by his student Plato, and were developed further by Aristotle who established guidelines for their engagement. Flew writes that Grecian forms of dialectic may have originated in a debating game called *eristic* in which 'one person debated a thesis against an opponent who tried to get him to agree to statements that contradicted the thesis' (Flew 1979: 269).

Flew suggests that the Socratic method as developed by Aristotle proceeds by negation; positions are challenged and discarded by demonstrating their weakness and inadequacy. Karl Popper similarly proposed that knowledge proceeds through attempts to falsify propositions on the basis that truth can never be proved but only disproved. Locke, writing on Popper, comments that 'knowledge is advanced by finding out what is *not* so...we can not have the same certainty about corroboration as we do about falsification' (Locke 1994: 11).

The oppositional, or centrifugal model of dialectic proceeds through participants challenging each other rather than through questioning. The participants are more likely to be of (relatively) equal status and the purpose of the conversation is for one to persuade the other of the superiority of their argument. These challenges can take two forms; that of 'contraries' in which polar, or binary opposites are contrasted (such as east/west, hot/cold) or contradictories (good/not good). The superiority of the argument may rest on greater logical development, more valid premises or, as in some of the later writings of Plato, a closer resemblance between that which the premise aims to describe and the greater 'ideal' or form to which it refers (Flew 1979).

The Hegelian model of dialectic differs from the Grecian in that it seeks a synthesis between positions rather than the conquest of one by the other. How describes Hegelian dialects as a 'form[s] of thought or argument that explores the connections between opposites; it involves thinking back and forth between two opposing ideas in hopes of finding a third position that embraces, but also transcends both' (How 2003: 185).

Flew (1979) suggests that there may have been an earlier form of Socratic dialogue based on a model of iterative cycles of question and answer. This understanding of dialectic is not unique to Western traditions, as the model of question – answer – question also underpins many other philosophical traditions in which the student learns from the wise teacher through the posing of questions. This dialectical method emphasises the question, rather than the answer, as the means by which the student is encouraged to develop greater knowledge. The teacher is regarded as the wiser of the two participants, and the purpose of the dialogue is to encourage the student to refine their understanding (although Socratic questioning includes the method of posing the student with contradictions of previous positions). One example of this form of dialectic is the dialogue between Lord Krishna and Arjuna on the field of battle in the Hindu epic *Bhagavad Gita*.

The hermeneutic circle of explanation and understanding can also be understood as a dialectical process. Ricoeur writes, 'explanation is a necessary step for understanding. We always explain in order to better understand.... But the opposite is just as true. If understanding passes through explanation, explanation is completed in understanding' (Ricoeur 1992: 43). Cunliffe suggests that Ricoeur and Merlieu-Ponty both saw dialectics not as dualistic but as a 'continuous interplay of two opposing terms such that they both maintain their difference yet pass into each other' (Cunliffe 2008: 131). Mehta, a hermeneutic philosopher who drew equally on Eastern and Western traditions writes of:

> ...the spirit of joyous adventure which boldly marches out into the unfamiliar and the alien, without fear of self loss, and returns to itself with enhanced understanding of itself, changed and yet the same. Like all understanding, the understanding of our cultural tradition is inescapably *dialectical* in character and presupposes a going out of oneself, the encounter with the other and the strange and a return to oneself...the wandering out in the direction of what is different and question-worthy is not mere adventure but a homecoming. (Mehta 1985: 129 my emphasis)

Mehta's model of dialectic implies that the pursuit of knowledge is endlessly dynamic, always in movement, always in flux, never at a resting point. Furthermore, Ricoeur's 'understanding' and Mehta's 'joyous adventure' affirm the validity of forms of knowledge that are not solely abstract or cognitive.

The Hindu god Shiva, in his manifestation as Nataraja, the lord of the dance, is a symbolic representation of the model of dialectical dynamics as 'continuous interplay'. Nataraja is depicted in a circle of fire within which he is dancing into existence an endless cycle of birth, death and rebirth (although the gestures of his hands point the way toward transcending these cycles). Zimmer writes: 'the wheel of birth and death, the round of emanation, fruition, dissolution and re-emanation…is understood as applying not only to the life of the individual, but to the history of society and the course of the cosmos' (Zimmer 1992: 13).

Hindu cosmology suggests that all materiality emerges out of undifferentiated matter, *prakrti* through the power of *sakti*, creative energy (Pintchman 1994) and to that state of undifferentiated matter all will return. 'At the time of dissolution the order of emanation is reversed, and the entire cosmos withdraws back into the principle or principles from which it originally came' (Pintchman 1994: 78). This is a very old formulation of an idea that has remerged as an important element of complexity theory which seeks to explain how phenomena are 'no longer perceived as either ordered or disordered, either stable or unstable, either organized or disorganized but could paradoxically be both *at the same time*' (Shaw 2004: 20 emphasis in the original). Complexity theories, sometimes described as being on 'the edge of order and chaos' (Waldrop 1993) seek to understand how systems and patterns emerge and similarly, the 'force that is constantly pushing emergent, self organising systems towards the edge of chaos' (Waldrop 1993: 303). In dynamic processes that are still not fully understood, self-organising patterns (common examples are flocking patterns of birds and sand dunes) emerge but then dissolve, only for new patterns to emerge.

Chen and Lee (2008) suggest that the yin-yang symbol represents the Chinese understanding of dialectic, describing both the separation and also the interdependence of paired opposites, and continues to have a profound influence on Chinese philosophy and culture. They write that although there may appear to be a similarity between the Daoist pattern of yin-yang thinking and the Hegelian dialectic of thesis-antithesis-synthesis 'nevertheless, relative to the Western logic of reasoning, the Daoist yin-yang reasoning prefers an ideal state of the middle and harmonious co-existence of opposites' (Chen and Lee 2008: 19). However, while this harmonious co-existence may be the ideal, 'opposing forces are in constant change and their relative positions may evolve or even reverse when leaders seize or create the right conditions' (Chen and Lee

2008: 20). Synthesis differs from the harmonious co-existence of opposites to the degree that it requires fusion, or assimilation. Chen and Lee also suggest that the Daoist model of dialectic differs from the Hegelian model in its location within a more holistic model of cognition that 'attends to and assigns causality to the complete field, especially to the background and contextual factors rather than to the object or the actor' (Chen and Lee 2008: 190).

These Eastern models of dialectic propose an understanding of the pursuit of knowledge that is very much broader than that of the Grecian/Hegelian model of debate. The Western models of dialectical dynamics concentrate on oppositions, whether in terms of the oppositional pattern of formal debating in which one argument emerges as the victor, or in the more holistic models in which the focus is on the dynamic movement between the points of opposition. The Eastern models differ in that their focus is on the centre ground, Shiva in the centre of the circle of fire, the space in which a new idea, a harmonious balance or reformulation emerges.

To summarise dialectic 'works' by defining and responding to difference, Lorde writes: 'difference must not be merely tolerated but seen as a fund of necessary polarities between which our creativity can spark like a dialectic' (Lorde 1981: 99). The meeting of differences, whether physical elements or elements of thought, creates a dynamic movement, which may be centrifugal or centripetal; continual or bound by resolution. These dynamics are manifested, in part, through dialogue.

Dialectics and organisations/dialectics of organising

Dialectical creativity is also manifested in organisation. Organisations emerge out of public space; they are constituted dialectically by the thoughts, aspirations and actions of the members of a particular society at a particular time and place. Habermas conceptualises the public sphere as a space in which 'issues of public importance are explored, debated and resolved through open and undistorted dialogue amongst the citizenry' (Habermas 1981 cited in Kersten 2000: 235). Organisation is one such form of resolution.

Modood suggests that citizenship is 'a work in progress...dynamic and revisable...understood as conversations and re-negotiations' in which the subject has 'the right not only to be recognised but to debate the terms of recognition' (Modood 2008: 49). Modood's ideas on citizenship seem to build on the Habermasian dialectic of communicative action. Habermas conceptualised citizens as 'communicative actors' who 'must be "equipped with three world-concepts (self, other and social) and be able to apply them reflectively", suggesting that "the success of the communicative action depends on a process of interpretation in which participants come to a common definition of the situation within the reference system of the three worlds"' (Habermas 1981: 119 cited in Kersten 2000: 238). A 'society that works', according to Bohm (2008) is one that 'is held together by a "tacit ground" from which thoughts [Habermas's "common definitions"] emerge'. In this way, Tsoukas suggests, 'organisations reproduce the beliefs and institutional practices of the society in which they are embedded, and in so doing they help to perpetuate them' (Tsoukas 2006: 221).

Carter and Jackson write 'order/organisation is only a momentary achievement snatched from chaos, filtered through some kind of "sieve" – an ideology [one such is capitalism, they suggest], *a prioris,* assumptions, a regime of truth – which includes/excluded, bounds, prioritises, to create an illusion of consistency' (Carter and Jackson 2004: 122). Therefore, 'a dialectical approach to organisation studies examines the inherent tensions and contradictions between agency and structure, between the multiple interpretive possibilities that exist in every discourse situation and institutional efforts to impose or fix meanings in particular ways' (Mumby 2004: 242).

> ...the dialectical approach, then, recognises that resistance and domination are not simple binary oppositions but exist, rather in a mutually implicative relationship. As such, organisational discourse can be constituted simultaneously of moments of domination and resistance... Dialectical analysis of power and resistance thus suggest possibilities for multiple and contradictory meanings and realities existing in the same discursive space. (Mumby 2004: 242)

The dialectical approach sees organisations as emerging from dialogic activities within public space from which certain meanings inhere and are given structural forms; forms in which contingent understandings of power relationships are both reproduced and deconstructed dialogically. For example, voluntary organisations come into existence to resolve a contradiction between an existing, unsatisfactory condition and a desired one. The motivation may be to protest against a perceived wrong or social injustice, to create a new service which meets a hitherto unmet need, to create a space to explore through research and participation, how we can build a more just society. Examples of specific activities can range from a group of parents coming together to create a new play facility for their children through to a desire to eradicate child malnutrition through social and cultural change (Schwabenland 2006a). Voluntary organisations inhabit this space between the state and the private sectors, created by the free association of individuals and groups and filled, in part by their most deeply held aspirations about how to create a better world.

Critchley[2] (2007) and Shaw (2004) describe organisations as *conversations*. Davies (2007) also proposes that dialogue is not only something that organisations *do*, but something that organisations *are* although she regards this as being more applicable to certain kinds of organisations rather than organisation more generally (her research focusses specifically on quasi autonomous non-governmental organisations, generally referred to as 'quangos'). She argues that some forms of organisations could be categorised as 'dialogic intermediary organisations' or 'DIOs', which are characterised by being structured through 'lesser known organizational practices which articulate [their] relations with stakeholders, emphasising how these are discursively presented from within [the organisation] in ways that *both call forth and contain possibilities for dialogue*' (Davies 2007: 51 my emphasis) and in which 'there are opportunities for different kinds of knowledge to come into play (Davies 2007: 55). An organisation is 'dialogic' in Davies' terms if its work involves the design of:

> ...an on-going process that brings stakeholder interests into the organisation at all stages. Practices are put in place with the intention of calling forth a set of relevant stakeholders, generating agreement (as far as possible) on what is known and what is in contention, and striving to name a resolution that, if not finally accepted by all parties, is at least acknowledged by them as having been the result of a consideration of all relevant issues (Davies 2007: 61).

This includes the processes it designs to carry out its own internal operating functions as well as in the ways it engages in public space. Davies suggests that in DIOs '*dialogic processes...are built into a more enduring organizational design*' (Davies 2007: 62 my italics).

Davies' work is interesting in its exploration of the ways in which organisational form and function co-create each other and in her specific focus, which is on dialogue as one aspect of governance. However, in her suggestion that the DIO is a new organisational form she ignores the extent to which voluntary organisations, along with other lobbying groups have always occupied this mediating role not only in contributing to public governance but also to social governance through the ways in which they contribute to the imagining and re-imagining of society itself.

Each of the different models of dialectic also finds expression in internal organisational forms and practices. The approach that most commonly finds organisational form is that of the formal debate in which speakers argue for and against a proposition and aim to persuade the audience of the relative merits of their arguments. At the end of the debate a vote is carried out and one side declared the winner. Although formal debates are less fashionable than they once were (with the exception of the continuing popularity of the debates organised by the Oxford University Debating Society) this model of conversation continues to be very influential. It structures the ways in which legal trials are conducted and public debates on current issues presented. One of the most popular public affairs radio programmes in the UK, the Radio Four *Today* programme, regularly invites two speakers who occupy opposing positions to present their arguments which are then tested, usually fairly cursorily, by the presenters. (Often the interviewee with the loudest voice and the best media training has the 'last word'.)

A different example of an organisational practice and one that embodies the cyclical dynamic of dialectic is the *ringi*, a Japanese model of decision-making, in which a proposal is circulated amongst all the staff whose agreement is necessary for implementation. Each person can amend the proposal as it circulates, and there may be several iterative cycles until consensus is reached (Morgan 1986). In this model the aim is not for one participant to persuade the other of the superiority of their position, but for each to learn from each other and to develop a new position that would not have been possible without mutual engagement in understanding each other's position. In this model the movements between positions are neither centrifugal nor centripetal but cyclical.

A third model of dialectic underpins such organisational practices as creative brainstorming and action learning groups, in which people occupying different roles and/or perspectives come together to contribute their different voices to solving a particular organisational problem, or to develop a new approach. (This is also, of course, the model of the 'business case' for diversity, that of multiple voices leading to more effective decision-making, of which more in the following chapters.)

The social dreaming matrix is probably the closest embodiment of Bohm's (2008) model of dialectic. This is a model of group work developed by Gordon Lawrence and colleagues (working in the Tavistock group relations tradition) in which people come together to share their dreams and to associate to these dreams. Lawrence's underlying proposition is that dreaming has a social function as well as an individual one and that by hearing and associating to each other's dreams we can develop new insights about the social and institutional worlds we inhabit. Initially developed amongst groups of interested individuals, the model has been applied within organisational settings as diverse as senior managers' groups (Tatham 2003) and schools (Balamuth 2003). In a social dreaming group the chairs are arranged in a matrix pattern. Lawrence writes that 'matrix is the web of minds existing at any one time and which are harnessed to focus on a particular topic. A matrix continually moving, as it does in a non-linear way, lets loose thinking that could never have been predicted; serendipity and synchronicity become standard' (Lawrence 2003: 270).

Critchley (ibid) suggests that organisations are 'social processes of communication and interaction' which are 'unpredictable, uncontrollable and complex'. Some implications of this third model of dialectic, with its emphasis on *emergence* are, firstly, that the act of bringing people together may produce unpredictable results, secondly, that in contrast to the model of the formal debate, what emerges will not be the creation of one individual, or a representation of one position alone. As Bohm writes, 'such communication can lead to the creation of something new only if people are able freely to listen to each other, without prejudice, and without trying to influence each other...each has to be ready to drop his old ideas and intentions and be ready to go on to something different, when this is called for' (Bohm 2008: 3).

What all three models of dialectic share is the generation of new meaning through difference. Cunliffe writes that 'a sense of organisational life, of selves and of what needs to be done, is contested, negotiated and created inter-subjectively by people in their relationally responsive dialogical activities...managing is a relational and dialogic process' (Cunliffe 2008: 131). In the next section I want to explore this notion of 'management as a dialogic process' with specific reference to managing diversity.

Dialectics of diversity

> It's hard to see how any country whose political system uses the word 'dialectical' to label its philosophy can then execute those of its countrymen who disagree with the party line. (Milner 1989: 114)

Milner highlights (rather dramatically) one of the paradoxes of management: this is the co-existence of desire for, and resistance to change. If we agree that one aspect of diversity management is the redress of systemic discrimination in the labour market then ultimately its purpose is to achieve social change. The different models of dialectic also represent different theories about how social change occurs. Burrell and Morgan's (1979) work on sociological paradigms distinguished between those theories that focussed on stability and on society's 'underlying cohesiveness' from those (such as Freire's) that were concerned with radical change and 'man's (sic) emancipation from the structures which limit and stunt his potential for development' (Burrell and Morgan 1979: 17). The dynamics of 'radical' sociology are centrifugal; organisation creating disorganisation, while sociology of 'regulation' is structured through a centripetal dialectic.

In an earlier work (Schwabenland 2006a) I drew on these paradigms in analysing the ways in which voluntary organisations responded to the problem of the systemic marginalisation of certain groups from many aspects of society. These contrasting perspectives on social change were represented by a clear distinction between those organisations that focussed on achieving the inclusion of marginalised people into the existing structures of society and those that questioned and challenged those very structures. Managers made choices about whether to work from the inside or the outside, but also whether to aim for radical or incremental change. These contrasting approaches also find expression in the debate about the 'radical' or 'liberal' diversity agenda (Kirton and Green 2005).

A third perspective, drawing on complexity approaches, and echoing Bohm's (2008) model, suggests that diversity is itself the driver of social change. Diversity creates a transitional space by interrupting taken for granted patterns of relating and acting. Shaw (2004) maintains that change occurs when patterns shift, and patterns shift when *difference* is introduced. Stacey writes that 'diversity arises in the scope for different interpretations open to people communicating with each other. ...It is in these ongoing differences of interpretation that individual and collective identities are continually recreated and transformed' (Stacey et al 2002: 189). So diversity is *intrinsic* to change.

Dialectic is also of fundamental relevance to managing diversity because, at its heart, it defines the structures that affect the way we think about ourselves and about others. Ironically, much of the rhetoric about diversity tends to be framed in binary rather than polyphonic patterns. Issues and tensions are frequently presented in pairs of mutually antagonistic oppositions: diversity *or* equality (Wrench 2005), the business case *versus* the social justice case (Tomlinson and Schwabenland 2010, Due Billing and Sundin 2006), individuals *versus* collectivities. the liberal *versus* that radical agenda (Kirton and Green 2005). Kandola and Fullerton distinguish between inclusive and exclusive strategies and they create tables that contrast these different approaches, in particular, the 'managing diversity' approach and the 'equal opportunities' approach (Kandola and Fullerton 2003: 13 and 167). Other common examples of the binary trope include hard skills versus soft skills, compliance (with legislation) versus co-operation – the field is littered with examples.

What are some of the implications that follow from framing diversity issues in this almost ubiquitous construction? Meyerson writes that the very words we use can become 'a mechanism of control...when people talk exclusively in the language of the dominant culture they come to think that way as well' (Meyerson 2003: 149). The way that we think influences the way we act; our thoughts not only create representations of reality as we perceive it, they also create new realities – our worlds become what we imagine them to be. As Ricoeur (1992) points out, social reality is constituted by social imagination.

Positioning ideas in opposition to each other can be a useful device. It creates distance, it emphases differentiation. Without frameworks for creating coherence, we would have no way of making sense out of what Weick calls a 'flowing soup' (Weick 1995: 128). But Weick also cautions us to remember that all sensemaking is a form of invention, the frameworks are distortions, or fictions. The danger is in losing sight of their symbolic nature and coming to believe that they are representations of truth rather than of ideas. As previously noted (in Chapter 3), Darwish writes that 'identity is the distorted image in the mirror that we must break the moment we grow fond of it' (Darwish 2009: 156).

Aldrich (1992) criticised Burrell and Morgan's (1979) model of sociological paradigms, which they derived by constructing two contrasting binary axes, arguing that the paradigms are merely focussing on 'contrasting but related' aspects of complex reality and that their commonality is more striking than their differences. Dalal (2006) in his work on the dynamics of racism also suggests that in creating distinctions in our minds between certain aspects of identity these distinctions may, intentionally or otherwise function to mask the similarities between them. Therefore, one danger in binary thinking is that the emphasis on difference obscures similarity.

Postcolonial theorists have mounted another challenge to binary forms of thinking by demonstrating that these polarities are often not seen as truly equivalent but may be presented in such a way as to construct the second as inferior. In his book *Orientalism* Said suggested that the project of colonisation was carried out on an imaginative level through the constructing of just such a binary opposition between the West and the Orient in which the West was always positioned as superior. Prasad writes that 'the discourse of Orientalism constructed an elaborate architecture of hierarchical dichotomies by which...the West, was conceptually manoeuvred into a position of ontological superiority' (Prasad 2006: 123–124). In addition to the binary of coloniser/colonised some of these opposing characteristics that Prasad identifies that still have salience today include: developed/developing; nation/tribe; vanguard/led; secular/non-secular (Prasad 2006: 124).

In his seminal essay on the psychology of colonialism, *The Intimate Enemy*, Nandy suggests that coloniser and colonised are *both* victims of colonisation, that colonisation is a 'state of mind in the colonisers and the colonised, a colonial consciousness' (Nandy 1983: 1) in which each can only be understood in terms of the other, in which each is engaged in the reification of each other. Arguably it is this interdependence and interconnectedness that is masked by the presentation of these positions as oppositions. Butler, in her work on *Frames of War* suggests that the reason why one person is not free to destroy another is precisely because of this fundamental interdependence; 'the subject that I am is bound to the subject I am not... How that interdependency [between groups engaged in conflict] is avowed (or disavowed) and instituted (or not) has concrete implications for who survives, who thrives, who barely makes it and who is eliminated or left to die' (Butler 2009: 43).

One of the most commonly identified colonising strategies is that of the exoticising, but simultaneously also essentialising the Other (Frenkel and Shenav 2005, Said 2003, Gandhi 1998). Bhabha writes that 'an important feature of colonial discourse is its dependency on the concept of "fixity" in the ideological construction of "otherness"' (Bhabha 2003: 66). Any attempt to understand one's own identity necessarily involves some separation, or boundary marking between that which I am and that which I am not. But these boundaries are endlessly fluid and changing. Butler (2009) and Dalal (2006) note that the permeability of these boundaries is often perceived as an existential threat, the threat of invasion and destruction. From this analysis dialogue becomes a very risky proposition because if my understanding of you is likely to be altered through engaging in dialogue, so is my understanding of myself, and perhaps even my sense of existence.

Meyerson (2003) also points out that one can only be perceived, or perceive oneself as different if there is something to which one is being compared. One cannot be different in a vacuum. The notion of difference very often implies that there is a norm *against which* one is being defined. For example, in his analysis of the 2001 UK census categories Mason concluded that:

> Those who ticked 'white' were not required to further differentiate themselves.... At the same time, the other categories represent a curious mishmash of principles of differentiation. Thus, they mix, in a variety of inconsistent ways, skin colour, geographical origin, and nationality or citizenship categories. In practice, the only thing that unites them is that they are all presumed to capture the ethnic identities of those members of the population whose skin colour is thought of as not being white, Therefore, the apparent recognition of diversity is immediately undermined by their definition, in practice, by exclusion – they are not white. (Mason 2003: 14)

Beatty and Humphries were interested in why some groups are 'recognised' under the gaze of diversity management and others were not. In particular, they noticed that indigenous groups such as the Maori in New Zealand, are rarely mentioned in the diversity discourse and they conclude that 'the act of defining diversity groups reinforces existing power relationships. This process is embedded when scholars focus their gaze on the legally defined diversity categories without challenging how they have been defined and to what effect' (Beatty and Humphries 2007: 1). They continue: 'The categorising of all species and placing them into relationships to one another has preoccupied humanity in all cultures...once sorted and ordered into groups, based on a specific and supposedly shared characteristic these can then be ranked in order of most or least in need, or most or least useful to the status quo – the functional needs of society. This categorising and ranking is not a politically or power neutral process' (Beatty and Humphries 2007: 6–7).

Centrifugal dialectics, as manifested in binary thinking, can thus entrench the position of the unexamined norm while also ensuring that, through its very invisibility it remains unavailable to challenge. However, these processes of naming and labelling are also essential sensemaking devices. Resisting the dangers inherent in these processes requires an ability to handle multiple, sometimes paradoxical concepts in mind, to develop the mental flexibility and agility to move from either/or thinking to the both/and patterns of thinking created through centripetal dialectics. Gutman writes:

> Full public recognition as equal citizens may require two forms of respect: (1) respect for the unique identities of each individual,

regardless of gender, race or ethnicity, and (2) respect for those activities, practices and ways of viewing the world that are particularly valued by, or associated with, members of disadvantaged groups, including women, Asian Americans, African Americans, Native Americans and a multitude of other groups in the United States. (Gutman 1994: 8)

This quotation comes from the introduction to a series of essays and commentary written in response to Charles Taylor's influential essay on *Multiculturalism and the Politics of Recognition*. Gutman's use of both/and thinking in his notion of the 'two forms of respect' seems to share affinity with Dubois's concept of 'double consciousness' (Gordon 2007) and also resonates with that of the postcolonialist theorist Dipesh Chakrabarty, who also writes about 'a consciousness that was inherently double' (Chakrabarty 2000: 240) in his description of the ways in which intellectuals from the global South develop an awareness of different modes of being, 'the infinite incommensureables through which we struggle...to "world the earth" in order to live within our different senses of ontic belonging' (Chakrabarty 2000: 254).

Double consciousness is a product of both/and thinking. However, I would distinguish it from metaphorical thinking, which I have described in the previous section of this book in very similar terms, because metaphor works by holding these different ideas and concepts in an irresolvable tension, while in these examples there is a dialectical movement; a fluidity being maintained between the different positions.

Meyerson coined the phrase 'tempered radicals' to describe people who 'want to succeed in their organisations yet want to live by their values or identities...[tempered radicals] want to fit in *and* they want to retain what makes them different' (Meyerson 2003: xi emphasis in the original). This label seemed to resonate with the people she interviewed. Meyerson's 'tempered radicals' bear close affinity to Perriton and Reynolds' (2004) 'teachers who refuse'. Perriton and Reynolds, in their analysis of critical management education, drew on the postcolonial critic Memmi's notion of the 'coloniser who refuses', the 'individuals who worked within the colonial state apparatus *despite* being politically uncomfortable with the idea and reality of colonial rule' (Perriton and Reynolds 2004: 72). Tempered radicals and managers who refuse locate themselves within a dialectic of challenge and collusion.

Managing this dialectic calls for what Creed and Scully (2000) termed 'micro-mobilisation', the strategies undertaken by workers who mobilise their social identity 'in ways they hope will advance social change projects' (Creed and Scully 2000: 392). Their study focussed on lesbian, gay, bisexual and transgendered employees whose social identities, as people with a minority sexual orientation, are often invisible. Acting as insiders seeking to effect social change, these employees would make strategic decisions about when and how to deploy their identities. Creed and Scully identified three distinct, albeit overlapping strategies of 'claiming' identity, using identity to educate others and using identity to advocate on behalf of themselves and others of their group. They write that 'claiming as a way to reduce stigma is partly about claiming common ground and showing alikeness, even in simple things. At the same time, truly speaking about an identity is *also* to highlight its distinctiveness' (Creed and Scully 2000: 399 my emphasis).

In their relationships with governments, voluntary organisations can find themselves playing a similar role. Many voluntary organisations are formed out of a strongly felt desire for societal change, usually on behalf of a marginalised group, often a group which may be a focus of diversity initiatives (such as people with disabilities or from minority ethnic groups). Many of these organisations direct their efforts at the state, either in terms of advocating for better services or legislation, or in the provision of services. The dilemmas that such organisations find themselves in when the government of the day seeks to work with them (or co-opt them) as willing partners in a shared endeavour, are heartfelt and well documented (see for example, Schwabenland and Tomlinson 2008, Rosenmann 2000).

Despite the obvious difficulties in occupying these highly ambiguous roles, the proposition that boundaries of ideology, positioning, sectoral interests and expertise (to name but a few) can be easily transcended seems to lie at the heart of much of the rhetoric about partnerships and coalitions of shared interest, whether they are public/private initiatives, multi-agency task forces, regeneration consortia, conflict resolution initiatives at an inter-organisational level; or action learning groups, group relations events and intra-disciplinary teams within organisations.

Noumair (2004) described a project she developed to explore diversity issues within a university, using the model of the group relations conference (as pioneered by the Tavistock Institute) over a period of years. She found that the conferences did provide a space in which some of the inherent contradictions in the university's own practices could be identified (and could thus be regarded as an initiative of tempered radicalism or refusal, in itself). However, the conflicts and contradictions within the group were not unproblematic. One of the challenges the groups encountered was a difficulty in conceptualising collaboration other than within an opposition of domination or submission. She writes that 'when we attempted to shift from monologue to dialogue we learned that the gap between these two approaches was too wide and too soon – rather what we needed was a transitional space in which the old could be maintained while learning about the new. What remained unclear, however was what such a transitional space would look like in group relations terms' (Noumair 2004: 74).

How can managers create such 'transitional spaces' in which multiple realities can be accommodated? Shaw, also drawing on Habermas, uses the metaphor of 'ensemble improvisation' as 'an organising craft of communicative action' (Shaw 2004: 164). In the quotation below, taken from an interview in a previously published study of the founding of voluntary organisations, I give an example of the way in which such communicative action, in this instance the founding of an organisation to bring together people working in the field of residential care, which was at that time a very marginalised activity, led to a new understanding of the way in which they were constructing the meaning of their work:

My understanding is that it [the organisation] was just a talking shop of various organisations providing residential care, about what they thought they were about, what they were doing, why they thought they were doing it, what was the purpose of residential care, should you train your staff, was it a vocation or was it a profession, or was it just a way of earning a living? (CEO of an association working with providers of residential care, cited in Schwabenland 2006: 93)

In summary, dialectical dynamics underpin the ways in which we construct our relationships with each other. These dialectics create patterns of thought, whether they be the oppositional binaries of self/other, the accommodations of 'refusers' or 'tempered radicals' or the creating of new understandings in the crucible of a transitional space. Each of these models of dialectic function, as do metaphors, to illuminate and obscure; each can also both disrupt and maintain the complex power relationships that sustain patterns of marginalisation.

Conclusions

In this chapter I have argued that dialectical dynamics structure the ways in which we think about ourselves and each other, by determining the ways in which we are similar and in which we are different. Engaging in dialectical modes of thinking is not an option, it is inevitable, and it is that which structures thinking itself. I have made a similar claim about metaphorical forms of thinking as well, of course, in the earlier chapters of this book. But metaphorical thinking proceeds through association while dialectical dynamics proceed through differentiation. And thoughts are immensely powerful. As Butler points out, 'the "frames" that work to differentiate the lives we can apprehend from those that we cannot...not only organise visual experience but also generate specific ontologies of the subject...such that our very capacity to discern and name the "being" of the subject is based on norms that facilitate that recognition' (Butler 2009: 3–4). She argues that 'if certain lives do not qualify as lives or are, from the start, not conceivable as lives within certain epistemological frames, these lives are never lived, or lost in the full sense' (Butler 2009: 1).

The Palestinian poet and activist Mahmoud Darwish wrote:

> The casualties/martyrs don't resemble one another. Each of them has a distinctive physique and distinctive features, different eyes and a different name and age. The killers are the ones who all look the same. They are one being, distributed over different pieces of hardware pressing electronic buttons, killing and vanishing. He [sic] sees us but we don't see him, not because he's a ghost but because he's a steel mask on an idea – he is featureless, eyeless, ageless and nameless. It is he who has chosen to have a single name: the enemy. (Darwish 2009: 26)

Darwish's description of the 'Othering' of the enemy here is particularly interesting because he is writing from the perspective of the oppressed; the rhetoric of the 'Other' as non-human, is more often used to justify the violence of the aggressor towards the (constituted as non-human) victim.

The ways in which we come to frame our understanding of each other may ultimately determine who lives or dies. Less dramatically, they determine who is heard in an organisation and who is not, who is seen and who is invisible and, of course who is included or excluded. In the UK researchers regularly carry out an experiment in which Curricula Vitae (CVs) are sent out to potential employees. The CVs are comparable in terms of the levels of education, skills and relevant experience of the applicants. Only the names are different. One name indicates that the applicant is probably white British, another name is ostensibly Muslim and a third is African. Each time this experiment is carried out the results are depressingly similar; the applicant with the white British name is very much more likely to be invited to interview than the others.[3] It is clear that the employers' response is influenced by the dialectics of difference – what is different (their names) becomes more significant than what is shared (the applicants' qualifications and experience).

Obviously more could be said about this example. But if such small differences, names, can outweigh the much more significant similarities, then whatever the diversity rhetoric says, there is a long way to go before differences are seen as something to be valued, let alone a source of competitive advantage.

Kersten writes that 'US society reflects racism not only structurally, through its patterns of exclusion and marginalisation, it also reflects racism in the subtle patterns of everyday reality, that take white norms of behaviour, interaction and perception as its not-so-subtle standards for normality, beauty, properness, professionalism and everything else' (Kersten 2000: 239). Oppositional dialectics position the non-white against this presumed norm of whiteness.

In this chapter I have presented some alternative models of dialectical dynamics such as the cyclical models that are represented in Eastern philosophical systems and within the Western tradition, those of Habermas's dialectics of communicative action, Bakhtin's model of polyphony and Bohm's model of emergent meanings. These models all propose less oppositional ways of working with difference. However, in her critique of Habermas's model Kersten argues that communicative action may be relatively straightforward when unexamined assumptions are shared between members of a group, but much more difficult when there are major differences. In these circumstances dialogue requires 'a critical and reflective understanding of one's own world, an empathetic grasping of the world of the other and the shared building of a joint world based on an undistorted social consensus' (Kersten 2000: 239). Kersten concludes that communicative action requires 'not only the willingness to critically examine one's own worldview but also the necessity to be open to, and transformed by the potentially radically different worldview of the other' (Kersten 2000: 239).

Kersten's suggested preconditions for dialogue echo Nussbaum's much cited capacities needed to live in a pluralistic democracy: 'the capacity for critical examination of oneself and one's traditions' and 'the ability to see [ourselves] as…as human beings bound to all other human beings by ties of recognition and concern' (Nussbaum 2007: 291–294). What are the factors that inhibit such engagement? Firstly, if there are significant inequalities between participants there will be major barriers to genuine participation.

Kersten argues that 'dialogue is only possible and effective if it manages to break through the ideological and structural parameters that define our racial positioning in society' (Kersten 2000: 236). Power dynamics are an intrinsic element in determining the direction of the dialectics.

Secondly, there is the contestation of public space. A current example is the debate about the wearing of the veil, currently being rendered illegal in some European countries. This demonstrates the difficulty of achieving the necessary 'consensual norms' (Warner 2010, Butler 2009) that Habermas suggests is necessary for communicative action to take place. In this particular instance Nandy (2002) argues that the public sphere must allow for continuous dialogue amongst religious traditions and between the religious and the non-religious, an accommodating of religion within public space rather than its exclusion.

Thirdly there is the barrier created by fear of difference. McCreary, writing about communal tensions in Northern Ireland during the Troubles, comments that 'those who are different to us have to always be part of our consciousness in a society where the other, at best, has often been seen as the other who is out to "threaten" me...or the other...who is out to kill me' (McCreary 2007: 104). In such situations fear of the other is not necessarily irrational. But fear can manifest itself in other, less dramatic ways. The anxiety that can accompany a loss of certainties and the decentring of one's own assumptions can be profound.

Fear of the other can also be experienced as a fear of being taken over by the other, a fear of the loss of self. This kind of fear can manifest itself by a dialectic of attraction and repulsion from the threat of pollution. Nussbaum writes that 'in many ways our social relations...are structured by the disgusting and our multifarious attempt to ward it off...most societies teach the avoidance of certain groups of people as physically disgusting, bearers of a contamination that the healthy element of society must keep at bay' (Nussbaum 2006: 72).

From a psychoanalytic perspective fear of the other is often motivated by a desire to repress unacknowledged and unbearable aspects of ourselves, which we then project onto the other (Dalal 2006). Creating a fear of the other then becomes a way of managing our fears of ourselves. To return to the quotation that I used to open this chapter, the 'exchanges with strangers and things alien' are encounters with the alien self. An awareness of the different dialectical ways in which we develop our understanding of self and other can help us to manage and transcend the more frightening aspects of these encounters.

6
Polarities, Paralysis and Paradox: Centrifugal Dialectics

> Which, of a multitude of differences between people justify us in treating them differently and which similarities justify similar treatment? (Edwards 1987: 45)

Introduction

The quotation above from Edwards is one that I have used a lot in teaching. It is a deceptively simple question that goes to the heart of the dilemmas of managing diversity. This chapter is going to concentrate on difference and how it is constructed within organisations and by organisations. In this, and subsequent chapters, I am drawing on Bakhtin's distinction between the centrifugal and centripetal dynamics that underpin dialectic. In a centrifuge rapid motion separates substances into components of different densities. Centrifugal force is that which propels these substances away from the centre. Centrifugal dynamics is a powerful metaphor for capturing some sense of the patterns of thinking that create notions of difference.

Difference depends on similarity – difference and similarity are two sides of the same coin. To determine how one thing is different from another depends on there being some similarity between them, whether that is the similarity to be found amongst entities that share the differentiating attributes or the similarity amongst those that do not. When I say that I am a vegetarian I am at the same time claiming commonality with other vegetarians and differentiating myself from people who eat meat. This example demonstrates that the processes of defining characteristics of difference and commonality happen simultaneously. To affirm commonality is to affirm difference, and vice versa.

In a centrifuge difference is determined by density. In relationships between people difference is determined through the identification of characteristics that can be used to categorise them into different groups. Categorising things, people or ideas stems from our need to impose some kind of order out of chaos and is at the heart of consciousness itself. Psychoanalytic theory has contributed greatly to our understanding of this process and suggests that it may originate with the experiences of a baby when s/he begins to comprehend that s/he is not a part of the mother but a separate being (Milner 1996). This increasing awareness may be accompanied by complex emotional responses including a greater sense of security, of knowing where and what you are, but also of anxiety and loss.

Foucault (2002), in his introduction to *The Order of Things* gives a wonderful example of the desire to impose order in the famous classifications of animals, sometimes attributed to an ancient Chinese encyclopaedia *The Heavenly Emporium of Benevolent Knowledge*[1] in which they are divided into 'a) those that belong to the emperor; b) embalmed ones; c) those that are trained, d) suckling pigs; e) mermaids; f) fabulous ones; g) stray dogs; h) those that are included in this classification; i) those that tremble as if they were mad; j) innumerable ones; k) those drawn with a very fine camel's hair brush; l) etcetera; m) those that have just broken the flower vase; and n) those that from a long way off look like flies' (Foucault 2002: xvi).

Foucault writes that when he encountered this set of categories it 'shattered...all the familiar landmarks of thought – *our* thought...breaking up all the ordered surfaces and all the planes with which we are accustomed to tame the wild profusion of existing things and continuing long afterwards to disturb and threaten with collapse our age old definitions between the Same and Other' (Foucault 2002: xvi). Windschuttle's (1997) suggestion that Borges actually invented this taxonomy does not detract from its usefulness in demonstrating three important aspects of systems of categorisation; firstly, that they are culturally contingent even if they have a basis in empirical observation, secondly, that they all work on the basis of differentiation which requires the identification of characteristics that are shared and those which are not, and thirdly, that the processes by which such characteristics are identified are never value free.

The awareness of the separation of the child from its mother can create anxiety, frustration and distress. Encountering the Borges/Chinese system caused Foucault laughter. But when the systems that we create to differentiate ourselves from each other rest on unconscious or taken for granted assumptions, such emotional reactions may be buried very deeply, as is an awareness of the subjective nature of these systems.

Although the creating of order is an essential part of sensemaking, there are several important caveats that are particularly relevant to managing diversity. Firstly, as discussed in the previous chapter, Beatty and Humphries argue strongly that 'the diversity schema is based on a *flawed* theory of categorisation' (Beatty and Humphries 2007: 4 my emphasis). They argue that in any system of categorisation there are inherent assumptions of value. The characteristics that define commonality and difference are rarely, if ever, seen as being of equal value. So, for example, in the distinctions between male/female, black/white, heterosexual/homosexual there are underlying assumptions that certain attributes are more valuable than others. Or, as Spivak puts it: 'when a cultural identity is thrust upon one because the center wants an identifiable margin, claims for marginality assure validation from the center' (Spivak 1993: 55). Spivak writes that 'the choice of a particular binary opposition…is no mere intellectual strategy. It is, in every case, the condition of the possibility of centralisation…and, correspondingly, marginalisation' (Spivak 2006: 153–154). From this perspective the discourse of diversity is inherently embedded in the very value system it purports to challenge.

Prasad (2006, 1997) further suggests that such flawed schema can promote essentialised understandings of self and other and he demonstrates how this process of creating categories is aided by a dialectic of oppositions. Writing specifically on the postcolonial context, Prasad appropriates Said's proposition that the 'Orient' is an imaginary creation, developed from the assumption that the 'Orient' and the 'Occident' are 'ontologically and epistemologically…binary opposites that do not share in the same humanness' (Prasad 2006: 123). The relevance of this observation to current diversity issues clearly goes beyond its historical significance.

Secondly, Beatty and Humphries suggest that these assumptions of value are themselves influenced by a hegemonic idealisation of the 'good society'. Beatty and Humphries equate this with the system of capitalism, however a different idealisation of the good society, and more relevant to Prasad's argument, is manifested by Samuel Huntingdon (1993) in his controversial essay, *The Clash of Civilizations*. Huntingdon suggests that the West and the non-West (specifically those countries with Muslim majorities) are engaged in a battle of irreconcilable ideologies, in this case cultural and religious rather than economic.

Thirdly, there is Hofstede. The field of cross cultural management has been strongly dominated by the work of Hofstede (1991, 2001) and, to a lesser extent, Trompennaars and Hampden-Turner (1997) who suggest that national cultures can be defined, measured and 'located' on 'dimensions' representing sets of values including attitudes to authority and uncertainty, affiliations to self or community and attitudinal affiliations towards 'masculine' or 'feminine' characteristics. This approach is definitely not without its critics who focus on issues such as methodology (McSweeney 2002), on Hofstede's essentialist perceptions of cultures (Kwek 2003) and his simplification of the complex dynamics between competing cultures particularly those of organisational culture, occupational culture and intra-organisational subcultures (McSweeney 2002).

In the same edition of *International Journal of Cross Cultural Management* two articles drew opposing conclusions about the relevance of national culture to organisational culture. Zander and Romani wrote that 'our results suggest that interpersonal leadership preferences related to national cultural values are *not* overridden by values acquired in an second (occupational) or third (organisational) level of socialization' (Zander and Romani 2004: 309 my emphasis). However, Sackman and Phillips concluded that 'in a multi-cultural and diverse society culture can no longer be implicitly defined as a substitute for nation, and members of such societies can no longer be assumed to identify solely, or most strongly with their country of national origin or citizenship' (Sackman and Phillips 2004: 384).

Despite these critiques, the 'cultural dimensions' approach is extremely influential; it is impossible to walk through any international airport in the UK without seeing adverts for HSBC bank that rely on a widespread understanding and acceptance of these dimensions. Also, in my experience, students love it. Even those who think that Hofstede's 'location' of their own country is simplistic often go on to apply his theories uncritically. Moreover, if we regard theory as not only reflective but also productive of reality then Hofstede's significance becomes even more important, as his dimensions have provided management theorists, managers and students with a popular heuristic.

In this chapter I explore some of these dilemmas in more detail. Centrifugal dialectics, emphasising separation and difference, promote ways of thinking about self and other that create dilemmas that influence the successful implementation of strategies to promote diversity as a positive force for good within organisations. The chapter is organised in three sections; the first looking at dilemmas for individuals, the second looking at some of the ways in which organisational processes *produce* difference and the third, looking at how organisations create and sustain constructions of difference within the wider society.

Dialectics of differentiation between individuals at work

Although I'm a black Briton when I'm in Shropshire I feel more black and when I'm in Hackney I feel more British.

This was a comment made by the *Guardian* journalist Gary Younge, at a conference on diversity at work in London, in October 2003 organised by the newspaper in conjunction with TMG Consultancy. Younge's remark demonstrates how much our environment affects the way we see ourselves. Often, if we feel a sense of commonality with the people in our immediate environment we may take those characteristics that we share for granted. However, when we become aware of some aspect of ourself that separates us from the others that awareness can be problematic and can affect the way we carry out our work roles. In this section I want to draw on several examples from research projects of my own and also projects carried out with a colleague, Frances Tomlinson. These demonstrate some of the complexities and dilemmas created by the intersection of personal and professional identity.

My first example comes from a small research project I carried out exploring the feasibility of introducing an element of peer assessment into postgraduate courses on diversity and cross-cultural management.

Deciding what methods of assessment to use is important, because 'assessment defines what students regard as important, how they spend their time and how they come to see themselves *as* students' (Brown et al 1977: 7 my emphasis). Therefore, a student's experience of assessment may be not only reflective of learning, but also *productive* of a certain sense of identity. The choice of assessment methods therefore influences not only what, or how the students learn, but also their very sense of self (Schwabenland 2006b).

Assessing your peers requires you to expose your shared and conflicting assumptions about the task, the criteria for making judgements and about what actually is good work. Students have to actively engage in negotiating boundaries between their professional and personal roles. Students have to become more aware of the responsibilities they have to the quality of the work and to each other. These are all highly useful management skills, and are particularly relevant to courses on diversity and cross-cultural management. Lange writes that 'critical transformative learning attempts to foster an individual's consciousness of himself or herself as situated within larger political and economic forces' (Lange 2004: 122) *and* to explore the potential for change. Discovering the different assumptions that colleagues have about what constitutes competent work opens up the possibilities for debate and for a mutual sharing of perspectives.

Peer assessment can also be related to Hofstede's dimension of 'power distance', which maps different underlying assumptions about hierarchy and authority within cultures. According to Hofstede, countries with 'low power distance' (such as Sweden) are more egalitarian than 'high power distance' countries such as India or China, where hierarchy is assumed (Hofstede 2001). Therefore, introducing peer assessment to a group of culturally diverse students needs to involve some consideration of these potentially divergent views about how power and authority can, or should, be wielded by students.

With this in mind, I convened two focus groups comprised of international students to discuss some of these issues. The first focus group, the students studying cross-cultural management, consisted of seventeen international students from Italy, Nigeria, Pakistan, Iran, Eire, Norway, Finland, Poland, China and Taiwan. The second group of students were studying diversity management: all were from minority ethnic groups and only two were residents in the UK. Only two of the students had any previous experience of peer assessment. At first, the majority of students in both groups reacted quite negatively. However, they became much more positive when I pointed out the relevance of peer assessment to management, and in particular, its relevance to managing people from diverse cultures and backgrounds. Some of the responses could be interpreted as supporting Hofstede's thesis by demonstrating that his dimensions of power distance and uncertainty avoidance were consistent with the students' national origins. The students who were least anxious were UK based (although from minority ethnic communities) and from Scandinavia (both categorised as low power distance and low uncertainty avoidance) while those who were most resistant were from countries such as China, Nigeria and some parts of Eastern Europe (high power distance, high uncertainty avoidance). For example, when a Polish student said *'the teachers know what to look for, students might be swayed by personal concerns'* it was a Finnish student who said, *'but you can find that problem with the teachers too'*. These different responses could be interpreted as representing different attitudes towards authority (Schwabenland 2006b: 103).

The following comment is particularly interesting:

We're all from different places – we write differently. The tutor can flow with what we're saying. But if you give it [work to be assessed] *to someone from China – they say religion isn't very important – to us it's very important so she'd just fail me. They have no experience to judge from.* (student from Nigeria cited in Schwabenland 2006b: 104)

The Nigerian student seems to be suggesting that the culturally determined values the students bring will influence their judgement, even where such values would seem to have little or no bearing on the coursework itself – to the extent that 'she'd just fail me'. She also seems to be assuming an absence of professional or ethical criteria from which to judge the work.

However, while I was undertaking this (admittedly very small) study a colleague who tutors nurses in professional health settings was also exploring their attitudes towards peer assessment and he found some quite significant differences. His sample of nurses were from equally diverse backgrounds but they were much less apprehensive. The only significant difference we could determine between his groups and mine is that the nurses regarded themselves as professionals, already working in a professional job while my students, although undertaking vocational courses, saw themselves primarily as students. Therefore, the students' perceptions of themselves as *students* may have been more significant than the cultural differences between them. My students demonstrated much greater enthusiasm about peer assessment when I drew parallels with the demands made on managers, especially those working in multinational companies. When they could see the relevance of it for their professional careers they became notably less anxious.

But this isn't to say that cultural difference plays no role and here again the Nigerian student's comment is illuminating, suggesting that without the trust in a shared sense of professional standards that comes with the occupancy of a professional role (illusory though that may be) students may become anxious and fall back on more atavistic fears of the 'other'. How else can we interpret her comment that the Chinese 'have no religion' when assessing student work on a management topic that seemed unconnected, in any obvious way, with religious belief? This example demonstrates that these underlying, and often unexamined assumptions carry their influence over from the personal to the professional domains.[2]

My next example comes from a set of interviews Frances Tomlinson and I carried out with managers and diversity specialists in voluntary organisations. The organisation referred to below provides services for people with disabilities, including personal care:

We have an issue there in that the male carers we bring on...the clients will say, as they have the right to say, I don't want a male carer...so sometimes it can be difficult to find work for male carers which is an equal opportunities issue we have. (CEO of a voluntary organisation cited in Tomlinson and Schwabenland 2010: 114)

While in the previous example the relevance of a religious identity (or lack of one) to the task of peer assessment seems extremely tenuous, in this example the relevance of gender identity to the provision of care becomes more complicated. Although in the West medical and care services have traditionally been provided without regard to gender, with women being cared for by male doctors or men being cared for by female nurses, this issue is made more complicated by our increasing awareness of different cultural prohibitions on the one hand, and the occasional incidences of non-professional conduct and even sexual abuse on the other. However competent the carer may be, if they are not of the same gender as their patient or user, that user may not regard the service they are providing as desirable, or even professional.

This example raises interesting questions about the intersection of identity and competence. While competence is usually understood as being about the ability to do a job or to carry out a role, increasingly aspects of identity are becoming commodified as attributes that either hinder performance (as in the example above) or enhance it, as in the previously cited example taken from an interview with a manager in a voluntary organisation working with ex-offenders.

I think what's positive about [the organisation] *is that...in terms of employment opportunities your offending background does not bar you from a job as a project worker or for any other position...sharing an experience with [clients]...may enable them to support their clients better...going to prison and com[ing] out and hav[ing] a job...it makes kind of like a role model, a standard to our clients...* (Project manager cited in Tomlinson and Schwabenland 2010: 112)

This example demonstrates the complex interweaving of attributes of doing and being. Here, it is not only the experience of having been in prison and overcoming the disadvantages such an experience confers that qualifies them for the job of support worker, but also their identity *as* an ex-offender; it is not only what the person has done but also who they are that makes it possible for them to act as a role model, to *be* an exemplar.

In Tomlinson's research into the experiences of refugee women working as volunteers she interviewed one woman who had later found employment in a refugee run organisation and who commented that voluntary work provided her with the confidence to present her experience of being 'different' (her identity as a refugee) not as a way of accounting for failure, but for her success in securing a job (Tomlinson 2005: 10).

Similarly, the next example cited below is taken from an interview I carried out with the manager of a community centre and in it she describes her strategy for ensuring that local people are prioritised over 'outsiders' for employment opportunities:

In terms of outsiders swooping in and taking the jobs, we've talked about how equal opportunities is about giving jobs on the basis of merit, but you know that's as objective as we say it is. I mean if you value local experience, experience of the service as a priority much more, the whole thing becomes much more equal opportunities.

This increasing commodification of being is developed further in the next example taken from an interview with a diversity specialist, working in a large, multinational voluntary organisation, in which she describes recent attempts to appoint new board members from more diverse ethnic backgrounds.

…last time we did get one BME person, that was the first. This time we're going to advertise again…we're also seeking a new chair this year and we've put in an advert for a chair…and I know there's a kind of desire for, you know, a BME female etc etc…

Taken as a group, these examples trace an interesting continuum from the valuing of experiences which may endow the individual with a particular set of perspectives that could be useful to the organisation, through, in the last quotation, to the valuing of certain aspects of identity simply for themselves. Identity in this last example has become objectified, it is not something that is performed (pacé de Beauvoir) but simply, is.

However, all of these examples concern aspects of identity that represent value to the organisation. In the example below the manager of an organisation providing services to disabled people describes her conflict about whether an employee should be given time to travel to an LGBT (lesbian, gay, bisexual and transgendered) staff affinity group meeting, or not.

Staff are there to provide a service and I think we sometimes forget that... where we're taking people away from their work...for a meeting they may be talking about aspects of their work [but] *which may not necessarily be particularly relevant to what they're paid to do, or what they're funded to do.* [The funding body] *gives us a two million pound grant to deliver a service in Essex, not to shape national policy up in Manchester!* (Senior manager cited in Tomlinson and Schwabenland 2010: 116)

This last quotation, as with the Nigerian student cited earlier, illustrates one of the potential dilemmas that can arise from the desire to find expression for an aspect of personal identity that either conflicts, or is perceived as irrelevant to the professional identity. However, determining relevance is also not always straightforward, as demonstrated by one of my students, a lesbian, reflecting on her experiences of a seminar covering gay and lesbian rights at work. She writes:

...the lecture left me with questions of how it is that I was the only one that was visible. I know that in a room of 200 I am not the only one. I did not want to speak out but I know without someone speaking out, showing others that it is okay, others may not and [that] *makes me feel sad, especially in one module on equality and diversity.*

The intersection between individual aspects of identity, who we are, and the roles we are required to carry out at work is a complex one and the terrain is much contested. Many of the managers we interviewed recognised that certain identities, such as those which established commonality with user groups, could be very useful to the organisation in its tasks of presenting its users with role models. In these examples the emphasis is not only on *being*, but on *doing*; specifically, on how an individual may have responded to, and perhaps overcome, the challenges of that shared history of disadvantage. In other examples the advantage that certain aspects of identity confer is more nebulous and, arguably more problematic. What, exactly, is the advantage that a 'BME woman' would confer to the Board of the multinational voluntary organisation referred to above? One possible answer is implied in the observation made by the lesbian student in my *Managing Diversity* module, that of being visible, and visible in such a way that the culture of the organisation is changed, even if only subtly.

It is these subtle challenges to the dominant culture that make up the majority of responses of Meyerson's (2003) 'tempered radicals' who made 'small actions [that] proved that things could be different...the countless people who modelled alternative ways of doing things, chipped away at existing institutions, inspired others to act, and played crucial roles in generating the momentum for social change' (Meyerson 2003: 167).

Meyerson identified a number of specific strategies people chose to adopt, ranging from quiet resistance, leveraging small wins and finally to more radical forms of direct action. However, she suggests that 'perhaps the most important way tempered radicals "lead" is by creating supportive social contexts and nurturing relationships with their peers and employees' (Meyerson 2003: 167). This may be especially important when working within systems that may, however unintentionally, reproduce rather than challenge disadvantage. These dilemmas are the subject of the following section.

Dialectics of differentiation in organisational processes

...if you do identify people as being different then they're are not included, they are automatically excluded in some way...the whole language you use talks about them in those terms. (MA student, focus group of students running organisations for refugees)

One of the most problematic examples of an organisational practice that can reproduce the very conditions of disadvantage that it is intended to challenge is that of diversity monitoring. Being asked to fill out monitoring forms that ask for ethnicity, gender, disability and a variety of other markers of identity has become a taken-for-granted and integral aspect of most, if not all encounters between individuals and organisations in the UK and the US. By contrast, in France, at the time of writing, monitoring by ethnicity is illegal. In my experience, just telling my students about the French policy has an interesting effect; monitoring practices here are now so ubiquitous that many students cannot quite imagine how organisations might manage without them. Comparing the UK approach and the French approach also requires some exploration of the different underlying assumptions about the nature of the (unwritten) social contract, and contrasting the French emphasis on the *egalitie* (and *laicite*) of all its citizens within the public sphere with the UK model of multiculturalism that seeks to recognise (and codify) plural allegiances and identities.

However, although managers, and management students seem to accept, pretty much unquestioningly, the idea of monitoring per se, the practice of it is much more problematic. For one thing, these processes are increasingly time consuming as demonstrated in the example below, in an interview with a voluntary sector manager working in a rural area.

In terms of employment, the job of monitoring through equal opportunities forms – that's a lot of onerous work, I...understand lots of people sort of baulking about having to compile all the information because equal opportunities forms get bigger and bigger, and it's difficult – particularly in an area like [rural county]...and if you've got 2% minority ethnic population and you employ 200 people well if you've got 4 people [that] would be reasonable number of minority population to employ, but how many people do you have to go through the employment process to actually monitor such a tiny figure?

Recently my colleague, Frances Tomlinson and I ran an action learning group with voluntary sector managers who had specific responsibility for implementing diversity initiatives within their organisations. The topic of diversity monitoring dominated many of the sessions.

[Diversity monitoring] *is well intentioned because the, the desire is to encourage and to increase the number of people with those difficulties participating, and the starting point being to try and count them. But it's a bit like all of the monitoring...we have a standard monitoring form that we give to all our clients, it's a membership requirement we have to do it, where we have to ask them what ethnicity they are and a whole load of other things besides – you know some people just put 'human' on it as a protest – resisting that sort of categorisation, but it's unsolvable really because if you want to address it in a proactive way you've got to start counting somehow – so that's very much the tension...* (Voluntary sector manager)

Monitoring practices are seen as an essential component of diversity initiatives because, as the manager above acknowledges, if you don't know what the makeup of your client group or staff group is, how can you begin to develop strategies to redress any imbalances? And once those strategies are in place, how can you measure progress? These are important questions. However, it is much less often publicly acknowledged that these practices also institutionalise a paradox. This is the paradox that was described by the student cited earlier, when she said that identifying people as different means that they are then perceived as different. Markers of difference are socially constructed, never value free, and can result in reinforcing exclusion.

Whether a group constructs its own identity or has that construction thrust upon it, and what meanings inhere to these constructions, are two of the most challenging issues raised by these practices of monitoring, as is demonstrated in the following quotation from a student studying community work in India:

...formal social work education...treats all human beings as people with problems. (MA student, Indian focus group)

One of the most important activities that many voluntary organisations engage in is the challenging of stereotypes that represent disadvantaged people as victims, and even more insidious, as somehow deserving of their exclusion. Reversing this stereotype Kretzmann and McKnight (1993) suggest that we re-conceptualise our idea of 'community' to one in which:

...even the poorest neighbourhood is a place where individuals and organisations represent *resources* upon which to rebuild. (Kretzmann and McKnight 1993: 5 my emphasis)

This is a notion of community that many people working in the voluntary sector would recognise and support. However, there are pressures on managers that militate against its achievement. For example, Beazley et al (2004) critique government regeneration initiatives because they are based on the idea of a community of problems, made up of deficits that need to be 'corrected' before the individuals within it can play an active role in community building. This deficit model is constructed on three levels; the individual is constructed through the lens of pathology, the group through notions of social exclusion and the community through the evocation of the 'democratic deficit' (Beazley et al 2004: 1). To challenge these constructions managers need not only to draw on different languages, different images and assumptions about the people they are working with, but also to balance these competing ideologies. And this raises a number of questions. How easily are these skills learned and nurtured in the individual worker? And, of broader concern, what is the wider impact of colluding with deficit assumptions? Managers may find themselves negotiating trade-offs between the conflicting desires of an individual to receive support services that are only available to the 'most in need' and their desire both as an individual and as a member of a marginalised group, to challenge the constructions that construct their exclusion.

In a discussion about these very dilemmas another manager suggested that some of these paradoxes are even inherent in the ways that anti-discrimination legislation itself is framed; for example the introduction of the regulations banning discrimination on the basis of age have led to his local municipal authority removing the subsidy that enabled older people to attend evening classes more cheaply on the grounds that it was ageist:

It's often a multi-layered thing. Yes it's right for the local authority, probably, not to subsidize older people...because that is making them different to younger people who ought to have equal access to those courses; on the other hand you're over fifty and you want to apply for a grant to have a degree or something like that then you get rejected automatically because you're too old to do it. And what I find is that legislation tends to be quite selective, quite discriminatory in its own right. So that makes it difficult.... I don't really know what the answer is. I think, I think it would be good to think about it as a sort of progression; that we start off with legislation for excluded and disadvantaged groups to give us a framework so that we can start to work with people in an ordinary living mode, and then over a period of time we move away from legislation towards change within society, which means that the law becomes redundant and we can forget about it... (Manager of a local community advice based organisation)

This example demonstrates the complex dilemmas and contradictions that need to be managed. One of these is the tension between representing difference as a source of strength or of vulnerability. The risk of mismanaging this tension is that it may become more difficult to challenge negative assumptions. Managers' efforts to move away from the 'deficit' model (Beazley et al 2004) may be undermined by circumstances and pressures that result in the client group being maintained in a construct, or hermeneutic of deficiency rather than being seen as people with something to offer.

Unfortunately, there is some evidence to suggest that these tensions are not always effectively challenged through the panoply of practices that are designed to promote equal opportunities, but actually increased. One way in which this can occur is through the imposition of a fairly crude and simplistic construction of a client group that may be at odds with the organisation's more nuanced understanding. Here is a further example of one way in which such distortions are maintained. The quotation below is taken from an interview with the manager of a project for homeless ex-offenders:

...they [local government commissioners] want [us] to monitor how many – how many tenants we have, how many have an action plan, how many have been reviewed – are we actually reviewing them, so we're constantly monitored how many have been reviewed and we review them every 3 months; now they want to know how many BME groups have a support plan that's been reviewed... (Voluntary sector project manager)

Although the speaker cited here begins by implying that the local government commissioners are interested in all of the clients, there is a subtle shift in emphasis to 'BME groups'. This phrase is used as shorthand to signify individual clients ('how many BME groups have *a* support plan'). The purpose of having all these individual action plans is, presumably, to emphasise the *individual* needs of each person, but the elision of some individuals into the marker of 'BME group' serves to reinforce, however subtly, the impression that it is this group that is particularly needy. This example demonstrates how even well intentioned actions can result in reinforcing and fixing a particular identity within a construction of deficiency.

And what are the effects of these processes on the monitored themselves who are captured in this hermeneutic of difference? A few years ago I taught a student who worked in the public sector in London. He told me that his employer had developed a management-training programme specifically designed for staff from under-represented groups, to enable them to compete more effectively for upcoming management vacancies. My student put his name forward for the scheme but was told that his ethnicity – he came from one of the countries that had been part of the former Yugoslavia – was not on the list of under-represented groups, and therefore he was not eligible for the course. A year later he applied again and this time was successful – because in the intervening months the employer had revised their monitoring systems and his ethnicity was now included on their list! In this case the story has a happy ending in that following his year on the management-training course he successfully applied for a more senior position within the organisation. This example simultaneously demonstrates the provisional nature of the markers of identity that are used and how they can become fixed and stabilised – and also how they can function to exclude.

Are these unintended consequences inevitable or can we find ways around these dilemmas? In the action learning group that Frances

Tomlinson and I ran we debated whether an organisation's members and clients could participate in the discussions about the kinds of markers of identity that were important to them and also about the information that would be important to collect about the experiences of the individuals within the groups that these markers created. Drawing on models of participatory research might offer ways of making monitoring an empowering process rather than an excluding one. Taking on a particular label can be empowering, if it is a desired label that one has chosen for oneself. One of the participants commented:

There're different ways people do self-define, I mean...I was going to give my example...sometimes I might say black African...then I might say black British because I was actually born in this country, OK I moved out for a while and came back to the UK, and my children, sometimes they actually go between black African and black British...people self-define in different ways at different times...people have a right to self-define.

As do organisations. A long established voluntary organisation in the UK described itself, for many years, as offering services 'to lonely people'. One of the participants in the action learning group worked for an organisation that supports very poor people. For him the most important 'marker' of identity is how much income a person has.

...less than £16,000 you're into benefit territory. People out of work can survive six months, a year whatever it is, on their savings. But as they're out of work and they're paying the bills and trying to do all the dutiful things that they want to do, their savings are rocketing through a hole in the floor and suddenly they're in a position – crumbs I've never been in this one before I'm needing advice...it's the £16,000 limit, bang you're into this benefit, that benefit, the other benefit...[whereas for] other people when their savings rocket through the hole in the floor, hang on a second, welcome to the party there's loads of stuff available for you...

Creating opportunities for individuals and organisations to determine their own categories and markers of difference is an important way in which the processes of monitoring can be more empowering than they are at present. But there will always be a tension between the categories that are seen as important at a local level and those that are required by government bodies needing to demonstrate progress nationally.

I definitely had a bit of an arched back [about being asked to fill out monitoring forms] *and if I sort of look at why I might I have had an arched back, about why are they asking me this, it's around a sort of a historical context...the reality is that we do carry our history with us and that in the past being labelled or fitting yourself into a label would count to your detriment, so it might be an area to think about...not actually are the statistics used, or this or that but...the communication around the ethos of diversity and equality and where the organisation is maybe wanting to go with it.* (Voluntary organisation manager)

The paradox that is maintained in the organisational processes discussed in this section is that the very measures that organisations have adopted to overcome the systemic disadvantage that certain groups experience, may reinforce the perception that they are still, in whatever way, 'different'. For this participant in the action learning group, reminding herself about the history of the struggles that underpin the legislation helped her to manage this tension. The relationship between the organisation and its location within a historical and societal context is explored further in the following section.

Dialectics of differentiation within the wider society

The centrifugal dialectic between commonality and difference that structures an organisation's internal monitoring processes is also manifested externally. In profit making organisations this is demonstrated in the measures it takes to represent itself as unique, which it may do primarily through its branding. In voluntary organisations campaigning and advocacy activities are specifically aimed at promoting the aspirations and the challenges facing people who are, in some way, disadvantaged or marginalised. Therefore, the tensions between the countervailing forces of similarity and difference, assimilation and separation could be said to be inherent in voluntary sector organising, and sometimes resulting, however unintended, in the concretising of signifiers of difference. When people from marginalised groups who have taken up power to define their own needs and solutions found organisations, this action legitimises the perspectives of the creators but can also serve to reinforce their *exclusivity*. Therefore these complex dynamics of difference are intrinsic to the processes of voluntary organising from their very inception. Creating the organisation involves establishing a boundary and once that boundary is drawn procedures usually follow that determine how insiders are to be privileged over outsiders. Solidarity itself creates a boundary and a separation (Schwabenland 2006a: 49). Narayan puts this well:

> ...discourses of 'difference' often operate to conceal their role in the production and reproduction of such 'differences', presenting these differences as something pregiven and prediscursively 'real', that discourses of difference merely describe rather than help construct and perpetuate. (Narayan 2000: 82)

And these tensions, between the 'production and reproduction of difference' on the one hand and the desire for inclusion and, indeed, invisibility of many of its client group continue to influence the organisation throughout its development. As many organisations are established to represent the special interests of a particular group, if the organisation 'succeeds' too well it can no longer claim to be unique nor the interests any longer 'special'; if it fails, it is likely to become as marginalised as its constituency. This dilemma was expressed by one CEO of a well-established organisation working in the field of child protection:

> *How do we live with the fact that although we have been in existence for*
> *over 113 years and yet there is more child abuse now than ever before?*
> (Voluntary sector CEO cited in Schwabenland 2006c: 66)

This confusion is reflected in the social capital debate, the focus of much current voluntary sector research (and public policy debates as well). Social capital is a rather nebulous concept and is open to appropriation by policy makers, politicians and academics from across the political spectrum.

> Social capital refers to the institutions, relationships and norms that shape the quality and quantity of a society's social interactions. Social capital is not just the sum of the institutions which underpin a society – it is the glue that holds them together. (The World Bank[3])

The idea has gained prominence that voluntary organisations are intrinsic to social capital because they bring people together, foster ties of relatedness and cohesion from which can grow trust and a shared sense of commonality with others. Social capital is a metaphor that allows people to acknowledge the importance of quite intangible aspects of society which are not only highly valued but also often seen as threatened. The metaphor has been most prominently developed by Robert Putnam who holds that social capital is in decline (Putnam 2000) for reasons that appear, on the face of it, to amount to a critique of Western, postindustrialised society in which people work too many hours in paid employment to have any time left over for local and neighbourly involvement, and where television has replaced shared activities such as bowling (*Bowling Alone* is the title of the book in which he develops these themes accompanied by an impressive array of supportive statistical evidence).

However, Putnam distinguishes between 'bonding' capital which reinforces the ties that bind people together from 'bridging' capital which brings people together across traditional cultural or geographical allegiances. Bonding capital also has the potential to reinforce bigotry, prejudice and exclusion while bridging capital can promote superficial acquaintances in which differences between people are exoticised, in a kind of locally based version of orientalism, as perhaps reflected in the story below, cited previously in the third chapter, about an organisation that worked with the travelling community:

We had a project, the Gypsy's Wish which was set up with travellers, the local Romany theatre…they produced a seventeen minute film based on the experiences of travellers…looking at some of the barriers they face, whether it's at school, outside the school…and then we showed it as part of the conference…they also had two travellers there from the community that actually was involved in the film and had a free for all question and answer session. It started off very slowly at first… I figured some of the voluntary organisations have probably never engaged with travellers before – there's this vision of them being 'well, they're X, they're Y, they're Z, there's all these assumptions…so it gave them a chance to actually ask them – by the time we got to the end of the forty minutes there was so many questions that luckily we had a break afterwards…and it was one of the feedbacks that got the highest – on the conference was the fact being that they could actually go up to them and find out something they didn't know about the travelling community before. (Organisational support worker)

Both bonding and bridging capital have the potential to create change or reinforce the status quo. A report on research into refuge organisations concluded that:

> …new associational forms are developing – social capital is apparently being created. But these organisations perform an essentially defensive role in an environment of hostile immigration policy.

> They may resist participation in formal institutional frameworks. We contend, therefore, that this social capital constitutes the currency of differentiation, fragmentation and exclusion, not a vehicle of social cohesion that Putnam's concept implies. (Zetter et al 2006: 11)

These findings are echoed in another research report on women's social capital that also concluded that it is more likely to be of the 'bonding' variety rather than 'bridging'.[4]

Zetter et al go on to include 'celebrating and reinforcing different cultural identities' and 'establishing an identity and presence in order to define a negotiating position vis-à-vis other groups or institutions and agencies who may control public resources' in a list of motivations for immigrant communities to come together and form associations (Zetter et al 2006: 14). However, Ackah's historical study of black organisations in the north of England argues that 'the "traditional" community organisation that catered for the general needs of a particular ethnic group has become outmoded...certain types of black community organisations...are in danger of becoming irrelevant and detached from the communities they serve' (Ackah 2006: 1).

Celebrating different cultural identities is hard to do without reinforcing difference. And from reinforcing difference it is a very short step to subjectifying, or essentialising difference. Putnam followed *Bowling Alone* with an article in which he concluded that 'in the long run...immigration and diversity are likely to have important cultural, economic, fiscal and developmental benefits. In the short run, however, immigration and ethnic diversity tend to reduce social solidarity and social capital' (Putnam 2007: 137). This article attracted a huge amount of debate and controversy (much of it centring on questions of methodology and replication Krotowski (2010) interestingly suggests that Putnam's analysis underestimates the growing significance of the internet in forging new bonds both within and across communities).

When we researched diversity management in voluntary organisations we identified many instances in which not only the identities of the people who were the subject of the organisations' efforts, became essentialised but also the organisations themselves (Schwabenland and Tomlinson 2008). One interesting example of how this process worked could be seen in the use of the label 'hard to reach' which we heard many times in our interviews and is also very common in policy discourse. Voluntary organisations are often celebrated for their achievements in reaching these 'hard to reach'. The label works through the representation of certain groups of people as, by virtue of sharing a certain identity, invisible and inaccessible by ordinary means and many organisations take pride in their successes in overcoming these difficulties while others regard it as an important challenge.

I wanted to look at our own equality work in terms of very hard to reach groups and disabled people...minority ethnic communities are staggeringly difficult to find, anywhere...in [a rural county] *where you're talking about 2% of the population it's difficult even for – people from ethnic communities to actually come together as a group, they're disparate right across the entire county and, er, the question we have* [is] *where are all the disabled people from these communities?* (Manager of an organisation set up by disabled people cited by Schwabenland and Tomlinson 2008: 328)

Usually this rhetoric seems to be accepted uncritically, although the support worker working with the traveller community seemed to invoke a degree of perhaps intentional irony:

...what the Travellers' Support Group is looking at, at the moment in terms of a project is...saying well look, a lot of them are in our community already. The ones that have had to actually come away from their travelling lifestyle are possibly living next door to you, you don't realise it. (Organisation support worker cited above and in Schwabenland and Tomlinson 2008: 328)

The following example demonstrates the essentialising not only of the identity of the 'hard to reach' but also of particular kinds of organisations, in this case organisations established and run by people from black and minority ethnic groups, the 'BME' organisations.

Lots of BME organisations are actually very good at reaching women within their homes because that's where, they've got the kind of cultural know how. (Manager of a voluntary run grants programme cited in Schwabenland and Tomlinson 2008: 328)

The following example is particularly interesting because here the speaker demonstrate ambivalence about the reduction of 'diversity' to 'BME' and as a euphemism for race but her ambivalence does not seem to extend to the essentialising of identities per se – note her use of the term 'special needs'.

And lots of people, when they talk about diversity in the voluntary sector, actually mean BME people, simple as that, and actually they don't really often think, and lots of people don't see beyond that. ...Or, they tend to talk about BME and Special Needs, and lump everything together under special needs, so of course you get huge figures for special needs and it seems to count as having a special need within the voluntary sector world where you have to meet certain targets. (Development manager in a support organisation cited in Schwabenland and Tomlinson 2008: 328)

This example demonstrates not only the essentialising, but also the *conflating* of the identities of BME and special needs, which is itself a euphemism for people with a very wide range of learning or physical disabilities. The essentialising of identities such as these works to fix their subjects in an identity of difference, even if that difference is seen as valuable (as in the case of the desirable BME trustee). These different dialectical dynamics may work to reinforce each other and can result in capturing the organisation (and people from the communities with which it works) within a double, or multiple bind. To accept these essentialised identities may bring recognition to the organisation and its members, and perhaps also access to desperately needed services. But in the long term such acceptance is likely to work against the organisation, and this is the double bind; if the organisation succeeds in reaching the hard to reach they are by definition, no longer unreachable and the already reached become even more undermined – how can they speak for the hard to reach when they are no longer so marginalised themselves – by the very fact of their being reached. The organisation has succeeded, but by virtue of that very success it has failed. There is no obvious way out of this dilemma (Schwabenland and Tomlinson 2008).

Campaigning and advocacy activities also raise some of these same tensions. For example, the advocacy group People First who were founded and run by people with learning disabilities, produced tee-shirts printed with the slogan 'labels are for jars not people'. This exactly illustrates the dilemma many organisations find themselves in. If people do not wish to be identified by a marker of difference such 'disability' that has historically brought with it mostly negative connotations, then how can an organisation or pressure group design a campaign to advocate for better services? A similar dilemma is commonly faced by staff designing fundraising campaigns that rely on photographs portraying people with disabilities as incapable, or of starving and otherwise suffering children, to appeal to the compassionate instincts of the financially better off.

These images are often strongly resisted by the very people the organisations are established to serve, who contest the representation of themselves as victims. Some organisations have responded to these criticisms by developing banks of photographs showing people overcoming disadvantage and taking an active role in all sorts of activities from which they have traditionally been excluded, from jobs to sports to the arts. These images are likely to be much more effective at challenging negative stereotypes. The evidence from my students that I presented in Chapter 4 about the way in which listening to Evelyn Glennie changed their attitudes about disability supports this. But I was not aiming to raise money for an organisation, or to influence government thinking about the need for a particular policy initiative, or to advocate for someone who is being denied a service they need.

Conclusions

'Identitarianism' as Spivak writes, 'can be as dangerous as it is powerful and the radical teacher in the university can hope to work, however indirectly, toward controlling the dangers by making them visible' (Spivak 1993: 54). Identitarianism 'works' through centrifugal dialectics in which certain characteristics are identified and, once named, create processes of thought that reinforce those characteristics as differentiating principles. This centrifugal dialectic creates a number of dilemmas for managers. Some of these have already been discussed; for example, that policies to 'celebrate' diversity and policies to implement equality initiatives may be in conflict, that diversity as a management strategy may work to institutionalise a system of control rather than empower the excluded and create structural reform, that labels that create commonality also reinforce difference.

The tension between protecting workers' freedom of religious expression and protection for gay, lesbian and bisexual workers from religiously inspired homophobic bigotry is a manifestation of another dilemma that managers have to surmount; that markers of difference not only tend to reinforce the exclusion of the minority from the majority, but also their exclusion from other minorities. The Ladele versus Islington Council case is a good example of the intense confusion that surrounds these debates. Lillian Ladele, who worked in the council registry was disciplined for refusing to carry out civil partnership ceremonies on religious grounds. She took the council to a tribunal, alleging that Islington was putting barriers on her freedom to practice her religion. She won her case but it was overturned on appeal (*Personnel Today*). Such contradictory legal judgements fail to establish either a clear precedent or to provide managers with a framework for making sense of competing claims.

How can managers navigate this contested terrain? Firstly, following Spivak, we can to try to make it possible for students, managers and employees to become more aware of their/our participation in these processes of identification and distanciation. The provisional and contingent nature of these allegiances to certain markers of identity creates opportunities to disrupt and interrogate the processes that construct them as they are happening. Spivak suggests that the dialectic of identification and distanciation may actually function as 'a philosophical dominant that disqualifies and excludes the inconvenient as its other and vice versa' and she goes on to cite Hindess and Hirst:

> Concepts are deployed in ordered successions to produce [the] effects [of analysis solution]. This order is the order created *by the process of theoretical work itself:* it is guaranteed by no necessary 'logic' or 'dialectic' nor by any necessary mechanism of correspondence with the real itself (Hindess and Hirst cited in Spivak 1999: 316 emphasis in the original).

Our desire to impose coherency and order may, therefore, lead us to ignore, or misrepresent the 'inconvenient'. However, once the 'taken-for-granted' nature of these processes is disrupted we create some space, some manoeuvring room, however small. Meyerson's descriptions of the strategies adopted by her 'tempered' radicals demonstrate how resourceful individuals can be, and also that in many cases, the cumulative effect of individual actions sometimes leads to significant social change.

The following example is an interesting description by a manager working with people with a history of substance abuse about how she struggles within this dialectic:

A single white male who is a drug user and who is homeless doesn't get any more access to housing than someone who isn't using drugs... So we exploit [their] vulnerability to try and advocate for them to get what they want, so if they've got HIV, if they've got hepatitis C then we'll use those things...rather than the discrimination thing... So it's almost like we probably add to [their] stigmatisation]...in the way that we try and use, get services and advocate for our clients.

When asked how she manages this tension she went on to say:

I suppose how you work with it. I suppose using a different language about how you talk to someone [or] to how you talk about them, which in some ways is not very congruent. But I think we subconsciously all do it. If I'm filing out a disability living allowance form for a client then I'm playing up how much their hepatitis C affects their life. But if I'm working with the client then I'm trying to support the client to live with their illness in a different way, being more empowering, So it's quite a, it is quite an incongruent way of working.

I asked her if she thought this was okay:

Ah. Well, I think it is. The services we are trying to get for our clients is ultimately to link, to support, you know the end is the same point...if they're getting a benefit that allows them to have a carer come to their home, to support them to do an activity, then ultimately that's the same goal. It's just that because resources seem to be tightening in so many areas then we have to advocate for our client group as a group, and say that they need things as much as other groups that are competing for the same resources. (Voluntary sector manager cited in Schwabenland 2011: 146–147)

This manager's solution to working within these tensions is to 'speak different languages' to different audiences while maintaining a clear vision of what she is trying to achieve: 'the same point', 'the same goal'. What she is describing seems to demonstrates Kohn's (1990) identification of the capacity not only to perceive the other as self and the self as other but also to hold these perceptions in tension. In this example the speaker is holding multiple perspectives in tension; the user's need for a service, the user's need for dignity and respect, the service providers' need to rationalise services and make sure that they are directed towards those most in need and her own perspective as a worker.

Finally, it may be helpful to frame these dilemmas as paradoxical, rather than problematic or conflictual. Bohm (2008) suggests that once we frame a situation as a problem we locate it within a dialectical dynamic that seeks for a solution. But some of the dilemmas that have been described in this chapter are not so easily amenable to resolution. Also, 'resolution' may not be desirable if it means one side 'winning', or demonstrating greater power of one kind or another. Bohm prefers paradoxes to problems because while problems look for solutions paradoxes can only be transcended.

7
Hybridity and Synthesis: Centripetal Dialectics

> ...in an age of exclusivist jihads to east and west the notion that people can reconcile more than one cultural identity may have much to recommend it. (Foster cited by Heaney 1996: 202)

Introduction

Centripetal dynamics propel the different elements in the centrifuge towards a 'centre' and away from the margins; it is a harmonising, or homogenising force in which separate ingredients are combined into something new. Centripetal dialectics aim for the resolution of differences, whether by fusion (as in a magnet, where the two elements are indistinguishable from each other) or into a new, hybrid entity.

In a metaphor the space between the two concepts remains open, the two concepts may be seen to 'act' on each other in that as we contemplate the metaphor our understandings of its two elements each refine our understanding of the other. The more I contemplate the rose-like qualities of my lover, and the loveliness of the rose, the deeper my understanding becomes of both. In this sense the space between the concepts of the rose and of love is a vibrant space. Charles Taylor writes that when the social imaginary is transformed 'people take up, improvise or are inducted into new practices...made sense of by the new outlook' (Taylor 2005: 29). And these new practices and understandings 'work' on each other, very much in the manner of a metaphor. 'The new practice', writes Taylor, 'with the implicit understanding it generates, can be the basis for modification of theory, which in turn can inflect practice, and so on' (Taylor 2005: 300).

In Chakrabarty's (2000) example of the 'double consciousness' required to 'provincialise Europe' the tension between different ways of seeing the

world provide the basis from which action must be taken. It is not possible to live in a state of passivity; the dynamics of the dialectic demand
action, life must always be lived. Spivak writes:

> ...'holding the positive and negative within a single thought without
> attenuating any of the force of either judgement' resembles an aporia
> more than a cognitive mapping. But an aporia discloses itself only as
> a crossing. And anyone programmed into this civil society has already
> crossed over. The dynamic of the dialectic...will not allow the work
> of the negative to stand still 'within a single thought' (Spivak, com-
> menting on an observation by Jameson 1999: 326 my emphasis).

In the previous chapter I suggested that some of the dangers inherent in
the differentiating dynamics of centrifugal dialectics include an increased
sense of distance between people and an essentialising of the markers of
identity that reinforce that distancing. On a societal level such dynamics
can lead to segregation and the creating of ghettos. 'Parallel communities'
is the phrase that the Cantle report used to describe the communities
in three cities that had seen inter-racial rioting in England in 2001[1] to
describe its finding that people from different ethnic or cultural groups
were living side by side but without communicating with each other.
However, the dangers inherent in centripetal dialectics are those of
assimilation and the denial of difference.

Centripetal dialectics underpin two practices that are of particular
relevance to managing diversity; one of these is partnership, or collaborative working and the other is the 'business case' for diversity.
The idea behind partnership working is that that organisations and
sectors will achieve better results if they can pool their resources and
expertise. Partnership is very much in vogue at the moment; public
policy discourse is redolent with collaborations, consortia, strategic
alliances and joint ventures. In some of these the partners come from
the corporate and public sectors (as in public private finance initiatives,
known as 'PPIs') in the UK. Others also include voluntary and community groups and international NGOs in initiatives such as community
regeneration projects and international aid. The underlying assumption seems to be that by bringing together organisations with different
areas of expertise shared objectives can be met, objectives that might
not be achievable, or not so effectively, *without* such collaborative
working. However, as Vangen and Huxtable note, while 'rhetoric about
the benefits of partnership working is endemic...so are complaints
about the difficulty of partnership working in practice' (Vangen and

Huxtable 2003: S62). Tomlinson's (2005) study of partnerships in organ-isations working with refugees suggested that the participants moved rather uneasily between competing discourses that represented the partner-ships as alternatively idealistic and realistic. As Vangen and Huxtable point out, 'reports of unmitigated success are not common' (Vangen and Huxtable 2003: S62).

The idea that bringing together people with different experiences and perspectives can lead to new ideas and better decision-making is, of course, also one of the principal tenets of the 'business case' for diversity. The shift from equality to diversity is characterised by the idea that organisations should not seek to ignore, or eradicate dif-ferences between employees because those very differences can be an asset to the organisation. For example, the Business Link website says that the 'benefits of building a diverse workforce include having a wider range of resources, skills and ideas among your employees that you can tap into...' (www.businesslink.gov.uk). Proponents of *managing* diversity differentiate their approach from that of equal opportunities on the grounds that the latter was too much focussed on the treatment of groups and collectives rather than of individuals, and too narrowly concerned with just those differences covered by anti-discrimination legislation (Kandola and Fullerton 2003). Managing diversity discourses have therefore appropriated the notion of multiplicity.

A more heterogenous workforce brings a greater range of opinions, perspectives and ideas. But in order to take advantage of these benefits this diverse workforce needs to be able to participate in decision-making processes that are open to being influenced by these different perspectives and receptive to alternative, perhaps unexpected, or apparently idio-syncratic contributions. To assume, therefore, that the greater parti-cipation of people bringing alternative perspectives in decision-making can lead to better policies and strategies overall, presents some specific implications for the people managing these processes. These include a commitment to their involvement throughout the organisation, the skills and imagination to encourage that involvement, the vision to encompass different ideas and the flexibility to be able to put them into action. It requires an active commitment to the necessity of doing things differently.

The business case for diversity also seems to share some theoretical ground with the postcolonial notion of hybridity.

>...internal hybridity is the *necessary* correlative to a greater open-ness to external difference and is the *necessary* condition of a more

porous and less rigidly policed boundary around whatever is defined as the home community. (Morely 2000: 6 cited in Kalra et al 2005: 95 my emphasis)

Hybridity, in the postcolonial context, emerges as a consequence of the colonial project in which new forms are created out of the encounter between different cultures. Hybridity as a concept has itself been extensively theorised (see Kalra et al for an interesting review of some of this work). One interesting and highly relevant debate is whether hybridity can be the result of a meeting of elements of equal strength and value (Kalra et al 2005) or whether it necessarily must involve unequal power relationships (Prasad 2003). Bhabha suggests that a 'passage between fixed identifications opens up the possibility of a cultural hybridity that entertains difference *without an assumed or imposed hierarchy*' (Bhabha 2003: 4 my emphasis). This latter notion of hybridity seems directly relevant to diversity.

In the following sections I look in more depth in how these processes of centripetal dialectics are being realised in organisations; firstly in terms of the ways in which individuals relate to each other, secondly by looking at some of the organisational practices that foster hybridity and thirdly, at the impact organisations have in transforming the social imaginary.

Dialectics of convergence between individuals at work

Habermas writes that the condition for equal participation of all members of a society is that discourses remain 'porous, sensitive and receptive to the suggestions, issues and contributions, information and arguments that flow in from a discursively structured public sphere, that is one that is pluralistic, close to the grass roots and relatively undisturbed by the effects of power' (Habermas 1996: 82). This halcyon state of affairs is not easy to realise in the wider society and arguably, even less so in organisations where power dynamics are inescapable. However, the business case for diversity requires just this, that people will feel able to contribute their ideas, that managers will listen and take them seriously and that organisational processes are responsive and open to change.

Is diversity management really just about talking about respecting all individual differences? If so, this is problematic and cannot in its present form lead to inclusive organisations. There is a real danger in seeing differences as benign variation among people. It overlooks the role of conflict, power, dominance and the history of how

organisations are fundamentally structured by race, gender and class.
(Nkomo, cited by Wrench 2005: 82)

'Double consciousness', as briefly mentioned in Chapter 5, is a phrase that is generally first attributed to W.E.B. du Bois in his writings on the experiences of Black Americans which he used to capture the sense of living in more than one world; the world of your cultural heritage and the world of the hegemonic culture. Power, alongside its dialectic partner marginalisation, is inherent in du Bois's conceptualisation of double consciousness. Gordon writes that 'whites and blacks internalise British culture differently depending on whether we are the recipients of white or black socialisation' (Gordon 2007: 102). And this difference is one in which descendents of enslaved Africans, citing Du Bois, '"have no true self consciousness" because they are only allowed to see themselves "through the revelation of the other world"' (Du Bois cited in Gordon 2007: 102). It is for this reason that Spivak maintains that the subaltern cannot speak.[2] Spivak's argument is that the only language and concepts that are available to represent their voices are themselves the products of elite consciousness.

However, Chakrabarty's interpretation of double consciousness seems more nuanced. He suggests that the ruptures, or dissonances that may arise from the realisation of a confrontation between different cultural ways of being 'refer us to the plurality that inheres in the constant fragmentariness that constitutes one's present' (Chakrabarty 2000: 243). He gives the example of an Indian scientist who was both astronomer and astrologer and managed the tensions between these disciplines through a 'strategy for living precisely in a "now" that lacked totality' (Chakrabarty 2000: 253).

The dilemma that is posed for managers and employees working within organisations, is whether it is possible to find a position that resists both the essentialising and the denial of difference; a position where it is possible to act from an awareness not only of multiple standpoints but also of the impossibility (and undesirability) of finding totality. Some of the examples that follow describe different strategies adopted by managers, and management students to manage multiple ways of being and knowing.

My first examples come from students' reflective reports and they demonstrate some of the ways each have developed their own approaches to working together with people from different communities. In the following quotation it is the awareness of the similarities between them that creates a sense of 'shock':

We were introduced to different poems written by people with various beliefs. Our task was to guess what religion they are about. I was shocked how difficult it was. Something that sounded as Islam happened to be a Catholic poem etc. People who associated themselves with a particular religion had difficulties to recognise their own religion. For me this experience was shocking. I did not realise how big the similarities between various beliefs are. It helped me to understand how pointless religious discrimination is if we could not even tell the difference in such a small thing as a poem…segregating people into categories and putting labels on them is pointless.

However, in the following example it is the awareness of differences that leads to growth. This student was writing about the challenges of participating in a group that had to create an assessed presentation:

Working in a group opened up different perspectives of looking at the subject. I remember that at our first session [I had] a clear idea of what topics we should cover and what structure the presentation should follow. As it turned out we all had different ideas and points of view. What was extremely impor-tant was the ability to stay open about the rest of the group's ideas but making sure that we contribute from our own perspective. I often feel very strongly about my own views [but] sometimes it is better to move back and allow yourself to see the subject from someone else's perspective; it takes you out of your box and brings the subject to a totally different level.

For me, what distinguishes this story from many similar accounts of group work is this student's recognition that trying to understand the subject from another point of view has enhanced her own understand-ing, taken it to 'a totally different level'. As previously cited, Barenboim comments that 'if you wish to learn how to live in a democratic society then you would do well to play in an orchestra. For when you do so you know when to lead and when to follow. You leave space for others and at the same time you have no inhibitions about claiming a place for yourself' (Barenboim in Barenboim and Said 2004: 173). My student seemed to have learned when she should lead and when she should listen to others and this allowed the group to create, if not a symphony then at least a good presentation, and one that transcended the possibilities available to each as individuals.

In the next example a student describes her growing appreciation that it is not only the products of groups, such as presentations (or concerts) that result from working together, but also increased self-understanding:

One thing I learned was that identity is not all about who I am. At first it might appear to be about personality, where you come from, what sort of person you are but I learnt that sharing an identity suggests some active engagement on my part. [The exercise] *addresses the relative importance of structures, the forces beyond our control which shape our identities. Identity requires some awareness on our part.*

This idea that identity is created collectively is echoed in the following example, taken from an interview I carried out some years ago with an Indian community activist who described a project of community exchanges her organisation had run. These involved taking a group of people from the National Slum Dwellers' Federation in India to meet a group of people living and working in Soweto.

The other thing is the mirror image we use, especially with our exchanges when communities talk to other communities. We say it is like a mirror...because when you go, you can actually look at yourself, when other people are reacting and see how you look, so it's like a mirror when one community shares its experience with another community. And that in itself makes you grow, because then you know what you look like, what you feel like. (CEO of an Indian voluntary organisation cited in Schwabenland 2006a: 64)

Double consciousness, experienced when there was a need to work across different worlds was referred to by all the students from the management programme for people working in refugee organisations. This is, of course, not surprising because many of the people that use, work or volunteer in refugee organisations are likely to retain strong links with the country they have left as is demonstrated in the example here where the speaker shifts from talking about 'their own' to 'our own' country system, demonstrating how she, as well as her client, is balancing these conflicting loyalties and identities:

But there are some things that I found they have to change. For example punctuality. You cry for the punctuality. You cry for it that please, please, please come on time. Attend the meetings. You say it is 3 o'clock, the staff come at 3:30. They follow their own – including myself, follow our own country system. (Student from refugee organisation cited in Schwabenland 2011: 147)

For one of the respondents empathy provides the bridge in which these different worlds are brought together, many of the staff having been refugees themselves.

They went through the same sort of experience, they have got that sort of feeling, that when any new arrival with no English come they treat them very nicely, they feel, you know, that they have that sort of empathy and they remember their own time when they arrived and no English, culture shock.

However, empathy was also seen as an important ingredient of the commitment of staff who had not shared those experiences:

Some people, they have it here [points to heart]...*Can I give a practical example? In my organisation I've got some volunteers that are very successful, very active, very committed. I find the reason why, is because most of them they travel to war zone countries...they notice how vulnerable these people are in these war zone countries. They came with that sort of mentality. When I interviewed them, why do you want to do voluntary work, they say look, I had a very kind of comfortable life in this country, when I went I saw these things. That's why it made my conscious awake so that I have to go and help these sorts of people.*

The ability to experience empathy, as Kohn (1990) suggested, is an important capacity for living in a plural society. Empathy offers us one resource to help us in managing our own awareness of double (or multiple) consciousness. Empathy has rarely been presented as a core competence of management, but it has recently begun to come into vogue partly because it is a core component of what Goleman et al (2002) term 'emotional intelligence' and also because empathy is the main focus of Simon Baron-Cohen's (2011) recent study on autism in which he argues that an inability to experience empathy may be one element in its development.

In the following example a student of mine wrote about empathy in her reflective report when she remembered her experience of watching a video about the struggle for integrated education in the US civil rights era.

The topic of this week was one that I know well and have studied often, but have never felt a strong tie to. Perhaps being of white European decent I have been fortunate enough not to be personally affected by issues of race. We watched a video in class where at one point the cameras take the viewer to a university in the south of the US. White students, talking about fellow students, black students, as if they had the plague, expressing relief that these students were thankfully sat far enough away so that they don't catch this phantom disease that they must have had. For the first time I can remember I was able to link racism to something more personal in my life. Being Jewish, I grew up with stories of the Holocaust, the pain, the suffering, the abuse and the strength it took to rise out of the ashes of a nation destroyed like an elegant phoenix... I understood that the oppression and segregation of a race (or a religion) has only made people stronger, better fighters.

These different strategies: finding commonality with others, developing the ability to balance your own contribution with others, seeing yourself in others, experiencing empathy with others are each useful ways for working within the liminal space where self and other meet. These are the strategies of individuals working together. The deeper questions of systemic inequality raised by Nkomo (cited in Wrench 2005) and Gordon (2007) are the subject of the following sections.

Dialectics of convergence in organisational processes

Nkomo's challenge to the mainstream diversity discourse is that it writes out issues of conflict, power and dominance, and in particular, how these combine to reproduce systemic discrimination (Nkomo cited in Wrench 2005). In other words, there is a danger that in the desire to establish commonality differences are rendered either invisible or benign. Butler writes that 'the forms the subject takes as well as the life-worlds that do not conform to available categories of the subject emerge in light of historical and geopolitical movements...[but] such new formations can "emerge" only when there are frames that establish the possibility for that emergence' (Butler 2009: 138–139). Can organisational processes create those frames, and make spaces for not only the recognition of available categories but also for the emergence of newer forms of identity construction? In this section I want to return to the two organisational practices shaped by centripetal dialectics that create the vibrant, or liminal space in which there is the possibility of new formations, the business case and the creating of hybridity and that of action learning groups as dialectical engagement.

The 'business case' and hybridity

In the introduction to this chapter I suggested that the business case for diversity shares some common ground with the notion of hybridity insofar as each is dependent on the creating of something new out of the encounter between different elements. The new formations of the subject that Butler alludes to can also be regarded as examples of hybridity. But the question that Spivak (1999), Prasad (2003) and Nkomo (cited in Wrench 2005) raise is whether or not the processes that create the possibilities of hybridity can ever be separated from the dynamics of power and conflict that set those processes in motion and shape their trajectories.

Voluntary organisations offer a particularly interesting arena to pursue these questions because they are often created to respond to the particular needs and aspirations of groups of people occupying marginalised positions within their societies and have a long tradition of doing things differently. Their capacity for innovation and creativity is highly valued. For example, in 2002 Douglas Alexander, a junior minister in the UK government's Department of Trade and Industry proposed that voluntary run social enterprises:

> provide *new models* of new and socially responsible business. ... Indeed mainstream business can learn a lot from social enterprises; about being close to customers, and responsive to their needs; about employment diversity; *about doing business better* (http://www.dti.gov.uk my emphasis).

There are many examples of innovative services and practices that voluntary organisations have developed that are responsive to the aspirations and needs of their users. In a recent research study my colleague, Frances Tomlinson and I found examples of diversity manifested at all levels of organisations, from the ways in which they delivered services, their internal management practices and also in the ways in which they went about encouraging greater involvement and participation throughout. The following extract comes from an interview with the manager of an organisation set up by people with disabilities:

Our original service, our disability advice service, the majority of people who work there – actually I think all of the people who work there now I think of it – are disabled and the reason is, is that to work in benefits advice you have to really know your stuff and the people who really know their stuff are the people who've gone through the mill trying to get their benefits in the first place. (Manager of an organisation established by people with disabilities cited in Schwabenland and Tomlinson 2008: 323)

Similarly in the next example, a home care service, the connection between the quality of the service and its management by disabled people is directly stressed in the interview with its chief executive:

The expectation from the client group at the very beginning is that that home care agency will provide best possible practice, because it's run by disabled people who receive domiciliary home care and they know what they like and they know what they don't like.

Having user involvement in the management of the organisation as a priority can also lead to innovations in management systems as is described in the following example:

Certainly if you look at financial management, and also at organisational management generally, there are smaller voluntary sector organisations out there that are very light touch in terms of their financial management and their accounts are what we have spent and what we have left in the bank. And there's a simplicity to that which really enables the people within the organisation and people looking at the organisation to understand the financial state and viability of that organisation. (Manager of a voluntary run grants programme cited in Schwabenland and Tomlinson 2008: 324)

My final example demonstrates that the belief in the importance of creating systems that allow greater involvement in the organisation is extended to participation within the wider society. This quotation comes from an interview with a manager who was responsible for developing a 'supported' volunteering scheme that makes it possible for people with learning disabilities to play a greater role in their community.

The [examples of good practice] *that work most successfully are the supported volunteering projects...where the person volunteering has a buddy, and where there are few examples where the buddy themselves has had a learning disability but has been volunteering for a certain period of time, or their learning disability isn't as great as the new volunteer's. And those work really well actually. Because they are empowering for absolutely everyone.* (Project manager cited in Schwabenland and Tomlinson 2008: 324)

In each these innovations, in which new, hybrid models of service delivery or management systems are the direct result of the involvement of the people for whom the service is intended, we can see centripetal dialectical dynamics at work in creating the conditions that make it possible for people who come from marginalised groups, people with learning or physical disabilities, women from minority ethnic groups, to be directly involved in planning and delivering these services. These examples all support the 'business case' for diversity, namely that greater involvement in decision-making can lead to innovation.

In these examples any underlying issues of conflict or coercion seem to be relatively benign. However, in our research we also heard many accounts of managers experiencing highly coercive pressures to conform to externally imposed, hegemonic discourses of good management. The following example was one of the most evocative and it comes from an interview with the chief executive of a well-established organisation. He told me that when he first joined the organisation he tried to develop a management system that would allow some flexibility so that local managers could adapt it as they saw fit:

About four years ago...we tried to develop something called 'Same but Different'. And the idea behind Same but Different, which I still maintain was the right thing to do and I think deep down inside of myself still believe that it is till the way we ought to be looking at ourselves but we're not, is that it allowed the organisation to find different ways of doing things. So the 'same' part was the values, our commitment to people with learning disabilities, the things that bind us, the glue that binds us. And the 'different' bits of it were an attempt to give people local freedom. [But] *What we found was that it resulted in anarchy. But not a negative or an aggressive anarchy, it was just the fact that we lost control. Everybody was doing things completely differently in different parts of the work, in terms of the actual areas in which we work. So we had to kind of rein that back.*

I asked him why he felt that he needed to reassert control.

...we've had to introduce standard recruitment processes, standard sickness and absence management processes, standard performance management processes around supervision and appraisal, all those sort of things to ensure that those things are delivered in a consistent way. (Chief executive of a disability organisation cited in Schwabenland and Tomlinson 2008: 324–325)

We found that many of the people we interviewed talked in similar terms about pressure to standardise management practices, even to standardise the way in which the service was being delivered. As in the example above, it was not always clear where this pressure originated although in come cases it was clearly attributed to government commissioners or to regulatory bodies. In other cases the source of the pressure seemed to be more intangible and was sometimes attributed to the need to demonstrate that the organisation was effectively managed. This coercive pressure creates a homogenising effect, standardising practices and reducing flexibility and local responsiveness – it directly mitigates against the achievement of the supposed benefits of diversity. The chief executive cited above concluded:

I think that over the last five years, organisations that have attempted to remain small and local and connected have struggled. They struggle to keep pace with the extraordinarily changing and challenging financial environment, the regulatory environment, human resource environment in terms of, you know, new legislation coming in, having to compete for staff, having to retain staff, and I think that over the next three to five years a number of those small organisations, through no fault of their own, are going to either wither on the vine, or have to find safe havens within a larger organisation that can provide some of those support and infrastructure areas.

Banerjee and Linstead (2001) write that '*local knowledge*...is both in opposition to the universalising tendencies of global knowledge, and part of it' (Banerjee and Linstead 2001: 690 emphasis on the original). But some localities are more equal than others. And although there are still many good examples of the creation of hybrid models of management, and despite the government rhetoric that valorises the voluntary sector for just those achievements, organisations are experiencing growing pressures towards conformity. In these examples the coercive pressures inhibit rather than support the creation of hybridity.

Action learning groups: Creating a dialogic space

Action learning is another practice that has been developed to encourage organisational actors to share insights and develop new ideas. There are many different models and approaches to action learning but all share a commitment to collaboration amongst group members who may come from very diverse situations and roles. The different approaches go by such names as action learning, action research, experiential or reflective learning; participatory, collaborative and co-enquiry research, education for social change, education for liberation and popular education to name but a few. Action learning and action research (the distinctions between these terms are often quite blurred) build on the experiences and aspirations of groups of actors and use them as the basis for related activities of education, organisation and social change. However, the different approaches and models are underpinned by quite different theoretical orientations which can be located on a continuum from least to most radical. For example, Kemmis's (2001) typology ranges from the technical to the critical, or emancipatory which 'aims to connect the personal and the political in collaborative research and action aimed at transforming situations to overcome felt dissatisfactions, alienation, ideological distortion, and the injustices of oppression and domination' (Kemmis 2001: 92).

Cassell and Johnson's (2006) typology specifically explores differences in the theoretical and philosophical groundings. While theoretically most seem (to varying extents) to assume a relativist ontology, Marsick and O'Neil (1999) characterise the 'scientific school' (in which they include approaches derived from the work of Lewin and Revens) as having a basis in scientific method, a problem solving epistemology and a 'rational' discourse. The scientific school is popular in management courses and consultancy and emphasises problem solving while the more radical approaches, aiming for deeper and systemic social change have been taken up by people working in the global south and in community organising. In these, the emphasis on listening, even privileging the voices and perspectives of marginalised groups leads to a questioning of hegemonic assumptions of more powerful theories and perspectives and respect for, and interest in alternative forms of reality creation and inter-pretation. Lather comments that 'dialectical theory building is more appropriate in this context than theoretical imposition' (Lather cited in Cassell and Johnson 2006: 801). The model of dialectics that Lather refers to is centripetal rather than centrifugal as participatory research methods work polyphonically.

Frances Tomlinson and I recently experimented with these models when we established a group with people working in the voluntary sector in order to share and develop learning about how people are cur-rently experiencing and struggling with diversity issues. Drawing on Lather, we did not seek to impose a particular model although we were in sympathy with the critical stance. We were not, however, seeking to privilege the voices of the marginalised as our participants were located in fairly senior roles, although as our only criteria was that participants regarded themselves as having a significant responsibility for imple-menting diversity initiatives in their organisations, it would have been possible, (and desirable) to have included a wider range of organisational actors.

Over the six months that the group ran there was a consistent core of attendees, one of whom commented towards the end of the time:

I want it to keep going! I've found it so useful...and the growth I've been able to get out of being in this environment with people who do have to deal with it [implementing diversity initiatives] *and that are constantly faced – and just hearing people's experiences and it's helped me so immensely...to just put perspectives on things or to open my mind on how I approach situations and I found it so useful, OK it's unfortunate that it's finishing...*

The participants each took responsibility for identifying a current issue that was important for them and where they felt they might benefit from the opportunity to discuss it with people from different organisations, but working in similar roles. Although there was quite a range of topics discussed we gained a real appreciation of how different processes were interconnected, and how these interconnections could facilitate or impede their effectiveness, which we felt might not have emerged from a different approach. There were a number of examples where participants discussed how initiatives taken in one part of the organisation might work against the realisation of other ones. For example, one member of the group commented that:

...for me I think today's been really interesting particularly around the whole systemic kind of things and the fact that systems can often perpetuate the situation...and the other thing was the whole thing of when two equality things kind of clash and how do you deal with that and the whole issue of whose rights do you protect or – which equality strand is – not more important – but you know there's that hierarchy I suppose which I found quite interesting – yeah I'm still thinking about that...

The different topics chosen also revealed significant tensions between practices that encouraged changes in attitudes, the 'hearts and minds' approach, and those based on coercion. For example one participant commented:

You do want people to take it upon their own initiative but equally, if you look back, again looking back at lessons that we've learned, like if you're changing mind sets sometimes it doesn't happen, like it's not going to happen like that and sometimes what you need in order to kick start that, like an enforcement of it – so a no tolerance policy to you know certain types of language...

A number of other tensions were identified – the labels people chose for themselves versus those that are chosen for them, the needs of the users versus the needs of the organisation (or between the organisation and government), conflicts between the different 'strands' as mentioned above (most commonly between sexual orientation and religion), and also between front line staff and people with a specialist responsibility for the organisation's diversity work. But the group seemed to provide an opportunity for people to explore the possibilities of transcending some of those dilemmas. For example one participant from a charity working in the area of cancer prevention and treatment commented:

I started thinking what is the diversity dimension to cancer and suddenly thinking well of course there are millions of – lots of different kinds of cancers which probably have quite different profiles amongst different groups – there's obviously gender – but there may be all sorts of things to do with life style and poverty or what sort of food people eat or whether there's a hereditary element with certain kinds of cancers so there's probably some really interesting connections there which really bring together – thinking around diversity with what the group – what the organisation's actually really there to do…

Action learning is not a panacea for all situations however. It was notable that several people who came to the initial sessions then dropped out. We speculated that the group may have been generating its own, unwritten and unspoken criteria for membership, its own dynamics of inclusion and exclusion. However, when we carried out follow up interviews with the participants who had attended most regularly, six months after the group had finished, they all spoke very enthusiastically about its usefulness in creating the space for them to reflect more deeply on their work. One participant told me that:

One of the biggest things that I gained from it was two very valuable contacts that are, we're constantly in e-mail contact with each other, I mean if one of them has a question and needs ideas, or if I have a question, it's just like more heads to tackle certain solutions and exchange ideas, and that's been really beneficial to have that. It's like helped me to move things forward.

The examples of the 'hybrid' practices developed by voluntary organisations working with, as well as for the people who will use those services, and the examples from the action learning group cited above demonstrate that the dynamics created by bringing people from different backgrounds together to work for mutually desired aims, *can* result in new ideas and ways of doing things that incorporate, but also transcend the needs of any one individual or group. However, these interviews also reveal the conflicting and coercive pressures that make this much harder to achieve.

Dialectics of convergence within the wider society

In developing new models of management and service delivery, organisations are effectively changing the ways in which we imagine social space and the institutional arrangements that create and sustain it. However, many organisation also deliberately set out to achieve social change, often by carrying out activities such as campaigning, lobbying and advocacy which, as I suggested in the previous chapter, are largely underpinned by the dialectics of differentiation. Some activities that are shaped by the dialectics of convergence include collaborative working, promoting dialogue and conflict resolution. Each of these models of engagement works by bringing people and groups together to forge new relationships and promote mutual understanding. The organisations that Davies (2007) categorises as dialogic intermediary organisations, DIOs, work through practices such as creating the conditions in which dialogue becomes possible, working dialogically with people and groups representing multiple and often conflicting interests, and contributing to the frames of public discourse.

In this section I aim to illustrate some of these activities in more detail, drawing primarily on material from a small research project I carried out with voluntary organisations that had been established to work across divided communities in India, Israel/Palestine and Ireland.

To create the conditions for dialogue, voluntary organisations can play a catalytic role in bringing people together and facilitating dialogue between them and this is one of the most familiar and recognised ways in which organisations influence the public debate. The excerpt cited below, from an interview with the chief executive of an organisation based in Ireland illustrates one such initiative.

...we had a project last year enabling women to talk about the Troubles and the impact that it had on their lives, and we had groups from across the North, weighted Protestant and Catholic, urban and rural, 117 women, I think took part in that, and you know, at first saying that no-one had asked them before, and saying well I wasn't affected by it, thinking well, unless my husband had been shot or something, but then, you know, they realised they had been deeply, profoundly affected by it. So it was a very structured series of programmes and they were enabled to talk about their experiences...then they came together and met other groups in a residential and were able to continue the conversation but hear the other group's experiences, and then we had a big conference at the end where they heard from a consultant with a

draft about their views and they were able to meet everyone who'd been involved.

This quotation describes a model of working that is fairly well established but there are some interesting things to note in this particular example. For instance, the observation that 'no-one had asked them before' demonstrates how the activity acts to legitimise the views of people whose contribution to the public discourse had hitherto been non-existent. Perhaps more interesting, the project also had the effect of helping the participants realise *for themselves* the extent to which they had rendered their own experiences invisible.

The second example concerns the founding of an organisation in Israel that runs integrated schools for Jewish and Arab children.

...in 1997 we began to think that firstly, if you really want to change something you should go the way of education, second you should bring the engaged to learn together. Because there is nothing like that, that Jewish and Arabs grow up together. And we emphasised the issue of equal meeting. Because we want really sharing civilities, not just to...you know, we want to really change the situation between the two groups...

In this example the organisation itself is functioning as a mechanism to bring people together. All the classes aim to have equal numbers of Jewish and Arab children and all the teaching is bi-lingual:

...because you know the situation here in Israel is that you could say most, you could say all of the Arab minority, they are bilingual, they speak Hebrew very well...but the Jews don't learn Arabic. This is part of the tragedy. We are looking at language as more than just a tool to communicate between people. It's more than identity. And I think this is one of the unique things in [the organisation]. *Language in the way, you know, it expresses, we can see, the share of power inside the societies.*

In these examples from Ireland and Israel the organisations are not seeking to influence a particular policy or campaign but rather to create the possibility that new ideas or new answers may emerge from the encounters. The co-founder of the Jewish Arab schools goes on to say:

...if you ask any Palestinian on the Arab side of Israel, how do we want to be equal? What is the meaning of 'equal'? How could we be equals? How could

we share civility between the two sides? And there are no, maybe, good answers.

The next two examples provide more detail about the ways in which such organisations working dialectically. They come from very different organisations working in different parts of the world. The first is based in Haifa, in Israel and the second is a grant-making trust in the UK. However, there is an interesting similarity in their approach. Each talks about working 'holistically' and in each it is the connections and inter-relations between individuals and their wider society that form the basis of their analysis. These extracts are worth reproducing at some length because of the insight they provide into their working processes.

We encourage Jewish and Arab mayors to work together, we establish frameworks, and working groups and we encourage them to work together because we think that the resources, not just at the national level should be allocated equally, but also the regional resources should be allocated equally. [He goes on...] we believe in the holistic way, that means we should work in all levels to ensure tangible results and one level supports the other level, okay? [For example] we are gathering Arab academicians and Arab activists and they get a lot of knowledge about the Israeli system, history, politics, economics, all the substantive materials that leaders should know about the situation...after that they are mapping the needs of the region and we chose two or three from each village in the same region and they chose a collective project that they want to achieve. ... we try to establish frameworks to empower, to strength the community or the officials or the mayors and to build those frameworks and to ensure their sustainability, that they can continue when we leave the area.

The second example, from the UK based organisation, reflects a similar philosophy but demonstrates some of the difficulties in enacting it:

What the BME organisations and the refugee and asylum organisations do is that they see the person and the totality of all the issues that that person is dealing with, and they seem to be about helping that person to have a better life, with all that that involves, whereas it's true that lots of other, of the white organisations will be focussed on a single issue. It's a different approach and it's probably a better approach in terms of the joined up-ness. The extent to which it works better, I'm not sure that it necessarily does. And it's not because it shouldn't work better, and probably if it was a well enough funded organisation it would work better because you'd have the skills and the knowledge to really do it, but because we're only talking about very small organisations, I'm not sure that in those circumstances it does work better.

In this example what is being presented as a better approach is a different way of conceptualising problems and solutions, a conceptualisation that sees an individual as a totality and as *connected* to their environment, in a way which allows multiple identities to be recognised, and not only a different but 'probably a better way of working' albeit one that is threatened by the lack of resources. I describe these examples as instances of organisations working dialectically because these different methodologies are underpinned by an interest in the connections between individuals, identities, functions and roles, and a desire to bring these together for the betterment of the organisation's members and clients.

Butler (2009) writes that the issue of the visibility or, more to the point the invisibility, of particular groups is a significant part of the normalising of the discourse of violence. Several of the organisations I have been researching were working in societies where there is a high level of communal violence between groups of people whose identities are being constructed through different markers of culture, ethnicity or religion. These organisations could be regarded as working at the sharp end of diversity, where discrimination can lead not only to unemployment, but to death. Studying their practices provides a particularly acute insight into the dilemmas of diversity but also into the creative ways in which organisations respond.

One of the organisations I visited had been founded specifically out of a concern about the *absence* of outrage after a particularly horrific outbreak of violence between different religious groups. In telling the story of the founding the project managers said:

You know, that essentially kind of makes you think that there is something that is not quite right here. If people are reacting they are reacting in a certain way, and if they are not reacting, why are they not reacting? Why are they not questioning?

The organisation works with children and teachers, in their own offices and also in schools. They run programmes of workshops for young people who decided together on themes they would like to explore and then fashioned works of art, such as theatre, photography, video making around the themes. The themes they chose to work on included issues around gender, poverty and human rights. The children come from different castes, classes and religions and are encouraged to voice their fears and hopes and to work together to create a project that expresses some of the ideas they have been working through together. In this way the organisation hopes to encourage people to speak out and give voice to their feelings, rather than to respond to horror with silence.

My next example is a story that was told to me by the director of an organisation providing welfare services for children who lost their families in the earthquake in Pakistan. This organisation is an off shoot of a large, international NGO established by a Hindu religious leader to promote peace and dialogue across religious communities, although the specific project that my respondent was working on had chosen to focus primarily on relief work. She describes the suspicion with which some of the local Muslims initially viewed her work:

Initially when we started this project, they [local people] *were very sceptical about what is my agenda. So one day on a Thursday night in a mosque, one of the mosques, they said 'we are going to go and shut down this lady's unit'. So they came in a truckload of people. Firstly they had five punctures along the way…they were to come at 10 o'clock in the morning, by the time they reached it was Friday, the next day, and they reached at 2 o'clock in the afternoon. Now 2 o'clock on a Friday is a very special prayer. That is what they call the 'namaaz', the Jaama, Friday, namaaz. And as luck would have it, the children were out in the garden, with their little carpets spread out, and they were doing their prayers. And there was a Maulvi, that means their own religious person was there, helping them out at that time. And so of course their faces fell in shame and they said 'oh we should be doing what you are doing'. I said 'you are welcome to take over, I am ready to go back and do some other work'.*

In each of these examples the work of the organisation has altered the public discourse in some small way; in the first by the challenging of silence and in the second by demonstrating that belonging to one religious group does not inevitably have to lead to the denial of recognition of other groups. Neither of these examples could be described as campaigning or advocacy, because they are not seeking to represent the views of one particular group, but to create the possibilities for multiple voices to be heard. These small projects are more akin to Modood's (2008) conceptualisation of 'coalitional citizenship' in which subjects negotiate and influence the terms of recognition, or to Habermas's 'communicative actors' working to bring together the three worlds of self, other and social (Habermas 1994). What all of these examples have in common is a desire to renegotiate and transform the power relationships that mediate contested social space, the liminal space where individuals, groups and organisations cross and overlap, and to do so in ways that create possibilities beyond assimilation and the denial of difference.

Conclusions

> A dialogue of cultures – or of utopias, visions and faiths – is a dialogue within each participating culture among its different levels and parts. This second dialogue could be articulate, well-defined or central to the culture; it could be inarticulate, ill-defined or marginal. Some cultures hide their most profound experiences at their peripheries but all cultures have the capacity to use creatively the intersecting demands of such outer and inner dialogues. (Nandy 1999: 17)

Of cultures, so too of individuals and organisations. Nandy summarises the quintessential dilemma that underpins the dialectics of diversity; organisations may chose to articulate and harness the creative possibilities that are inherent in a plural workforce comprising people from different perspectives and experiences, or they may chose to marginalise or deny them.

In this chapter I have presented a number of examples of different ways in which managers, primarily in voluntary organisations, are working within the dynamics of centripetal dialectics. These dynamics create a momentum towards coming together in shared space to create new approaches to what are sometimes regarded as intractable problems. They can also create pressures towards uniformity, assimilation and the negation of difference. At an individual level we see managers struggling to maintain an awareness of working across different discourses and needing to move from one 'language' to another as they work within and across these sometimes competing worlds. For some managers being able to experience empathy is a necessary capacity for working within this liminal space.

At an organisational level these dynamics are often conceptualised as underpinning the business case for diversity. Bringing together people who have different perspectives but a shared interest in the issue being addressed in order that a creative solution, a hybrid, may emerge is a pattern of organising that finds expression in action learning and action research groups, partnerships, coalitions, collaborative agreements and multi-disciplinary work teams. Some of the differences that are represented in these temporary working groups are differences of function and role but the principal has been extended, in the rhetoric of the business case, to differences of identity. Voluntary organisations have a long history of working dialogically in order to create new models of management systems, services and even organisational models that manifest hybridity (Billis 2010).

Within the wider society many organisations in the public and voluntary sectors are explicitly working in the areas of peace building initiatives and conflict resolution by bring together different communities to promote dialogue and shared understanding. They create the conditions for people to come together. They also work at the symbolic level by developing and promoting the creating of joint artistic endeavours. But however inspirational these examples may be, they are hard won. Each of the people interviewed for the research projects that provided these examples spoke eloquently of the tensions and struggles they faced.

Many writers challenge the notion that heterogenous teams actually do make better decisions; less still decisions that lead to improved productivity (Wrench 2005, Ho 2000). In fact, not only has any direct, causal relationship been exceedingly difficult to prove (Wise and Tschirhart 2000) there even seems to be evidence that heterogenous teams can lead to increased conflict and *reduced* performance (Ho 2000). Although the rhetoric of diversity is often promoted as if it were unproblematic, this rhetoric may function to mask the fear that actually it might not work.

Another criticism that is often made of the diversity rhetoric (Wrench 2005) is that it obscures underlying issues of systemic exclusion, oppression and poverty. Interestingly, a similar charge is sometimes made about the concept of hybridity (Kalra et al 2005). The different participants in the joint ventures are treated as if they have equal standing and equal capabilities. However, this is seldom the case. Both of the managers I interviewed in Israel were eager to emphasise that without equality the conditions for dialogue do not exist – equality is a *precondition* for co-existence.

Some years ago I facilitated an action learning group for students working with small organisations, generally run by refugees or people from BME groups. One student described his role as the sole employee of a forum that had been established to co-ordinate representation from smaller, locally based groups working with people from a number of different African countries who were living with HIV. The purpose of the forum was to bring these groups together to advise the health authority in commissioning culturally appropriate services. Therefore, the original idea in establishing the forum was that these groups were a resource for the health authority because they possessed particular knowledge that the authority could not easily gain for itself.

However, as time had gone by, there had been a subtle shift. The funding for the post of forum co-ordinator specified that his role was to provide capacity building support to these organisations. This funding came from the same source as the money that funded the various groups – and it was in short supply. So the effect of defining the forum co-ordinator's role in this way was to create competition not only between the groups themselves but also between the groups and the forum that was meant to represent them. Furthermore, this forum now saw *itself* in the role of expert – an expert in the management systems that the smaller organisations were now being defined as lacking. Thus two shifts had occurred; the smaller groups' expertise in understanding the needs of their members had been obscured by their objectification as needy and inadequate in managing themselves. And the role of the forum officer had shifted from that of being their representative to being an expert advisor – but an advisor who was in competition with them (as they were with each other) for funding. Interestingly, when the student presented this story his initial concern had been to understand why the groups seemed to be resistant to all his efforts to offer them his services, organisations that he described as lacking in leadership. This is an interesting example, because it illustrates a shift from a dialectics of convergence, where groups were originally valued for the specialist contribution they could make to the common good, to a dialectics of differentiation, in which they were essentialised as needy and inadequate and forced into competition, rather than collaboration with each other – a competition which each organisation could only 'win' by recourse to a statement of its own uniqueness.

We can see these contradictions at play in the relationship between funders or policy makers and the voluntary organisations they support, when the later are characterised (as they often are) as inferior and indisciplined. This characterisation is maintained not only through the allocation and regulation of funding but also through the collusion of voluntary organisations themselves in their internalisation of this construction. The collusion is maintained, in part, through the fostering of a spirit of competition which acts as a colonising mechanism of divide and rule by which co-operation and collaboration loses out. Thus, 'a flattening of differences is secured at the very moment that celebrates difference and the creative productivity of new mixings' (Kalra et al 2005: 100).

This example suggests one way of understanding why the appropriation of the concepts of diversity and plurality into the discourse of management is inherently problematic. Valourising diversity and plurality cannot help but undermine the idea that there is just one good management, or one good model of civilisation. The voluntary sector is a site in which these competing discourses of the management of diversity are played out; one understanding of diversity being that in which the valuing of differences leads to the creation of hybridity, and the other understanding in which it is subsumed into the discourse of the one good management. And Frenkel and Shenav (2005) demonstrate that the discourse of rational, Western management is intimately bound up with notions of superiority. They further suggest that the myth of the supposed 'western-ness' of management and its equally supposed superiority over other models is sustained through the 'writing out' of inconvenient histories that might undermine that idealised image. And challenging hegemony, whether it is the hegemony of universalising management models or of powerful vested interests is very risky indeed. de Peuter writes:

> the dialogical challenge is to expose the monologue of centripetal superiority as an interpretive discourse constructed in the service of Western domination, and to unveil the construction of the centrifugal 'other' as a *serviceable* other...it is by defining centrifugal tendencies as forces to discipline and manage that centripetal forces gain their definition and privileged status. (de Peuter 1998: 41)

But the dialogical challenge is more than this. Each dialectical dynamic, whether towards the centre or away, towards convergence or divergence, masks as much as it reveals. There are always messy bits, fragments, ideas, parts, people who don't fit.

8
Cacophony or Polyphony?
Concluding Thoughts

...it's all about the stuff that is nothing which is something...

Introduction

This book is based on the proposition that metaphor and dialectic are patterns of thinking that help us to structure our thoughts and that these patterns are particularly powerful in shaping our thinking about how we perceive similarity and difference. Thinking, as Lawrence writes, 'is a defining characteristic of the life and work of the people in an organisation' (Lawrence 2000: 3). Our thoughts drive our actions, even if much of this happens at an unconscious level. The options available to us for taking action in organisations are determined by the limits we set ourselves in our thinking. Armstrong suggests that these limits are, in part, mediated through the ways in which we imagine ourselves in role: 'the idea or conception in the mind through which a person manages himself [sic] so as to further its aim or purpose' (Armstrong 1988: 5).

But the reverse is also true; 'action shapes cognition' (Weick 1995: 12). Weick gives an example of what he calls 'a wonderful account of sensemaking' in a quotation from Graham Wallas about a little girl who, on being cautioned that she should be sure of her meaning before she spoke, replied 'how can I know what I think until I see what I say?' (Wallas cited by Weick 1995: 12). Our actions also drive our thoughts. Thinking is a complex business. Lawrence identifies four different modalities of thinking; thinking as being, thinking as becoming, thinking as the unthought known and thinking as dreaming (Lawrence 2000).

Weick's quotation identifies one of the central problems about thinking – we do not always (or often?) know what we think, or even what we are thinking. The psychoanalyst Marion Milner kept diaries for years in which she charted her many and diverse efforts to follow her own processes of thinking. She observed that 'having once found out that writing down whatever came into ones' head, however apparently nonsensical, could reveal a meaning and pattern that one would never have guessed at, so I had now thought that drawing without any conscious intent to "draw something" might also be interesting' (Milner 1983: 4) – presumably as a means for revealing Lawrence's 'unthought known'.

But if thoughts influence actions (and actions influence thoughts) then if we want to change our organisations in whatever way we think is desirable, we need to become more aware of what and how we are thinking about them, and to do so by drawing on the full repertoire of our thinking modalities. In this book I have concentrated on one aspect of organisational management, that of managing diversity, and suggested that metaphor and dialectic are two such modalities that are particularly relevant to diversity management because they structure our thinking about similarity and difference and it is this thinking that lies at the heart of the relationships we form with our colleagues at work. Metaphor and dialectic each create meaning out of the encounters between similarity and difference. Metaphor works by holding these elements in tension, dialectic by alternating dynamics of distanciation and convergence.

Moreover, metaphor and dialectic can be particularly helpful in enabling us to discover our 'unthought knowns'. Throughout this book I have given examples that demonstrate that each of these modalities of thinking can function in ways that can be either creative or degenerative. Metaphor allows us to apprehend hitherto unappreciated aspects of similarity; metaphor also creates stereotypes of the 'other' that can have enormously destructive consequences. Stereotypes can kill. Dialectic recognises difference, allows us to exchange positions of centrality and marginality and creates possibilities of multiple, hybrid forms of knowing and being to be interwoven polyphonically – but dialectic can also reinforce essentialism and binary forms of knowing that reproduce disadvantaged positioning. Discrimination *is* dialectical.

Therefore, what this book is arguing is that metaphor and dialectic are not simply tools we should adopt to help us to manage more productively. We don't make choices to think metaphorically or dialectically, we are participants, both actively and unconsciously in these processes. We are made by our thoughts and our thoughts follow trajectories underpinned by the dynamics of metaphor and dialectic. So, what is important is that we become more conscious of ourselves as thinkers, more aware of our own patterns of thinking and how these influence the actions we take.

In the preceding chapters I have drawn on examples from some of my work with student managers and with managers working in voluntary organisations. In several of these projects, including the research projects that Frances Tomlinson and I developed together, there has been an explicit intention to create the conditions in which these metaphorical and dialectical patterns of thinking could be exposed, so that not only the products, but the processes of thinking could be recognised and engaged with. I have also included some excerpts from follow-up interviews, both with students from my *Managing Diversity and Equality* postgraduate module (where I developed a series of exercises designed to promote metaphorical thinking) and also from the action learning group that Frances Tomlinson and I ran (which represented a dialogical space in which multiple meanings could emerge polyphonically). These interviews suggest that the participants found their experiences in these events to be valuable and memorable. This extract is taken from one of the follow-up interviews with a student manager:

…although it's the most theoretical module [of her MA course] *for me it's been the most practical. Which is weird. Because in theory it shouldn't be. But I've just found it the most practical in terms of day to day use…. No, actually…I don't think the word theoretical is correct. It's more philosophical I should say, rather than theoretical…well the problem is, is that with learning you can sit there and say well this is the right way to do things, but you have to learn the right way for yourself. Otherwise it's not there, is it? And* [the module] *enables you to do the right thing for yourself, which is, that's what makes it practical.*

The next extract is taken from an interview with one of the participants of the action learning group:

I feel as though I've found myself. I've really had the time to reflect. And I [already] *had a really good understanding of what I think equality and diversity is, and I think without that I wouldn't be able to carry it forward, I wouldn't be as passionate, I wouldn't be that trainer who you can look at and know that I actually believe the words that are coming out of my mouth, you know?… So it probably would have happened anyway. But it probably happened faster… So it's just great. It's an opportunity to speak about the sort of more philosophical kind of components, which equality and diversity really is. It's all about the philosophy, it's all about the perspective, it's all about the stuff that is nothing which is something. You know? So yeah, it's great. I got so much out of it.*

I have taken one line from this extract for the quotation that opens this chapter; 'the stuff that is nothing which is something'. To me, this conveys something of the sense of the ephemeral, fragile, yet utterly powerful nature of thought. I have also chosen these two quotations in particular, because in each the participants have drawn a direct connection between the philosophical and the practical (and without any prompting from me!).

I want to use the rest of this concluding chapter to return to two of the main themes that have resonated throughout the book; the role of poetry in social change and the necessity of the dialectical imagination in creating a better world. However, before moving on to these rather abstract topics I want to revisit some of the current debates and dilemmas around managing diversity that I identified in the opening chapter.

Metaphor and dialectic in Managing Diversity

In the first chapter I identified some of the current debates and concerns about the desirability and efficacy of the diversity paradigm. These included the debate about whether the diversity paradigm represents an advance on the equality approach, questions about whether the business case for diversity conflicts with the social or moral justice case and whether diversity is something that can be *managed*. Now, having developed my argument about the relevance of metaphor and dialectic in structuring our thinking about diversity over six chapters, it seems important to revisit these debates in the context of this emerging understanding.

Revisiting the debate about the diversity paradigm

The debates about the diversity paradigm concern the question about whether the diversity approach represents an advance on the 'older' equality approach. Does valuing a diverse workforce lead to greater equality between individuals from marginalised and non-marginalised groups? Or is it irrelevant? Or worse, does the emphasis on diversity mask underlying issues of systemic oppression, reproduce them and thereby *increase* inequality?

These are important and serious questions. If we start to address them, as suggested in the previous section, by attending to the ways in which we think about diversity and equality, can we find new ways of approaching them?

We might begin by positioning diversity and equality in a metaphorical tension; diversity *is* equality; equality *is* diversity. Metaphors are not truth claims, they represent associations of similarity and difference. In what way is diversity similar to equality? In what way is it different? How does positioning it in a metaphorical tension with equality enhance our understanding of diversity? Engaging with these questions within the specific context of a particular organisation might yield interesting insights. For example, one organisation may be particularly good at creating systems that enable people with disabilities to contribute equally but have a very poor record of promoting people from minority ethnic groups into senior positions. Another may value the contributions that people from different cultural backgrounds bring, but find it hard to work with differences of political perspectives. And a third might recognise the benefits of marketing its products to a diverse customer base but fail to appreciate a similar diversity amongst its workforce or its board. Clearly, not all aspects of diversity are equally valued; nor are all employees from the same ethnic, gender or cultural group equal in terms of their role, their contributions to the organisation, their competence. But asking to what extent the metaphor is 'true' and to what extent is it not, is itself a process that may be fruitful.

If diversity and equality are considered to be in a dialectical relationship with each other different questions emerge. Are diversity and equality binary oppositions? If so, what are the elements that make them so? And does thinking of them in such terms reinforce these polarities? Occupational segregation might be thought of as an example of diversity without equality (and equality without diversity). Or is the organisation's capacity for innovation dependent on the diverse perspectives of its employees and other stakeholders? Following Bohm (2008) if we reframe potential problems as paradoxes are there possibilities of transcending them?

The answers may come down to a question about the kind of organisation (or society) that we want to live in. In the third chapter I presented two very different pictures of mosaics. The first followed a fairly traditional pattern, where all the component parts, albeit of different colours, were combined in geometric precision. But the second, a mosaic by the Catalan artist Gaudi, is an almost haphazard assemblage of different shapes, colours, sizes, somehow held together in a happy, but precarious relationship. Similarly, if we draw on the metaphor of polyphony, do we think of it in terms of a piece of music such as Monteverdi's sixteen voice, a cappella harmonies or do we hear John Cage's *Imaginary Landscape No. 4* for twelve radios? Which is polyphony and which cacophony? Who decides?

I am raising a lot of questions and no answers. This is because I think the answers have to be found locally, in the context of specific organisations and the relationships they create. The answers may not be transferable or repeatable and they may be temporary and contingent. Even if you are a great fan of John Cage's music there may be times when you want to listen to Monteverdi. Valuing diversity may have the effect of reducing some inequalities while leaving others untouched or even unrecognised.

Revisiting the debate about the business case

The business case for diversity rests on the proposition that having good diversity practices is good for business. Many of the reasons given to support this claim are aligned to the HR function, for instance that having good recruitment and retention strategies in place will ensure the 'best' person for the job is selected and, once in post, decides to stay. People who feel they are undervalued or discriminated against are likely to start looking for a new job pretty soon.

But one of the other arguments of the business case is that having a more diverse workforce allows the company to develop a strategic advantage because people with different experiences and perspectives will be able to contribute new, and valuable insights into decision-making and product or service development. Critics of this argument suggest that it commodifies employees' experiences of oppression, harnessing them for the good of the company and exploiting their insights for profit.

Again, this is a serious criticism and one that warrants consideration. At the very least it would seem that the business case is not going to be equally relevant to every company. Wrench (2005) clearly makes the point that some companies are engaged in activities that would seem to be largely irrelevant – the example he cites is a Scandinavian auto-mated printing company. I sometimes made this point to students by commenting that lesbians and heterosexuals generally use the same kinds of paper clips. However, here again, much depends on how the company understands its role. Does it only see itself as producing paper clips, or does it see itself as contributing to the well-being of the community in which it is located?

In the previous chapter I discussed some research that my colleague Frances Tomlinson and I carried out into diversity management in the voluntary sector in which we explored the relevance of the business case to organisations whose 'business' was social justice and found that although there was no clear consensus as to how these issues were framed, nor of how to work creatively within the conflicts that pre-sented themselves between the aspirations of clients and the needs of staff, nonetheless there were clear examples of instances in which the moral, social justice and strategic priorities were aligned (Tomlinson and Schwabenland 2010). Perhaps a more useful way of exploring the relevance of the business case arguments is to ask *to what extent* the business case applies to a particular organisation, and *in what circumstances* is there a conflict?

Another key argument in favour of the business case rests on the proposed link between more diverse teams and organisational creativity. Chia and Holt contrast two approaches to strategy; the first is the more traditional in which 'the strategist is always looking at the world knowledgeably, on his terms; the task is to subject the world into a condition of pliant and communicable phenomena such that his reach, and the reach of his organisation, remains assured, governed and purposeful' (Chia and Holt 2011: 152). Within this understanding of strategy formation it is easy to see how identities become commodified and regarded as being within the organisation's control. However Chia and Holt propose an alternative model of strategy as artisanal crafting. Drawing on Heidegger, they describe the creative processes of a cabinetmaker who 'encounters things such as wood, tools, the equipmental demands of furniture without reducing these encounters to an entirely instrumental logic of pragmatic confinement; her identity is one of constant disclosure within this relational condition that she animates but over which she has no distinct perspective or control' (Chia and Holt 2011: 152). Chia and Holt's metaphor of strategist as cabinetmaker bears close affinity with Mintzberg's earlier metaphor of strategist as potter. Mintzberg wrote that crafting requires 'involvement, a feeling of intimacy and harmony with the materials at hand, developed through long experience and commitment. Formulation and implementation merge into a fluid process of learning though which creative strategies emerge' (Mintzberg 1987: 109). (Coincidentally or not, both Mintzberg, writing in 1987 and Chia and Holt over twenty years later, used the pronoun 'she' to describe their crafting strategists and either the male pronoun or none to represent the more traditional approach.)

There are two important aspects of the metaphor of strategist as craftsperson that have implications for business case for diversity. The first is that in this model the strategist develops a certain kind of intimacy as well as profound respect with the materials at hand. This relationship is presented as one characterised by 'consideration, curiosity and sensitivity' (Chia and Holt 2011: 152). Although one is using the other this is not an exploitative relationship. Secondly, the crafting process is envisioned as a dialectical one between the crafter and their materials. Thirdly, this creative process is not entirely in the control of the crafter. It is through contrast, through the unexpected and the ambiguous that art works its spell. Diversity is at the heart of creativity but it is not controllable or predictable.

Applying the metaphor of craft to strategy raises the interesting possibility that the problem with the business case for diversity is not that it isn't radical but that it is *too* radical. A diverse workforce may indeed hold the potential for creative expression and innovation – the proponents of the business case are not wrong about this. But they too often disregard the more difficult aspects of creativity; its uncertainties, anxieties and frustrations. Perhaps one of the challenges of the business case is that if it were to be taken really seriously, it might transform the way we work with people in organisations.

Revisiting the debate about whether diversity can be managed

Chia and Holt's critique of the planning model of strategy offers some interesting insights into why diversity initiatives so often fail. They write that 'the more directly and deliberately a specific strategic goal is single-mindedly sought the more likely it is that such calculated actions eventually work to undermine and erode their initial successes, often with devastating consequences' (Chia and Holt 2011: x). They argue that the traditional model assumes that the task of management is to shape, coerce and subjugate its resources to achieve a pre-determined outcome. However, the world is not so amenable to our manipulations, as climate change is forcing us to acknowledge daily. And not only do top down planning initiatives often have unintended and sometimes disastrous results, many of the most successful innovations come from small, local, idiosyncratic, ad hoc responses to day-to-day, lived events. Chia and Holt argue that the future is simply not knowable, predictable or controllable. Using this insight it is interesting to return to Czarniawska Joerges and Wolff's description of the tasks of leadership, management and entrepreneurship that I quoted in Chapter 1:

> ...leadership is seen as symbolic performance, expressing the hope of control over destiny, management as the activity of introducing order and co-ordinating flows of things and people towards collective action and entrepreneurship as the making of entire new worlds. (Czarniawska Joerges and Wolff 1991: 529)

This now can be read very differently. Leadership expresses hope of control over destiny, but that hope is an illusion. Management is the activity of introducing order, but we now know that order and disorder create each other. And entrepreneurship, or the making of new worlds, may be manifested in the small things – 'transformation, because it is continuous and operates at a mundane, everyday level, normally passes unnoticed' (Chia and Holt 2011: 192). Perhaps the question is not whether diversity can be managed but whether *anything* can be managed.

This conclusion sounds profoundly depressing. And indeed, Chia and Holt are unfashionably wary of hope. While hope has its uses it can distract us from fully living in the present. Hope can be a way of avoiding responsibility for things as they are now. And this brings us back to the two aspects of metaphorical thinking that Kohn (1990) advocates; the ability to see the world from someone else's perspective while not losing sight of our own, and the ability to experience the other's world through empathy. Perspective sharing and empathy are experiences that call us to the present.

As are the strategies of Meyerson's (2003) 'tempered radicals' who work quietly, often 'below the radar', carrying out their agendas through being *responsive* rather than through grand designs. Winning hearts and minds is not achieved in the future but through small, daily encounters in the present. Perhaps the challenge is not how to manage *diversity* but how to *diversify* our ideas about management. And this requires us to develop a wider range of approaches to thinking itself.

Metaphor and dialectic offer ways of working within competing truth claims. The plurality of competing voices can create polyphony or cacophony – but which we hear it as depends on us. Critical management theorists often suggest that the diversity rhetoric masks/obscures/rides roughshod over structural inequality (Zanoni et al 2010, Due Billing and Sundin 2006, Wrench 2005). But it is also possible to argue the opposite – that if diversity rhetoric is taken at its face value it is immensely radical.

In the previous chapters focussing on empirical data I have organised my findings around three themes; the individual, the organisation and the wider society. These different levels are, of course, deeply inter-related – Syed and Ozbilgin point out that 'the issues of diversity and discrimination that proliferate in the workplace have their genesis in...macro-contextual determinants' (Syed and Ozbilgin 2009: 2436). They point out that for interventions to be effective they need to consider what factors influence the different ways in which meaning is constructed at these different levels and '"the space between" where agency, action and structures have causal interdependence and where they intertwine and co-generate social interdependencies and inter-subjectivities' (Syed and Ozbilgin 2009: 2446). Metaphorical and dialectical forms of thinking offer a resource for helping us to bridge these different levels because they connect us with our contexts. In the next two sections I want to explore their significance as heuristics that help us to engage more fully with the societal issues that influence the success or failure of diversity initiatives in the workplace.

Metaphor, poetry and social change

'A metaphor is a poem in miniature' (Ricoeur 1991b: 316[1]); and 'all beautiful poetry is an act of resistance' (Darwish 2009: 130). I have used Ricoeur's observation in an earlier chapter and I quoted Darwish at the beginning of Chapter 2 to introduce the grouping of chapters on metaphor in organisational analysis. Ricoeur's proposition refers to poetry's associational structure; metaphor *is* poetry because it brings together different ideas in such a way that we see the world anew.

However, Darwish goes further when he explicitly draws a connection between poetry and social change, and here he is referring to the idea I explored briefly in the second chapter, that poets are, in Shelley's words, 'the unacknowledged legislators of the world' (Shelley cited in Reiman and Powers 1977: 508). But what exactly, does Darwish mean? *All* poetry? All *beautiful* poetry? If he means the former, then he is referring to the power of poetry itself; if the latter then it is the notion of beauty that has particular salience.

Let us explore each of these interpretations in turn. What is it about the way in which poetry works that encourages writers such as Darwish (2009), Ricoeur (1991b) and even Nietzsche (cited by Ricoeur 1991b) to say that poetry is *inherently* subversive?

Firstly, poetry is concerned with 'multiplicity not specificity' (Cunliffe 2008: 133). As Ricoeur writes: 'all poetry is by nature rebellious against this [reductionist] use of language' (Ricoeur 1991b: 449). In structure and in content poetry tells us that there is always more, there is always a surplus of meaning. This is what Ricoeur means when he says that 'it is the task of poetry to make words mean as much as they can and not as little as they can. Therefore, not to elude or exclude this plurivocity but to cultivate it, to make it meaningful, powerful...' (Ricoeur 1991b: 449).

Secondly, poetry 'disturbs certainties' (Ramsey 2008: 549). Spivak write that 'poetic and figurative gestures can be read as the conditions of the possibility of a stand against a "rage for order"' (Spivak 2006: 156). Spivak is referring to a poem by Wallace Stevens (The Idea of Order at Key West) and she interprets Stevens as arguing against what she calls the 'will to consistency' and in favour of those things that get lost, the 'ghostlier demarcations' when knowledge is 'totalised' (Spivak 2006: 156). This is a political stance – Spivak claims that 'your political allegiance can pretty well be plotted out in terms of which one you want to centralise, the concept or the metaphor' (Spivak 2006: 157). Spivak's position on the imposition of totalising systems of order, and the violence that they do to those who are either excluded or located in a peripheral or marginal position, has been discussed in Chapter 6.

Although poetry resists any move or tendency towards reductionism and disrupts our taken-for-granted ways of seeing by presenting us with surprising, disconcerting and sometimes disorientating resemblances, poetry also creates a new order of association. Ricoeur again: 'the function of metaphor that we put above all other features – its nascent or emerging character – is related to the function of poetry as a *creative* imitation of reality' (Ricoeur 1991b: 317: my emphasis). But it is an imitation that presents us with a reality that is not as we thought. Edwards writes:

> Poetry enables the world to speak, to enter human language while remaining itself: it draws the world towards us, as it draws us towards the world. And in doing so it changes the world, or changes the way we perceive it... It seems to me that the one universal effect of poetry is this modification of reality, whatever the worldviews of the poets concerned. (Edwards 2011: 12)

The third function of poetry that can be linked to social change is its capacity to arouse our emotions, and, as described at considerable length throughout this book, promote empathy. Engaging with poetry draws us out of ourselves and into the poem.

> Poetry is more a threshold than a path, one constantly approached and constantly departed from, at which reader and writer undergo in their different ways the experience of being at the same time summoned and released. (Heaney 1989: 108)

Here again is the tension between awareness of self and awareness of the other. Heaney says that in encountering poetry we are *both* summoned *and* released into our engagement with it. We lose ourselves but we are not lost. What is important here is not simply experiencing empathy or identification, it is the ability to do that while simultaneously retaining the gaze of the outsider. Too much empathy is no more useful than too little. Poetry can help us to find the balance.

Therefore, we can conclude that poetry is inherently subversive in its capacity to disrupt the ordering of our perceptions, presenting us with alternative forms of interpreting our world and in so doing, reminding us that there is always more, that there is an infinity of possible truth claims and ways of seeing. Poetry contains the possibility of a measured experience of empathy; an experiencing of the other which changes the self but without entirely losing the self.

However, even if poetry is inherently subversive, that does not mean that society always changes in the direction we want it to go. Geary (2011) points out that metaphor is a highly effective weapon in the armoury of advertising, where its purpose is to solely encourage us to imagine our lives as lacking in ways that we had not hitherto thought them to be. (Geary also explores the use of metaphor in propaganda but this raises more complicated questions as to the extent to which what is being suggested in the metaphor is an alternative perspective or represents a deliberate attempt to deceive.[2]) Adrienne Rich, herself a poet, points out that 'a poem can be deep or shallow, visionary or glib, prescient or stuck in an already lagging trendiness. What's pushing the grammar and syntax, the sounds and the images – is it the constriction of literalism, fundamentalism, professionalism – a stunted language? Or is it the *great muscle of metaphor* drawing strength from resemblance in difference?' (Rich 2009: 142 my emphasis). Rich suggests that there are important distinctions to be made between 'those for whom language has metaphoric density and those for whom it is merely formulaic' (Rich 2009: 142) and between poetry's intention to control and to repress, rather than reveal difference.

Beauty, as discussed in Chapter 2, is much more problematic. Not all poetry is beautiful. Is Darwish's notion of the beautiful in poetry something that readers must decide for themselves, or is he referring to some more objective or absolute conception? Either interpretation contains some difficulties. Is the geometrically precise pattern in the first mosaic more or less beautiful than Gaudi's? Is Nussbaum's evocation of 'the *beautiful* chaos of an Indian city' (Nussbaum 2007: 334 my emphasis) an aesthetic judgement that all would share? Or is there a third possible interpretation, namely that for something to be perceived as beautiful it must contain, or give rise to some aspect of subversion?

The debates about whether or not art promotes morality are at least as old as Plato (Carey 2005, Schellekens 2007) and well beyond the scope of this book, but Carey's somewhat dismal conclusion is that 'the widely shared belief that art can instruct the public, and help to attain a better state of affairs, lacks any factual backing' (Carey 2005: 101). However, perhaps one way in which the beautiful retains its subversive power is in 'taking us away from our technologically ordered and intellectualised condition' (Chia and Holt 2011: 156). Beauty reminds us that there is an extra dimension to our existence, one where things command respect and attain value for qualities beyond the purely instrumental. Beauty just is. It doesn't need any more justification. It doesn't need to *do* anything. Beauty asks us to dwell in the moment in all its multifarious dimensions.

How does this help us in the tasks of managing diversity? Schellekens suggests that 'the experience of beauty…engages the imagination in such a way as to pull together actively the strands of a work into a coherent, aesthetic entity [including] the element of lived, personal experience' (Schellekens 2007: 144). In other words, appreciating beauty, in whatever way we do, helps us to create a kind of unity from diversity, through an awareness of the interconnectedness of the different levels of human experience, and it is this, she suggests that 'keeps the genuinely moral aspect of our deliberations alive, preventing moral life from collapsing into a set of ready-made propositions and decisions' (Schellekens 2007: 144).

If this seems a long way away from the day-to-day life of decision-making in organisations, Chia and Holt's (2011) book on strategy, while saying very little about poetry, contains a whole chapter on the relevance of Ruskin's thoughts on the differences between Gothic and Renaissance art and on Heidegger's appreciation of Van Gogh's painting of a peasant's clogs. And it is just these two features of the experience of beauty, its capacity to draw us into the present on the one hand, and to remind us of the interconnectedness of different dimensions of being on the other that they relate to the function of strategising. They write:

> What distinguishes the work of art from the entity we term a pair of clogs, therefore, is that whereas the clogs are brought forth in order that their nature be then ignored (they become serviceable pieces of equipment), or they are bought forth to be analysed in terms of their material forms and dimensions, Van Gogh's work brings forth something whose thingness is revealed by what is implied, rather than what is explicitly stated. It is this kind of paradoxically distanced emotional involvement, this near-documenting of things, this thoughtfulness and attunement that are required if we are to understand what we mean by the real experience of strategy. (Chia and Holt 2011: 156)

This kind of attunement, or appreciation of things as they are, is a much more respectful position than that in which people and their identities are regarded instrumentally, in terms of their usefulness to the organisation.

Chia and Holt draw extensively on Heidegger's concept of *Dasein*. Heidegger defines *Dasein* as 'this entity which each of us is himself and which includes inquiring as one of the possibilities of its Being' (Heidegger 1996: 28).[3] Heidegger's Being is full of restless curiosity and pursues its enquiry, he suggests, hermeneutically; a hermeneutics that takes being out of itself in order to find itself (Being) anew. And this process is, of course, what poetry can help us to do.

Therefore, beauty is subversive in that it draws us into an appreciation of things as they are, beyond any instrumental purpose, and this appreciation encourages a more respectful stance. The appreciation of beauty is a means through which we fulfil our inquiry of the possibilities of Being.

Individual transformation can lead to social change as each person acts on their imaginative constructions of the relationship between themselves and their environment. However, Shotter moves beyond the domain of the individual in his evocation of the concept of a *'social poetics'* that names the processes of inquiry in which, as 'we move from the "inside" to the "outside" of a disciplinary system, it becomes possible to sense how – from within the system – its metaphorical ways of talking seemingly entrap those within "its" reality'...a social poetics [being the task of] creating new networks of connections and relations between the events within them, thus to give those events new roles, new parts to play in our lives' (Shotter 1995: no page numbers). Social poetics, understood in these terms, extends the processes of the individual journey from being to Being to that of a collective journey undertaken by groups and organisations. In this sense social poetics offers us some assistance in surfacing and challenging enduring patterns of systemic discrimination.

To summarise: poetry can help to create the conditions for social change. Poetry presents us with multiple meanings and multiple ways of knowing that co-exist in an endless array of shifting relationships. Poetry manifests and celebrates plurality. Poetry disorders order and then creates new, and surprising connections, and in so doing, reminds us of the interconnectedness of all phenomena. Poetry is one way in which we are brought to an appreciation of beauty which in itself draws us out of ourselves and evokes a respectful stance for that which we regard as beautiful, a stance that takes us beyond a purely instrumental understanding of people, identities, objects, as simply resources to be used.

Finally, poetry can be gentle in its challenge. 'Poetry should be great and unobtrusive, a thing which enters into one's soul, and does not startle it or amaze it with itself but with its subject' (Keats 2009: 493). Poetry gives us some privacy and space and perhaps one of the most valuable uses of poetry is that it gives us ways in which the unsayable can be said.

Dialectic and the bridge between past, present and future

Having considered the role of metaphor in social change, we now turn to dialectic. Does dialectic also have a contribution to make in helping us to create a better society? In this section I want to consider the way in which the dynamics of dialectic structure our thinking about past, present and future. Our ideas about the future are often characterised by extremes; either in Malthusian doomsday scenarios in which climate change or the expanding birth-rate or the like has lead to the breakdown of social order, or in utopian manifestations of the good society. Whether we are predisposed to create doomsday or utopian scenarios they each have a similar function; they are imaginative constructs that allow us to step outside of the present in order to present it anew.

> This development of new, alternative perspectives defines utopia's most basic function. May we not say then that imagination itself – through its utopian function – has a constitutive role in helping us to *rethink* the nature of our social life? ...Does not the fantasy of an alternative society and its exteriorisation 'nowhere' work as one of the most formidable contestations of what is? (Ricoeur 1986: 16)

One function of imagining a utopia is to highlight what is believed to be wrong in the present and to provide some sort of picture, or imaginative construction, of what a better world would look like. Much (although not all) science fiction functions similarly. In this sense we can say that utopian thinking is dialectical; it proceeds by identification and recognition of difference, how the present differs from this idealised (or, in the case of doomsday scenarios, diabolised) state – it is *not* this, *not* that. A similar dynamic underpins our relationship with the past whether it is as remembered (or imagined) as a 'golden age' to be recovered or a nightmare from which we need to escape. These imaginative constructions, as Ricoeur suggests, influence our thinking about how we perceive our present.

In the third chapter I described a programme of exercises I devised to encourage my students to develop their capacity for metaphorical thinking. However, there was one exercise that I did not write about because it was not a success. The first time I experimented with the exercises I began by asking students to imagine a utopian future where diversity issues in the workplace were no longer problematic and where unfair discrimination on the grounds of gender, race etc. did not exist. The idea behind this was that we are more likely to be successful, in diversity initiatives as with any other organisational strategy, if we know where we want to go. But the exercise was a flop. After a few minutes I realised that although the students were chatting to each other they were not talking about diversity at all. When I asked them why they were not doing the exercise some just said nothing (itself, a form of resistance) but others said that they couldn't get their head around it. Others said that this 'utopian' future would be 'boring, confusing, robotic'. One said 'there'd be no conflict if people are equal'. Another said that 'we'd probably just create other differences like hair colour or something'.

When I reminded them that I had not said that there would be no *diversity* there was surprise. Most of the students said that they had 'heard' it as *equality* and associated equality with 'sameness', lack of variety – and with boredom.

This experience was interesting for a number of reasons. At the time what struck me most was the negative connotations that students had to their own conceptualisations of equality. They didn't like it. It wasn't attractive. This raises the issue of whether people are likely to strive to create a condition they don't perceive as desirable. (*Why* they don't see equality as desirable is another issue.) Since then I have also reflected on their inability to imagine what success in managing diversity might be like because this theme also surfaced in the action learning group that Frances Tomlinson and I ran. In the notes I made immediately after the first session I wrote:

After going around the group twice to discover what concerns or issues participants had a number of themes stand out. One of these is about how to 'make diversity real'; how to embed it in the culture, how to recognise, or envisage what a diverse organisation would look like, how to know when (if ???) you have 'achieved' it.

I think there is a problem here. Although 'diversity' in terms of an idealised workplace where people from many different backgrounds and perspectives are all valued, fulfilled and committed is obviously an unachievable goal (or only achievable for temporary moments in time), this inability to 'know what it is' or to recognise when progress has been made may be more characteristic of diversity initiatives than other organisational interventions. It may be overstating it to suggest that a great deal of energy and time is going into organisational initiatives that have been designed without any clear idea of what they are intended to achieve, but that is a feeling I often get when talking to people about how diversity is being thought about in their organisations.

In the action learning group this lack of understanding was sometimes projected on the other people as in the following examples from two of the participants:

I think that people don't understand what diversity is...

[There is] *a lack of understanding about equality and diversity in terms of how it relates to people in their job role and what it means in terms of the job they do, the services we provide and getting that kind of basic awareness across...*

But in other cases the lack of understanding was owned by the participants:

Equality and diversity...I can give you a definition but I can't actually see it, I'm not actually sure exactly what equality and diversity should look like for our organisation...so I'm aware that we're not doing enough in that area...

This last example demonstrates one of the reasons why I think this is problematic. Although the speaker acknowledges that he doesn't know what equality and diversity 'would look like' in his organisation he *does* know that he isn't achieving it. This does not seem to be a good place to be. Not only is there the obvious difficulty in designing initiatives to achieve an unknown and unimagined future, being in the rather Kafka-esque situation of having responsibility for achieving it is clearly going to be anxiety provoking. It is perhaps not surprising that fear was mentioned by all the participants at various stages over the duration of the group and in the last session, when we asked them to draw a map of how they 'saw' diversity and equality the word 'fear' appeared in all but one of the drawings.

Darwish writes:

What is meaning? I don't know, but I may know what its opposite is: thinking that nothingness is easy to bear. (Darwish 2009: 130)

And interestingly, although many people may have difficulty in imagining what diversity is, the negative dialectic is much more powerful – they are very clear what it is *not*. We can all identify the feeling of being devalued and discriminated against. So dialectical, thinking offers us a means to build on this knowledge to begin to create a clearer idea of what a better situation might feel and look like – *not* like this, *not* like that. However, it is also surely important to be able to flesh out the picture at the other end – it *is* like this, it *is* like that. Otherwise we are placing ourselves in a permanently reactive position; we know what we are against but not what we are for.

But a little caution is needed. Utopias tend to be very tidy and real life is not. Carey writes that 'anyone who is capable of love must at some time have wanted the world to be a better place, for we all want our loved ones to live free of suffering, injustice and heartbreak. Those who construct utopias build on that universal human longing. What they build may, however, carry within it its own potential for crushing or limiting human life' (Carey 1999: xi).

Chia and Holt (2011) also caution against overly grandiose and overly ordered blueprints. They write that 'ambitious strategic plans, the "big picture" approach that seeks a lasting solution or competitive advantage through large-scale transformations often end up undermining their own potential effectiveness because they overlook the fine details of everyday happenings at "ground zero" level' (Chia and Holt 2011: 18).

Carey also points out that the people who inhabit fictional utopias tend to differ from the rest of us, primarily in that they have overcome selfishness and any desire to harm their brethren and sistren or to indulge in any anti-social behaviour. People who exhibit undesirable characteristics are either not there at all, or the utopian residents have found some gentle way to control them.

Interestingly, a phrase that reoccurred in the action learning group was that of the 'right' people.

I think it's important to recruit the right type of people with the right kinds of attitudes...

Centrifugal dialectics would suggest that if some people are 'right' then others must be 'wrong'. As I quoted Spivak (in Chapter 6) 'the choice of a particular binary opposition...is no mere intellectual strategy. It is, in every case, the condition of the possibility of centralisation...and, correspondingly, marginalisation' (Spivak: 2006: 153–154). When utopian dialectics lead us to create imaginative constructions of a desired 'this' not 'that', we need to be alert to the consequences of these judgements.

On the other hand, centripetal dialectics draws oppositions back from their margins and into alliances, even if uneasy ones. According to Spivak, the task of deconstructing oppositions is that of radical politics (Spivak 2006). Centripetal dialectics also underpins her interesting (and amusing) observation about teaching (and which has particular salience for *management* education). In her somewhat opaque rhetorical style she writes that she is:

> ...interested in the theory-practice of pedagogic practice-theory that would allow us constructively to question privileged explanations even as explanations are generated.... It should be clear by now that I could not be embarked upon a mere role reversal – a more central-ising of teaching-as-practice at the same time as research-as-theory is marginalised. That slogan has led to the idea of teaching as the creation of human rapport or the relieving of anxiety and tension in the classroom that I have heard described as 'pop psych' teaching and that I myself call babysitting. (Spivak 2006: 159–160)

Centripetal dialectics bring us back to the present; the bridge between past and future. Questioning explanations *even as* explanations are generated calls for complex modes of thinking, the ability to dwell within the moment of construction while simultaneously deconstruct-ing the boundaries that define its existence. Max Black (1979) suggests that when you look at the famous picture of two faces/a vase it is poss-ible to see *both* the faces and the vase if you decide that the picture is of two faces pressing against a vase. But you can only see both images for a brief moment in time and once you relax your attentiveness one or other image tends to dominate.

Chia and Holt call this capacity to dwell in the moment of construc-tion 'strategic blandness'. They write that 'strategic efficacy is found in escape from positions, from commitment and from objectives. These establish opposition and separation from other systems and risk patho-logy whereas blandness is perception constantly opening up to new states, new paths, new things. This is the seat of creativity; the ability to absorb contradiction, to display an array of character and a multiplicity of traits, none of which dominate' (Chia and Holt 2011: 206).

Chakrabarty writes of 'possible thought practices in which the future that "will be" never completely swamps the futures that already "are"' (Chakrabarty 2000: 254). The future that 'will be' is that which results from intentional design and the future that 'is' is that which is inherent in day-to-day gestures, responses and actions; it is the future that unfolds from the present. The present is the moment where past and future meet; the challenge that Chia and Holt identify is to discover what it means to 'dwell' in that moment rather than to 'build' and to move from it by 'wayfaring' rather than 'navigating'. Chia and Holt advocate for a more passive alertness that Spivak's active questioning but each shares an emphasis on a mindfulness of the present as a point in time of infinite possibilities in which some are manifested and others rejected.

Younge writes that 'who we are is not simply a matter of our own creation' (Younge 2011: 66); our histories and those of the people who matter to us, whether because of our relationships with them or the power that they have to affect our lives, influence the ways in which we perceive ourselves and others. Dialectical thinking underpins these perceptions about individual identity as much as it shapes our wider, culturally shared ideas about the kinds of organisations and societies we wish to inhabit. Do we want a future that represents a return to a mythologised past, as so many do who argue for a 'return' to 'traditional' values? Or are we in thrall to a vision of an idealised future in which growth has 'tricked down', communities have been rebuilt from the grass roots up and wrinkles and cellulite airbrushed out of our photographs? Younge observes that that 'the most gruesome periods in history take place in the passive tense: "Jews were gassed", "Women were denied the vote" and "Africans were sold into slavery". Power, it seems has many parents but the brutality it takes to acquire it is an orphan' (Younge 2011: 57). Our imaginary constructs of past and future perform an invaluable role when they help us to re-evaluate our present situation but they can also direct our attentions away from the present's complexities and possibilities. Adorno is often quoted as saying that after Auschwitz poetry is no longer possible[4] but Hoffman reminds us that 'poetry existed in Auschwitz as well as Madjanek and was written in the Warsaw ghetto; for some it was almost as important as bread and water' (Hoffman 2004: 152).

Conclusions

[Studying] equality and diversity gave me a sense of how difficult it is to manage the two side by side…

Finally, how does this exploration of metaphor and dialectic contribute to our understanding of managing diversity? To speak of managing diversity is to present a metaphorical tension between the wayward, endless fluidity of diverse identities on the one hand and the centrifugal notion of harnessing these trends towards some collective enterprise. To speak of managing diversity is to speak of hybridity, of managing a metaphor, of arresting a dialectic.

No methodology is value free. Metaphor and dialectic work in different ways but they share some important characteristics. Firstly, they create meaning through making connections. Metaphorical thinking creates meaning through the associations and resemblances it suggests between elements hitherto thought of as disparate while dialectic creates meaning through defining the relationship between them. Dialectic works through reference – one thing becomes known by its relations to another – this not that, text to context, inside to outside, centre to margin, past to future. This is, of course, one of the reasons why metaphor and dialectic are so relevant to managing diversity. Diversity has no meaning in itself; one cannot be 'diverse' in isolation but only in relation to others. Metaphorical and dialectical modes of thinking focus on those relations and how they are constructed.

Within the field of organisational analysis, therefore, metaphor and dialectic as methodologies share some affinity with systemic approaches in their emphasis on the interconnectedness of the different elements of the system and of its interaction with the environment. Although systemic approaches to management have their advocates, they remain a minority interest. The more prevailing tendency is towards separating out and breaking down elements, functions and roles into their component parts – a kind of centrifugal dialectic but one in which the individual parts are rarely reconnected. Recently the UK Home Secretary argued in favour of proposed cuts to the funding of the police force, suggesting that the cuts would have no effect on the delivery of policing on the street because they could be made through efficiency savings in back room functions.[5] This is a good example of this more atomised form of thinking. Whereas, if she were to take a more systemic approach she would have to acknowledge that intervening in one part of the system is bound to affect the whole. There is a relationship between the back room functions and the delivery of services to the public that will be affected in some way.

Secondly, metaphor and dialectic represent the possibility of multiple interpretations. They are manifestations of a pluralist epistemology. There are infinite meanings that can be created through associational thinking, there are endless ways in which elements can diverge and converge. The meanings that emerge from these modes of thinking are not fixed, but in flux. They deconstruct certainties. Ricoeur wrote that 'the discovery of the plurality of cultures is never a harmless experience...suddenly it becomes possible that we ourselves are an "other" amongst others' (Ricoeur 1974: 278). In terms of approaches to organisational analysis this feature of metaphor and dialectic argues against the universalist, or 'monological' idea that there may be one 'best' way to manage, and in favour of pluralist, contingent, local approaches.

Thirdly, metaphor and dialectic are complex forms of thought. Tsoukas suggests that sensemaking *is* organising; organising is a feature of our thinking *about* the world. He writes that entering 'the domain of the thinker thinking about complexity – raises issues of interpretation...the logic of complexity theory is entirely compatible with an interpretive approach' (Tsoukas 2006: 231). Speaking within a day or so of an outbreak of rioting in a number of English cities in the summer of 2011, David Cameron, the UK prime minister, said 'this was criminality, pure and simple'[6]. The desire to simplify in making sense of confusing, contradictory and challenging phenomena may be understandable, but it is reckless and wrong. We do not equip student managers with the skills they need to navigate (or 'wayfind' in Chia and Holt's terms) the complex terrain in which they will find themselves if we pretend that such complicated events can be reduced to 'pure' and 'simple' explanations.

Fourthly, metaphor and dialectic both legitimate emotional experience; metaphor through its aesthetic function in promoting the possibility of empathy; dialectic through recognition of the self in the other. Younge writes:

> It is difficult to relate to the very concept of empathy unless you recognise you have something to be empathetic with. It is also difficult to be empathetic unless you are capable of making a connection between your own experience and that of an other. Either way, without sympathy your empathy won't be worth much. For those who think that empathy is a bad thing, this is, of course, not a problem. For the rest of us, empathy has the potential to be the first, crucial step on the way to solidarity – not just feeling someone else's pain but working together to try and cure it. (Younge 2011: 62)

Empathy is important too because it offers a way of dealing with one of the most difficult aspects of encountering the other – repulsion. The fact that visceral feelings of disgust and repulsion may co-exist alongside more generous impulses is something that is hard to acknowledge and even harder to respond to. Arguably, disgust is the elephant in the drawing room of the diversity rhetoric. Psychoanalytic theory offers some way forward (primarily through framing disgust of the other as fear of the unwanted or unacknowledged aspects of ourselves) but there is mostly a resounding silence in the management literature about how to manage such controversial emotions. And yet, disgust is an important element in the ways in which the identities of people from marginalised communities are constructed, whether it is evoked through such referents as smell, ugliness, dirt or pollution. The idea that the very presence of some people is polluting is deeply disturbing but no less real for that. It is a common feature of the rhetoric of violence. We need to find ways of dealing with such visceral experiences and arguably, such emotional reactions can only be effectively challenged through empathy.

Applying metaphor and dialectic to the idea of diversity management then leads to the conclusions that as a concept it is rooted in the relatedness of people, roles, identities and institutions, that it emphases the interconnectedness of people and processes, that it is a relativist approach in which our emotions play a legitimate and valuable role in sensemaking. Many of these ideas are somewhat inimical to mainstream management theory. Managing diversity *is* inherently radical – which is why it is so often rendered impotent or marginalised into 'a way of making things look different and act[ing] the same' (Younge 2011: 15).

Young writes that 'ignoring rights, agency, authority or status makes a nonsense out of attempt to fathom consequence, outcome, effect or ramification. In short, to try to understand the role of identities outside of their power relationships is to misunderstand them completely' (Younge 2011: 179). I have written a little about power and more about systemic inequality but have primarily chosen to approach these aspects of diversity management more obliquely by focussing on the processes of individual sensemaking. I have written about metaphor and dialectic as though they have independent agency, separate to us, not in order to collude with the passivity that Younge criticises so robustly but to demonstrate that we are located in contexts that are not purely of our own making and that our thought patterns are not solely our own. However, the only way we can increase our agency is to increase our awareness of ourselves as thinkers and makers of our own meaning.

Notes

Chapter 1 Re-writing Imagination into Management

1 Statistics from the various reports of the Labour Force Survey and published by the UK Government Office for Statistics are available on http://www.statistics.gov.uk.

2 Race for Opportunity is a committee of Business in the Community, a membership organisation aimed at improving the social contribution of business.

3 *RfO Benchmarking Report 2009* is published by Race for Opportunity and is available on Business in the Community's website: <http://www.bitc.org.uk>

4 At a talk by Baroness Prosser, the Vice Chair of the Equality and Human Rights Commission to students at London Metropolitan University in autumn 2009, she credited lobbying pressure from the CBI with influencing the government's decision not to extend the positive duty to all sectors.

5 The comments by Bill Critchley are taken from a presentation he gave on the use of complexity theory in organisational consulting at a workshop I attended organised by OPUS (an Organisation for the Promotion of Understanding in Society) on *Exploring Complexity and Systems-Psychodynamic Approaches to Organisational Consulting* in London on 20/10/07.

Chapter 2 *'All beautiful poetry is an act of resistance'*: Introducing Metaphor

1 Darwish 2009: 130.

2 From <www.capabilitiesapproach.com> accessed on 02/02/08. This is the website of the Human Development and Capability Association founded by Martha Nussbaum and Amartya Sen.

3 Line 65 from By Blue Ontario's Shore by Walt Whitman in *Leaves of Grass*, edited by J. Valente, 1928 edition.

4 Lines 154 and 155: lines 160 and 161 from By Blue Ontario's Shore by Walt Whitman in *Leaves of Grass*, edited by J. Valente, 1928 edition.

5 Eagleton, T. (2007) 'The Original Political Vision: Sex, Art and Transformation', *The Guardian* 28/11/2007. http://www.guardian.co.uk accessed on 31/08/2011.

6 Scarry interviewed by David Bowman on 9/11/99 available on http://www.salon.com/books/feature/1999/11/09/scarry/, accessed on 18/01/08.

7 It is very important to note that Scarry is not equating 'fairness' with pale skin – she is drawing on early usages of the notion of fairness to mean 'pleasing to the eye' which include those from Sanskrit sources.

8 Scarry is referring to Rawls' definition of fairness.

Chapter 3 *Fireworks and Football Crowds*: Metaphor as Theory

1 In this and subsequent chapters, unacknowledged citations are taken from my students' reflective reports.

2 The poet, John Keats, writing on Shakespeare in a letter to his brothers, George and Thomas Keats dated 21 December 1817 (Keats 2009: 492).
3 There are two reasons for allowing students to choose who they want to work with. The first is that it is important to provide a degree of safety and security in any exercise that requires one to be attentive to the workings of ones' own unconscious. For that reason students are also told that they will only be asked to share as much or as little of their ideas as they wanted with the larger group. Secondly, many of my students are international and English is not their first language. Allowing them to work together with other students who share their language and culture makes it more possible for them to generate the metaphors that have meaning for them.
4 Inside the book it emerges that they are also using 'mosaic' as an acronym for '**m**ission and values, **o**bjective and fair processes, **s**killed workforce, **a**ware and fair, a**c**tive flexibility, **i**ndividual focus and a **c**ulture that empowers' (Kandola and Fullerton 2003: 166).
5 Gary Younge, speaking at a conference organised by *The Guardian* and TMG consultants: October, 2003.
6 Ricoeur is drawing here on Monroe Beardsley's (1981) analysis of metaphor in *Aesthetics: Problems in the Philosophy of Criticism* (114–164).

Chapter 4 *Listening to Evelyn Glennie*: Metaphor as Art

1 In the UK the phrase 'BME' standing for 'Black and Minority Ethnic' is a frequently used abbreviation, most commonly in the area of public policy. There is, of course, a history of how this particular label has come to dominate and also many critiques which are beyond the scope of this chapter.
2 Robert Whitfield's victory was reported by *Personnel Today* and details are available on <http://www.personneltoday.com/articles/2005/02/004/27835/tribunal-awards-35000-in-sexual-orientation-case.html>.

Chapter 5 *'Exchanges with strangers and things alien'*: Introducing Dialectic

1 Habermas 1994: 132.
2 Critchley 2007 (ibid): see Chapter 1 endnote 5.
3 When this experiment was carried out in 2009 applicants with 'white sounding names' were invited to interview after nine applications while candidates with names that sounded as though they were likely to be Black or Muslim were only invited after sixteen applications (*The Observer* 18/10/2009).

Chapter 6 *Polarities, Paralysis and Paradox*: Centrifugal Dialectics

1 Foucault's source for this list of categories is an essay by Jorge Luis Borges in which Borges maintains that he found this classification in a translation from the Chinese by Franz Kuhn but whether Borges actually made this up himself or found it in the earlier book is open to debate. See for example, the

debate on http://www.thenationalreview.com/15sept97/windschuttle091597. html accessed on 18/08/2010.
2   A longer discussion of this research project was published in Schwabenland, C. (2006b) 'The Influence of Cultural Heritage on Students' Willingness to Engage in Peer Assessment', *Investigations in University Teaching and Learning* 3/2: 100–108.
3   http://web.worldbank.org/WBSITE/EXTERNAL/TOPICS/ESTSOCIALDE accessed on 08/07/2011.
4   See *Understanding Women's Social Capital: 2005 Global Exchange Report* published by the Barrow Cadbury Trust, the Foreign Policy Centre and Women Acting in Today's Society (WAITS).

Chapter 7   *Hybridity and Synthesis*: Centripetal Dialectics

1   See Chapter 3 endnote 6.
2   I am referring here to Spivak's (1988) very influential essay 'Can the Subaltern Speak?' in which she challenged the project of the subaltern studies group that aimed to discover and rewrite history from the perspectives of the marginalised, the 'subalterns'.

Chapter 8   *Cacophony or Polyphony?* Concluding Thoughts

1   See endnote 11.
2   Yiannis Gabriel explores this issue of deliberate and non-deliberate deception in more detail in his essay on 'The Narrative Veil: Truths and Untruths in Storytelling' (Gabriel 2004: 17–31).
3   Heidegger (1996) distinguishes 'being' from 'Being' with Being representing the fulfilment of the searching for meaning that is inherent in existence.
4   As Adorno was writing in German this quotation is a translation and, as such, open to different interpretations. The most frequently cited example of Adorno's that conveys this idea is taken from an article in *Prisms* 10/a: 30 (1955). The full translation is usually given as: 'The critique of culture is confronted with the last stage in the dialectic of culture and barbarism: to write a poem after Auschwitz is barbaric, and that corrodes also the knowledge which expresses why it has become impossible to write poetry today'. http://marcuse.org/herbert/people.adorno/AdornoPoetryAuschwitzQuote.htm accessed on 24/08/2011.
5   As reported in BBC News 15/05/2011 http://www.bbc.co.uk accessed on 25/08/2011.
6   As reported in *The Guardian* 09/08/2011 http://www.guardian.co.uk accessed on 25/08/2011.

Bibliography

Abbs, P. (1996) *The Polemics of Imagination*, London: Skoob.

Abravanel, H. (1983) 'Mediatory Myths in the Service of Organisational Ideology', in Pondy, L., Frost, P.J. and Morgan, M. (eds) *Organisational Symbolism*, pp. 273–293, Connecticut: JAI.

Ackah, W. (2006) 'Struggling to Cope with Change; The Case of Unsuccessful and Unengaged Minority Ethnic Community Organisations in Liverpool and Manchester and European Structural Funds', paper presented at the NCVO conference *Researching the Voluntary Sector*, September 2006: Warwick.

Ahmed, S. (2004) *The Cultural Politics of Emotion*, Edinburgh: Edinburgh University Press.

Aldrich, H.E. (1992) 'Incommensurable Paradigms? Vital Signs from Three Perspectives', in Reed, M. and Hughes, M. (eds) *Rethinking Organisations*, pp. 17–45, London: Sage.

Alvesson, M. (1993) 'The Play of Metaphors', in Hassard, J. and Parker, M. (eds) *Postmodernism and Organizations*, pp. 114–131, London: Sage.

Anderson, B. (1991) *Imagined Communities*, London: Verso.

Appiah, K.A. (1994) 'Identity, Authenticity and Survival: Multicultural Societies and Social Reproduction', in Gutman, A. (ed.) *Multiculturalism: Examining the Politics of Recognition*, pp. 149–164, Princeton: Princeton University Press.

Argyris, C. and Schon, D. (1978) *Organizational Learning: A Theory of Action Perspective*, New York: McGraw Hill.

Aristotle (1996) *Poetics*, in Heath, M. (ed. and trans.) London: Penguin.

Armstrong, D. (1991) *The 'Institution in the Mind' Reflections of the Relations of Psychoanalysis to Work With Institutions*, London: The Grubb Institute.

Armstrong, D. (1989) *Names, Thoughts and Lies: The Relevance of Bion's Later Writings for Understanding Experiences in Groups*, London: The Grubb Institute.

Armstrong, D. (1988) *Professional Management*, London: The Grubb Institute.

Badrinath, C. (1996) 'Transcription of Dialogue Following a Lecture by K.M. Meyer-Abich "Towards a Physio-centric Philosophy of Nature"', in Surendra, L., Schindler, K. and Ramaswamy, P. (eds) *Stories They Tell: A Dialogue Among Philosophers, Scientists and Environmentalists*, pp. 147–168, Madras: Earthworm.

Balamuth, R. (2003) 'Childreamatrix: Dreaming with Preschool Children – or Bootlegging Dreams into School Years', in Lawrence, W.G. (ed.) *Experiences in Social Dreaming*, pp. 122–141, London: Karnac.

Banerjee, S.B. and Linstead, S. (2001) 'Globalization, Multiculturalism and Other Fictions: Colonialism for the New Millennium?', *Organization*, 8/4: 683–722.

Barenboim, D. and Said, E.W. (2004) *Parallels and Paradoxes: Explorations in Music and Society*, London: Bloomsbury.

Barfield, O. (1999) *Fundamentals of Poetry*, New Delhi: Shubhi Publications.

Baron-Cohen, S. (2011) 'I Know Just How You Feel', *The Observer*, 27/03/2011: 37–42.

Bate, W.J. (1939) *Negative Capability: The Intuitive Approach in Keats*, Boston MA: Harvard University Press.

Bauman, Z. (2003) *Community: Seeking Safety in an Insecure World*, Cambridge: Polity Press.

Baxter-Magdola, M.B. (1992) *Knowing and Reasoning in College: Gender-related Patterns in Students' Intellectual Development*, San Francisco: Jossey Bass.

Beardsley, M. (1981) *Aesthetics: Problems in the Philosophy of Criticism*, Indianapolis: Hackett.

Beatty, J. and Humphries, M. (2007) 'Diversity and Defining the Other: The Power of Naming and Claiming Control', paper presented at the 5th International Critical Management Studies Conference, 11–13 July, Manchester, UK.

Beavis, A.K. and Ross Thomas, A. (1996) 'Metaphors as Storehouses of Expectations', *Educational Management and Administration*, 24(1): 93–106.

Beazley, M., Griggs, S. and Smith, M. (2004) *Rethinking Approaches to Capacity Building*, Birmingham: INLOGOV.

Bhabha, H.R. (2003) *The Location of Culture*, London: Routledge.

Bhavnani, R. (2001) *Rethinking Interventions in Racism*, London: Trentham.

Billis, D. (ed.) (2010) *Hybrid Organisations and the Third Sector: Challenges for Practice, Theory and Policy*, Houndsmills: Palgrave Macmillan.

Black, M. (1979) 'More About Metaphor', in Ortony, A. (ed.) *Metaphor and Thought*, pp. 254–283, Cambridge: Cambridge University Press.

Bohm, D. (2008) *On Dialogue*, London: Routledge.

Boyce-Tillman, J. (2007) *Unconventional Wisdom*, London: Equinox.

Bronk, R. (2009) *The Romantic Economist*, Cambridge: Cambridge University Press.

Brown, G., Bull, J. and Pendlebury, M. (1977) *Assessing Student Learning in Higher Education*, London: Routledge.

Bruns, G. (1992) *Hermeneutics Ancient and Modern*, CT: Yale University Press.

Burrell, G. and Morgan, G. (1979) *Sociological Paradigms and Organizational Analysis*, London: Heinemann.

Burke, J. (2007) 'The Jihadist Next Door', *The Observer Magazine*, 20/10/08: 14–24.

Butler, J. (2009) *Frames of War: When Life is Grievable*, London: Verso.

Butler, J. (1997) *Excitable Speech: A Politics of the Performative*, London: Routledge.

Carey, J. (2005) *What Good Are the Arts?*, London: Faber.

Carey, J. (1999) 'Introduction', in Carey, J. (ed.) *The Faber Book of Utopias*, pp. xi–xxvi, London: Faber and Faber.

Carter, P. and Jackson, N. (2004) 'Gilles Deleuze and Felix Guattari', in Linstead, S. (ed.) *Organization Theory and Postmodern Thought*, pp. 105–126, London: Sage.

Cassell, C. and Johnson, P. (2006) 'Action Research: Explaining the Diversity', *Human Relations*, 59/(6): 783–814.

Cavanaugh, J.M. (1997) '(In)corporating the Other? Managing the Politics of Workplace Difference', in Prasad, A., Mills, A.J., Eames, M. and Prasad, P. (eds) *Managing the Organizational Melting Pot*, pp. 31–53, Thousand Oaks: Sage.

Cazal, D. and Inns, D. (1998) 'Metaphor, Language and Meaning', in Grant, D., Keenoy, T. and Oswick, C. (eds) *Discourse and Organization*, pp. 177–192, London: Sage.

Chakrabarty, D. (2000) *Provincializing Europe: Postcolonial Thought and Historical Difference*, Princeton NJ: Princeton University Press.

Chen, C-C. and Lee, Y-T. (2008) 'Introduction', in Chen, C-C. and Lee, Y-T. (eds) *Leadership and Management in China: Philosophies, Theories and Practice*, pp. 1–27, Cambridge: Cambridge University Press.

Chia, R. and Holt, R. (2011) *Strategy Without Design: The Silent Efficacy of Indirect Action*, Cambridge: Cambridge University Press.

Cohen, A.P. (1993) *The Symbolic Construction of Community*, London: Routledge.

Collins, P.H. (2009) *Another Kind of Public Education: Race, Schools, the Media and Democratic Possibilities*, Boston: Beacon Press.

Cornelius, N. (2002) *Building Workplace Equality: Ethics, Diversity and Inclusion*, London: Thomson.

Creed, W.E.D. and Scully, M.A. (2000) 'Songs of Ourselves: Employees' Deployment of Social Identity in Workplace Encounters', *Journal of Management Inquiry*, 9/4: 391–412.

Cunliffe, A. (2008) 'Orientations to Social Constructionism: Relationally Responsive Social Constructionism and Its Implications for Knowledge and Learning', *Management Learning*, 39/2: 123–139.

Curzon-Hobson, A. (2002) 'A Pedagogy of Trust', *Teaching in Higher Education*, 7/3: 266–276.

Czarniawska Joerges, B. and Wolff, R. (1991) 'Leaders, Managers, Entrepreneurs: On and Off the Organizational Stage', *Organization Studies*, 12/4: 529–546.

D'Addelfio, G. (2006) *The Educative Value of Empathy Within the Capability Approach* available on www.capabilitiesapproach.com/publist/php?pubtype+research accessed on 26/02/08.

Dalal, F. (2006) *Race, Colour and the Processes of Racialization*, London: Routledge.

Davies, C. (2007) 'Grounding Governance in Dialogue? Discourse, Practice and the Potential for a New Public Sector Organizational Form in Britain', *Public Administration*, 85(1): 47–66.

Darwish, M. (2009) *A River Dies of Thirst*, Cobham, C. (trans.), London: Saqi.

Darwish, M. (2007) *The Butterfly's Burden*, Joudah, F. (trans.), Northumberland: Bloodaxe.

Dentith, S. (1995) *Bakhtinian Thought: An Introductory Reader*, London: Routledge.

de Peuter, J. (1998) 'The Dialogics of Narrative Identity', in Bell, M.M. and Gardiner, M. (eds) *Bakhtin and the Human Sciences*, pp. 30–49, London: Sage.

Due Billing, Y. and Sundin, E. (2006) 'From Managing Equality to Managing Diversity: A Critical Scandinavian Perspective on Gender and Workplace Diversity', in Prasad, P., Pringle, J. and Konrad, A. (eds) *Handbook of Workplace Diversity*, pp. 95–120, London: Sage.

Dyson, M.E. (2004) *The Michael Eric Dyson Reader*, New York: Basic Civitas Books.

Eagleton, T. (2007) 'The Original Political Vision: Sex, Art and Transformation', *The Guardian*, 28/11/2007 http://www.guardian.co.uk, accessed on 31/08/2011.

Edgar, I. (2004) *Guide to Imagework: Imagination Based Research Methods*, London: Routledge.

Edwards, J. (1987) *Positive Discrimination, Social Justice and Social Policy*, London: Tavistock.

Edwards, M. (2011) 'Believing in Poetry', *Literature and Theology*, 25/1: 10–19.

Esslin, M. (1961) *Theatre of the Absurd*, New York: Anchor Books.

Flew, A. (1979) *A Dictionary of Philosophy*, London: Pan.

Foucault, M. (2002) *The Order of Things*, London: Routledge Classics.

Fredman, S. and Spencer, S. (2006) 'Delivering Equality: Towards an Outcome-focussed Positive Duty', submission to the Cabinet Office equality review, available on www.edf.org.uk/news/Delivery%20equality%20submission/200300606-fund-pdf, accessed on 15/05/2008.

Foldy, E. (2002) '"Managing" Diversity: Identity and Power in Organizations', in Aaltio, I. and Mills, A.F. (eds) *Gender, Identity and the Culture of Organizations*, pp. 92–112, London: Routledge.

Frenkel, M. and Shenav, Y. (2005) 'From Binarism Back to Hybridity: A Postcolonial Reading of Management and Organization Studies', *Organization Studies*, 27(6): 855–876.

Frost, R. (1931) 'Education by Poetry', Address given to Amherst College and revised for publications in the *Amherst Graduates' Quarterly*, February 1931, available from http://www.en.utexas.edu/amlit/amlitprivate/scans/edbypo.htm, accessed on 23/02/2011.

Gabriel, Y. (2004) 'The Narrative Veil: Truth and Untruths in Storytelling', in Gabriel, Y. (ed.) *Myths, Stories and Organizations: Pre-modern Narratives for Our Times*, pp. 17–32, Oxford: Oxford University Press.

Gadamer, H. (1993) *Truth and Method*, London: Sheed and Ward.

Gandhi, L. (1998) *Postcolonial Theory: A Critical Introduction*, New Delhi: Oxford India Paperbacks.

Geary, J. (2011) *I is an Other: The Secret Life of Metaphor and How it Shapes the Way We See the World*, New York: Harper.

Gergan, K.J. (1992) 'Organization Theory in the Post Modern Era', in Reed, M. and Hughes, M. (eds) *Rethinking Organizations*, pp. 207–226, London: Sage.

Gergan, K.J. and Gergan, M.M. (2004) 'Dialogue: Life and Death of the Organization', in Grant, D., Hardy, C. and Oswick, C. and Putnam, L. (eds) *Handbook of Organizational Discourse*, pp. 39–60, London: Sage.

Gibbs, R.W. (1994) *The Poetics of Mind*, Cambridge: Cambridge University Press.

Glennie, E. (1993) *Hearing Essay*, http://www.evelyn.co.uk/hearing_essay_aspx, accessed on 01/04/2011.

Goldberg, D.T. (1994) 'Introduction: Multicultural Conditions', in Goldberg, D.T. (ed.) *Multiculturalism: A Critical Reader*, pp. 1–41, Oxford: Blackwell.

Goleman, D., Boyatzis, R. and McKee, A. (2002) *The New Leaders: Transforming the Art of Leadership into the Science of Results*, London: Time Warner Paperbacks.

Gordon, G. (2007) *Towards Bicultural Competence: Beyond Black and White*, Stoke on Trent: Trentham.

Grant, D., Keenoy, T. and Oswick, C. (eds) (1998) 'Introduction', *Discourse and Organization*, pp. 1–13, London: Sage.

Green, T.F. (1979) 'Learning Without Metaphor', in Ortony, A. (ed.) *Metaphor and Thought*, pp. 462–473, Cambridge: Cambridge University Press.

Gutman, A. (1994) 'Introduction', in Gutman, A. (ed.) *Multiculturalism: Examining the Politics of Recognition*, pp. 3–24, Princeton: Princeton University Press.

Habermas, J. (1996) *Between Facts and Norms*, Cambridge MA: MIT.

Habermas, J. (1994) 'Struggles for Recognition in the Democratic Constitutional State', Nicholson, S.W. (trans), in Gutman, A. (ed.) *Multiculturalism: Examining the Politics of Recognition*, pp. 107–148, Princeton: Princeton University Press.

Hage, G. (1994) 'Locating Multiculturalism's Other: A Critique of Practical Tolerance', *New Formations*, 24/1: 19–34.

Heaney, S. (1996) *The Redress of Poetry: Oxford Lectures*, London: Faber and Faber.

Heaney, S. (1989) *The Government of the Tongue*, London: Faber and Faber.

Heath, M. (1996) 'Introduction', in Aristotle *Poetics*, pp. vii–lxxi, London: Penguin.

Heidegger, M. (1996) 'From the Introduction to Being and Time', in Kearney, R. and Rainwater, M. (eds) *The Continental Philosophy Reader*, pp. 23–52, London: Routledge.

Ho, C.D. (2000) 'How Does Diversity Affect Performance: A Mediating Process Model', *Working Paper in Human Resource Management, Employee Relations and Organisation Studies*, No. 16, University of Melbourne.

Hoffman, E. (2004) *After Such Knowledge; A Meditation on the Aftermath of the Holocaust*, London: Secker and Warburg.

Hofstede, G. (2001) *Cultures' Consequences: International Differences in Work Related Values*, London: Sage.

Hofstede, G. (1991) *Cultures and Organizations: Software of the Mind*, New York: McGraw Hill.

Horton, M. and Freire, P. (1990) *We Make the Road By Walking: Conversations on Education and Social Change*, Philadelphia: Temple University Press.

How, A. (2003) *Critical Theory*, Basingstoke: Palgrave Macmillan.

Huntingdon, S. (1993) 'The Clash of Civilizations', *Foreign Affairs*, 72/3: 22–49.

Illeris, K. (2002) *The Three Dimensions of Learning: Contemporary Learning Theory in the Tension Field Between the Cognitive, the Emotional and the Social*, Reader, D. and Malone, M. (trans.), Fredericksberg: Roskilde University Press.

Imel, S. (1998) *Transformative Learning in Adulthood*, ERIC Digest No. 200, www.ericdigests.org/1999-2/adulthood.htm, accessed on 12/12/2007.

Janssens, M. and Zanoni, P. (2004) 'Diversity Discourses as Control or Emancipation: The Role of Materiality and Agency', paper presented at the 200th EGOS Colloquium, Ljubljana, 1–3 July.

Johns, N. (2004) 'Ethnic Diversity Policy: Perceptions Within the NHS', *Social Policy and Administration*, 38/1: 73–88.

Joudah, F. (2007) 'Translator's Preface', in Darwish, M. *The Butterfly's Burden*, pp. xi–xvii, Northumberland: Bloodaxe.

Jung, H.Y. (1998) 'Bakhtin's Dialogical Body Politics', in Bell, M.M. and Gardiner, M. (eds) *Bakhtin and the Human Sciences*, pp. 95–111, London: Sage.

Jussim, L. (1992) 'Dissonance: A Second Coming?', *Psychological Inquiry*, 3(4): 332–333.

Kalra, V.S., Kaur, R. and Hutnyk, J. (2005) *Diaspora and Hybridity*, London: Sage.

Kandola, R. and Fullerton, J. (2003) *Diversity in Action: Managing the Mosaic*, London: CIPD.

Kay, R. (1991) *An Analysis of the Use of Metaphor in Voluntary Organisations*, unpublished PhD thesis, Cranfield University.

Keats, J. (2009) *'Bright Star' The Complete Poems and Letters of John Keats*, London: Vintage.

Kemmis, S. (2001) 'Exploring the Relevance of Critical Theory for Action Research; Emancipatory Action Research in the Footsteps of Jurgen Habermas', in Reason, P. and Bradbury, H. (eds) *Handbook of Action Research: Participative Inquiry and Practice*, pp. 91–102, London: Sage.

Kersten, A. (2000) 'Diversity Management: Dialogue, Dialectics and Diversion', *Journal of Organizational Change Management*, 13/3: 235–248.

King, N. and Anderson, N. (1995) *Innovation and Change in Organizations*, London: Routledge.

Kirton, G. and Greene, A.M. (2005) *The Dynamics of Managing Diversity: A Critical Approach* (Second edition), Oxford: Elsevier: Butterworth Heinemann.

Kociatkiewicz, J. and Kostera, M. (2010) 'Experiencing the Shadow: Organizational Exclusion and Denial with Experience Economy', *Organization*, 17/2: 257–282.

Kohn, A. (1990) *The Brighter Side of Human Nature: Altruism and Empathy in Everyday Life*, New York: Basic Books.

Kostera, M. (ed.) (2008) *Mythical Inspirations for Organizational Realities*, London: Palgrave Macmillan.

Kretzmann, J.P. and McKnight, J. (1993) *Building Communities From the Inside Out: A Path Towards Finding and Mobilizing a Community's Assets*, Evanston IL: Center for Urban Affairs and Policy Research.

Krotowski, A. (2010) 'Linked Out?', *RSA Journal*, Autumn: 28–31.

Kwek, D. (2003) 'De-colonising and *Re-presenting* Cultures Consequences: A Post-colonial Critique of Cross Cultural Management', in Prasad, A. (ed.) *Postcolonial Theory and Organizational Analysis*, pp. 121–146, Houndsmills: Palgrave.

Lakoff, G. and Johnson, M. (1980) *Metaphors We Live By*, Chicago: University of Chicago Press.

Lange, E.A. (2004) 'Transformative and Restorative Learning: A Vital Dialectic for Sustainable Societies', *Adult Education Quarterly*, 54/2: 121–139.

Lawrence, W.G. (2003) 'Some Thoughts on Social Dreaming', in Lawrence, W.G. (ed.) *Experiences in Social Dreaming*, pp. 267–272, London: Karnac.

Lawrence, W.G. (2000) *Tongued With Fire: Experiences in Groups*, London: Karnac.

Lehrer, J. (2008) 'The Eureka Hunt: Why Do Good Ideas Come To Us When They Do?', *The New Yorker*, 28 July, 40–45.

Letiche, H. and Essers, J. (2004) 'Jean-Francois Lyotard', in Linstead, S. (ed.) *Organization Theory and Postmodern Thought*, pp. 64–87, London: Sage.

Liff, S. (1997) 'Two Routes to Managing Diversity: Individual Differences or Social Group Characteristics', *Employee Relations*, 19/1: 11–26.

Lipner, J. (1997) 'Sankara on *Satyam Jnanam Anantam Brahma*', in Bilimoria, P. and Mohanty, J.N. (eds) *Relativism, Suffering and Beyond: Essays in Memory of Bimal K. Matilal*, pp. 301–318, Delhi: Oxford University Press.

Locke, M. (1994) 'Basics', in Pratt, J., Locke, M. and Burgess, T. *Popper and Problems, Problems with Popper*, pp. 8–14, Centre for Institutional Studies Working Paper 64, London: University of East London.

Lorbiecki, A. and Jack, G. (2000) 'Critical Turns in the Evolution of Diversity Management', *British Journal of Management*, 11: S17–S31.

Lord, C. (1992) 'Was Cognitive Dissonance Theory a Mistake?', *Psychological Inquiry*, 3(4): 339–341.

Lorde, A. (1981) 'The Master's Tools Will Never Dismantle the Master's House', in Moraga, C. and Anzaldua, G. *This Bridge Called My Back*, pp. 98–101, Watertown, MA: Persephone Press.

MacDiarmid, H. (1992) *Selected Poetry*, Riach, A. and Grieve, M. (eds) Manchester: Carcanet.

McCarthy, C. and Dimitriades, G. (2000) 'Globalizing Pedagogies: Power, Resentment and the Re-narration of Difference', in Burbules, N.C. and Torres, C.A. (eds) *Globalization and Education: Critical Perspectives*, pp. 187–204, New York: Routledge.

McCreary, A. (2007) *In War and Peace: The Story of Corrymeela*, Belfast: Brehon Press.

McInery, R. (undated) 'The Ancient Quarrel Between Philosophy and Poetry', available on http://www.nd.edu/~rmcinery/dg_background.pdf, accessed on 08/01/2010.

McIntosh, P. (2010) *Action Research and Reflective Practice: Creative and Visual Methods to Facilitate Reflection and Learning*, London: Routledge.

McIntosh, P. (2008) 'Poetics and Space: Developing a Reflective Landscape Through Imagery and Human Geography', *Reflective Practice*, 9/1: 69–78.

McIntosh, P. (2007) *The Puzzle of Metaphor and Voice in Visual and Literary Data*, unpublished paper shown to the author.

McSweeney, B. (2002) 'Hofstede's Model of National Cultural Differences and Consequences: A Triumph of Faith – A Failure of Analysis', *Human Relations*, 55/1: 89–118.

Mangham, I. (1986) *Power and Performance in Organizations*, Oxford: Blackwell.

Mangham, I. and Overington, M. (1987) *Organizations as Theatre*, Chichester: John Wiley.

Marsick, V.J. and O'Neil, J. (1999) 'The Many Faces of Action Learning', *Management Learning*, 30/2: 159–176.

Mason, D. (2003) *Explaining Ethnic Differences: Changing Patterns of Disadvantage in Britain*, Bristol: Policy Press.

Mehta, J.L. (1985) *India and the West: The Problem of Understanding:* Selected Essays of J.L. Mehta with an introduction by W.C. Smith, California: Chico Press.

Meyerson, D. (2003) *Tempered Radicals: How Everyday Leaders Inspire Change at Work*, Boston MA: Harvard Business School Press.

Milner, M. (1999) *A Life of One's Own*, London: Virago.

Milner, M. (1996) *The Suppressed Madness of Sane Men: Forty-four Years of Exploring Psychoanalysis*, London: Tavistock.

Milner, M. (1989) *Eternity's Sunrise*, London: Virago.

Milner, M. (1986) *An Experiment in Leisure*, London: Virago.

Milner, M. (1983) *On Not Being Able to Paint*, Los Angeles: J.B. Tarcher Inc.

Mintzberg, H. (1987) 'Crafting Strategy', *Harvard Business Review*, 7: 66–75.

Mohanty, C.T., Russo, A. and Torres, L. (eds) (1991) *Third World Women and the Politics of Feminism*, Bloomington: Indiana University Press.

Modood, T. (2008) 'A Basis For and Two Obstacles in the Way of a Multiculturalist Coalition', *British Journal of Sociology*, 59(1): 47–52.

Morgan, G. (1986) *Images of Organization*, London: Sage.

Morgan, G. (1980) 'Paradigms, Metaphors and Puzzle Solving in Organization Theory', *Administrative Science Quarterly*, 25: 606–662.

Mumby, D. (2004) 'Discourse, Power and ideology: Unpicking the Critical Approach', in Grant, D., Hardy, C., Oswick, C. and Putnam, L. (eds) *Handbook of Organizational Discourse*, pp. 237–258, London: Sage.

Murdoch, I. (1970) *The Sovereignty of Good*, London: Routledge and Kegan Paul.

Nandy, A. (2002) *Time Warps: Silent and Evasive Pasts in Indian Politics and Religion*, London: Hurst and Co.

Nandy, A. (1999) *Traditions, Tyranny and Utopias: Essays in the Politics of Awareness*, New Delhi: Oxford India Paperbacks.

Nandy, A. (1983) *The Intimate Enemy: Loss and Recovery of Self Under Colonialism*, New Delhi: Oxford University Press.

Narayan, U. (2000) 'Essence of Culture and a Sense of History: A Feminist Critique of Cultural Essentialism', in Narayan, U. and Harding, S. (eds) *Decentering the Center: Philosophy for a Multicultural, Postcolonial and Feminist World*, pp. 80–100, Bloomington: Indiana University Press.

Narayan, U. and Harding, S. (eds) (2000) *Decentering the Center: Philosophy for a Multicultural, Postcolonial and Feminist World*, Bloomington: Indiana University Press.

Nichol, L. (2008) 'Forward', in Bohm, D. *On Dialogue*, pp. xv–xxvii, London: Routledge.

Noumair, D. (2004) 'Diversity and Authority Conferences as a Social Defence', in Gould, L., Stapley, L. and Stein, M. (eds) *Experiential Learning in Organizations*, pp. 63–84, London: Karnac.

Nussbaum, M. (2007) *The Clash Within: Democracy, Religious Violence and India's Future*, Ranikhet: Permanent Black.

Nussbaum, M. (2006) *Hiding From Humanity: Disgust, Shame and the Law*, Princeton: Princeton University Press.

Nussbaum, M. (2004) *Liberal Education and Global Community*, published online by the Association of American Colleges and Universities, http://www.aacu.org/liberaleducation/le-wi04feature4.cfm, accessed on 11/12/2007.

Nussbaum, M. (2002) 'Education for Citizenship in an Era of Global Connection', *Studies in Philosophy and Education*, 21: 289–303.

Nussbaum, M. (1995) *Poetic Justice: The Literary Imagination and Public Life*, Boston: Beacon Press.

Oswick, C. and Grant, D. (1996) 'Introduction: Organisational Development and Metaphor: Mapping the Territory', in Oswick, C. and Grant, D. (eds) *Organisation Development: Metaphorical Explorations*, pp. 1–3, London: Pitman.

Perriton, L. and Reynolds, M. (2004) 'Critical Management Education: From Pedagogy of Possibility to Pedagogy of Refusal?', *Management Learning*, 35(1): 161–177.

Perry, W.G. Jr. (1999) *Forms of Intellectual Development in the College Years: A Scheme*, San Francisco: Jossey Bass.

Petrie, H. (1979) 'Metaphor and Learning', in Ortony, A. (ed.) *Metaphor and Thought*, pp. 438–461, Cambridge: Cambridge University Press.

Phillips, A. and Appignanesi, L. (2005) 'Free Speech: An Exchange', in Appignanesi, L. (ed.) *Free Speech is No Offence*, pp. 162–180, London: Penguin.

Pintchman, T. (1994) *The Rise of the Goddess in the Hindu Tradition*, Albany: State University of New York (SUNY) Press.

Pondy, L.R. (1983) 'The Role of Metaphors and Myths in Organisation and the Facilitation of Change', in Pondy, L.R., Frost, P. and Morgan, G. (eds) *Organisational Symbolism*, pp. 157–166, Connecticut: JAI.

Prasad, A. (2003) (ed.) *Postcolonial Theory and Organizational Analysis*, Houndsmills: Palgrave.

Prasad, P. (2006) 'The Jewel in the Crown: Postcolonial Theory and Workplace Diversity', in Prasad, P., Pringle, J. and Konrad, A. (eds) *Handbook of Workplace Diversity*, pp. 121–144, London: Sage.

Prasad, P. and Mills, A.J. (1997) 'From Showcase to Shadow: Understanding the Dilemmas of Managing Diversity', in Prasad, P., Mills, A.J., Elmes, M. and Prasad, A. (eds) *Managing the Organizational Melting Pot: Dilemmas of Workplace Diversity*, pp. 3–31, Thousand Oaks: Sage.

Punter, D. (2009) *Metaphor*, London: Routledge.

Putnam, R. (2007) 'E Pluribus Unum: Diversity and Community in the Twenty-first Century: The 2006 Johan Skytte Prize Lecture', *Scandinavian Political Studies*, 300/2: 137–174.

Putnam, R. (2000) *Bowling Alone: The Collapse and Renewal of American Community*, New York: Simon and Schuster.

Ramsey, C. (2008) 'Managing to Learn: The Social Poetics of a Polyphonic "Classroom"', *Organization Studies*, 29/4: 543–558.

Reed, B. (1995) *The Psychodynamics of Life and Worship*, London: The Grubb Institute.

Reed, B. (1978) *Professional Management*, London: The Grubb Institute.

Reedy, P. (2002) 'Keep the Black Flag Flying: Anarchy, Utopia and the Politics of Nostalgia', in Parker, M. (ed.) *Utopia and Organization*, pp. 169–188, Oxford: Blackwell.

Reiman, D. and Powers, S. (eds) (1977) *Shelley's Poetry and Prose*, New York: W.W. Norton and Co.

Reynolds, M. and Vince, R. (2004) 'Critical Management Education and Action-Based Learning: Synergies and Contradictions', *Academy of Management Learning and Education*, 3/4: 442–458.

Rich, A. (2009) *A Human Eye: Essays on Art in Society 1997–2008*, New York: Norton and Co.

Ricoeur, P. (2007) *The Rule of Metaphor*, Czerny, R. (trans.) London and New York: Routledge.

Ricoeur, P. (1992) *Hermeneutics and the Human Sciences*, Thompson, J. (ed. and trans.) Cambridge: CUP.

Ricoeur, P. (1991a) 'On Interpretation', in Blamey, K. and Thompson, J.B. (trans.) *From Text to Action, Essays in Hermeneutics*, London: Athlone Press.

Ricoeur, P. (1991b) *A Ricoeur Reader, Reflection and Imagination*, Valdes, M. (ed.), New York: Harvester Wheatsheaf.

Ricoeur, P. (1986) *Lectures on Ideology and Utopia*, Taylor, G.H. (ed.), NY: Columbia University Press.

Ricoeur, P. (1974) *Social and Political Essays*, Stewart, D. and Bien, J. (eds) Athlone: Ohio University Press.

Rosenmann, M. (2000) 'Morphing into the Market: The Dangers of Missing Mission', paper presented to the conference *Researching the Voluntary Sector*, 5–6 September 2000. NCVO: Birmingham.

Rowan, J. and Reason, P. (1981) 'On Making Sense', in Reason, P. and Rowan, J. (eds) *Human Inquiry*, pp. 113–137, Chichester: John Wiley and Sons.

Rumi, J. (2004) *The Masvani: Book One*, Mojaddedi (trans.) Oxford: Oxford University Press.

Sackman, S.A. and Phillips, M. (2004) 'Contextual Influences on Culture Research: Shifting Assumptions for New Workplace Realities', *International Journal of Cross Cultural Management*, 4/3: 370–390.

Samuels, A. (2008) 'New Developments in the Post-Jungian Field', in Young-Eisendrath, P. and Dawson, T. (eds) *The Cambridge Companion to Jung*, pp. 1–18, Cambridge: Cambridge University Press.

Said, E. (2003) *Orientalism*, London: Penguin.

Scarry, E. (2006) *On Beauty and Being Just*, London: G. Duckworth and Co.

Schein, E. (1991) *Organizational Culture and Leadership*, San Francisco: Jossey Bass.

Schellekens, E. (2007) *Aesthetics and Morality*, London: Continuum.

Schon, D. (1979) 'Generative Metaphor: A Perspective in Problem Solving', in Ortony, A. (ed.) *Metaphor and Thought*, pp. 254–283, Cambridge: Cambridge University Press.

Schwabenland, C. (2011) 'Surprise and Awe: Learning from Indigenous Managers', *Journal of Management Education*, 35/1: 138–154.

Schwabenland, C. (2009) 'An Exploration of the Use of Disruption as a Pedagogic Intervention', *Educational Action Research*, 17/2: 293–309.

Schwabenland, C. (2008) 'Representations of the Ideal as Symbols of Subversion', in Kostera, M. (ed.) *Mythical Inspirations for Organizational Realities*, pp. 88–99, Basingstoke: Palgrave Macmillan.

Schwabenland, C. (2006a) *Stories, Visions and Values in Voluntary Organisations*, Aldershot: Ashgate.

Schwabenland, C. (2006b) 'The Influence of Cultural Heritage on Students' Willingness to Engage in Peer Assessment', *Investigations in University Teaching and Learning*, 3/2: 100–108.

Schwabenland, C. (2006c) 'Stories, Mythmaking and the Consolation of Success', in Satterthwaite, J., Martin, W. and Roberts, L. (eds) *Discourse, Resistance and Identity Formation*, pp. 59–75, Stoke on Trent: Trentham.

Schwabenland, C. and Tomlinson, F. (2008) 'Managing Diversity or Diversifying Management?', *Critical Perspective on International Business*, 4/2–3: 320–333.

Shah, R.C. (1997) *The Voice of the Sacred in Our Time*, unpublished paper presented at the *Temenos* conference, January 1997, New Delhi.

Shaw, P. (2004) *Changing Conversations in Organizations: A Complexity Approach to Change*, Abingdon: Routledge.

Shotter, J. (1995) 'Wittgenstein's World: Beyond the "Way of Theory" Toward a "Social Poetics"', Spoken paper for *Social Construction, Culture and the Politics of Social Identity*, New School of Social Research NY: April 7, 1995, available on http://www.massey.azc.nz/alock/virtual/poetics.htm, accessed on 29/07/2011.

Shotter, J. and Billig, M. (1998) 'A Bakhtinian Psychology: From Out of the Heads of Individuals and into the Dialogues between Them', in Bell, M.M. and Gardiner, M. (eds) *Bakhtin and the Human Sciences: No Last Words*, pp. 13–29, London: Sage.

Smith, R. (1996) 'Dialectic and Method in Aristotle', paper presented to the APA Central Division, 27 April, available at http://aristotle.tamu.edu/~rasmith/APA-Central-1996.htm, accessed on 16/07/2010.

Spivak, G.C. (2006) *In Other Worlds: Essays in Cultural Politics*, London: Routledge.

Spivak, G.C. (1999) *A Critique of Postcolonial Reason: Toward a History of the Vanishing Past*, Cambridge MA: Harvard University Press.

Spivak, G.C. (1993) *Outside in the Teaching Machine*, New York: Routledge.

Spivak, G.C. (1988) 'Can the Subaltern Speak?', in Nelson, C. and Grossberg, L. (eds) *Marxism and the Interpretation of Cultures*, pp. 271–313, Houndsmill: Macmillan.

Stacey, R., Griffin, D. and Shaw, P. (2002) *Complexity and Management: Fad or Radical Challenge to Systems Thinking?* Abingdon: Routledge.

Stevens, A. (1994) *Jung: A Very Short Introduction*, Oxford: Oxford University Press.

Stewart, I. (1997) *Does God Play Dice?*, London: Penguin.

Sticht, T.G. (1979) 'Educational Uses of Metaphor', in Ortony, A. (ed.) *Metaphor and Thought*, pp. 474–485, Cambridge: Cambridge University Press.

Strati, A. (1999) *Organization and Aesthetics*, London: Sage.

Subramanyan, K. (1994) 'A Matter of Perspective and What Shall We Do About Culture?'. Two essays given as part of the series of S.G. Deuskar Lectures on Indian History and Culture, 1992 at the Centre for Studies on Social Sciences, Calcutta: Kolkata: K.P. Bagchi and Co.

Swan, E. (2010) 'Commodity Diversity: Smiling Faces as a Strategy of Containment', *Organization*, 17/1: 77–100.

Syed, J. and Ozbilgin, M. (2009) 'A Relational Framework for International Transfer of Diversity Management Practices', *International Journal of Human Resource Management*, 20/12: 2435–2453.

Taras, M. (2007) 'Machinations of Assessment: Metaphors, Myths and Realities', *Pedagogy, Culture and Society*, 15/1: 55–69.

Tatham, P. (2003) 'Social Dreaming and the Senior Managers' Programme', in Lawrence, W.G. (ed.) *Experiences in Social Dreaming*, pp. 179–188, London: Karnac.

Taylor, C. (2005) *Modern Social Imaginaries*, Durham and London: Duke University Press.

Tomei, M. (2003) 'Discrimination and Equality at Work: A Review of the Concepts', *International Labour Review*, 142/4: 401–418.

Tomlinson, F. (2008) 'Marking Difference: Placing the Category "Refugee" in Diversity Discourses', paper presented to the International Critical Management Studies conference, July 2005, Cambridge.

Tomlinson, F. (2005) 'Idealistic and Pragmatic Versions of the Discourse of Partnership', *Organization Studies*, 26(8): 1169–1188.

Tomlinson, F. and Schwabenland, C. (2010) 'Reconciling Competing Discourses of Diversity? The UK Non-Profit Sector Between Social Justice and the Business Case', *Organization*, 17/1: 101–121.

Trompenaars, F. and Hampden-Turner, C. (1997) *Riding the Waves of Culture: Understanding Cultural Diversity in Business*, London: Nicholas Brealey.

Tsoukas, H. (2006) *Complex Knowledge: Studies in Organizational Epistemology*, Oxford: Oxford University Press.

Turchi, P. (2004) *Maps of the Imagination: The Writer as Cartographer*, San Antonio: Trinity University Press.

Turner, B. (1992) 'The Symbolic Understanding of Organizations', in Reed, M. (ed.) *Rethinking Organizations*, pp. 46–66, London: Sage.

Vaill, P.B. (1989) *Managing as a Performing Art*, San Francisco: Jossey Bass.

Vangen, S. and Huxtable, C. (2003) 'Enacting Leadership for Collaborative Advantage: Dilemmas of Ideology and Pragmatism in the Activities of Partnership Managers', *British Journal of Management*, 14: S61–S76.

Waldrop, M.M. (1993) *Complexity: The Emerging Science at the Edge of Order and Chaos*, London: Viking.

Walker, M. (2006) *Higher Education Pedagogies: A Capabilities Approach*, Maidenhead: Open University Press.

Warner, R. (2010) *Secularization and its Discontents*, London: Continuum.

Weick, K.E. (1995) *Sensemaking in Organizations*, Thousand Oaks: Sage.

Whitman, W. (1928) *Leaves of Grass*, New York: Macmillan.

Windschuttle, K. (1997) 'Absolutely Relative', essay available on http://old-national-review.com/15sept97/windschuttle091597.html, accessed on 18/08/2010.

Wise, L.R. and Tschihart, M. (2000) 'Examining Empirical Evidence on Diversity Effects: How Useful is Diversity Research for Public Sector Managers?', *Public Administration Review*, 60/5: 386–394.

Wrench, J. (2005) 'Diversity Management Can Be Bad For You', *Race and Class*, 46/3: 73–84.

Younge, G. (2011) *Who Are We? And Should It Matter in 21st Century Britain?*, London: Penguin.

Zander, L. and Romani, L. (2004) 'When Nationality Matters: A Study of Departmental, Hierarchical, Professional, Gender and Age Based Employee Groupings' Leadership Preferences Across 15 Countries', *International Journal of Cross Cultural Management*, 4/3: 291–314.

Zanoni, P., Janssens, M., Benschop, Y. and Nkomo, S. (2010) 'Unpacking Diversity, Grasping Inequality: Rethinking Differences Through Critical Perspectives', *Organization*, 17/1: 9–29.

Zetter, R., Griffiths, D. and Sigona, N. (2006) *Immigration, Social Cohesion and Social Capital: What are the Links?* York: Joseph Rowntree Foundation.

Zimmer, H. (1992) *Myths and Symbols in Indian Art and Civilization*, Princeton: Princeton University Press.

Index